The Senate's War Powers

THE SENATE'S WAR POWERS

Debate on Cambodia

from the

CONGRESSIONAL RECORD

edited by

EUGENE P. DVORIN

California State College at Los Angeles

MARKHAM Publishing Company   Chicago

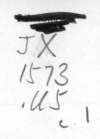

MARKHAM POLITICAL SCIENCE SERIES

Aaron Wildavsky, Editor

To
Janet and Miriam
In Memoriam

"Put it down, Mr. President!"

Preface

The theory of democratic representation through elected legislators is based in large measure upon an assumption of the educative
role of debate within legislative chambers. Untold numbers of students
have been told, "the debate is the important thing, regardless of the
final recording of votes cast." Where existing policy must be justified by those in power before the onslaught of those out of power and
seeking to displace them---with public opinion the ultimate arbiter---
there, so sayeth the Professor, democracy survives.

After two decades of teaching American government to a wide va-
riety of majors as well as "captives," I suspect I may have oversold
the educative role of the Congress, and this suspicion refuses to be
quelled. Debate from the floor may indeed prove instructive for members themselves. Yet, for millions of Americans directly affected by
the issues involved, the brief news article, the television news clip,
and the five-minute radio news summary of global, national, and local
affairs provide little education in the possible alternative paths of
a nation's public policy.

So much greater must the frustration be for classroom students of
political science who must dutifully note the educative function of
Congressional debate in their examinations but have yet to experience
even remotely the significance, drama, and anguish of truly great debate when national unease is laid bare. The Congressional Record,
that sometimes maligned and more often ignored compendium of legislative activity, does potentially allow the interested layman and
student the opportunity to follow public policy debate on the most
pressing issues of the moment. More realistically, however, the general unavailability of the Record precludes its widespread use as a
means by which Congressional debate informs and educates the nation,
even in the classroom.

For these reasons I have attempted to provide a more suitable
format by reducing the hundreds upon hundreds of pages of debate from
the Record to a more manageable and, possibly, more meaningful form.
In this way, I hope the educative nature of Congressional debate may
be more fully realized.

Aside from my own brief introductory comments and tentative concluding observations, the debate is presented as it evolved on the
floor of the U.S. Senate. Few who have followed the course of the
Cambodian debate through the nearly two months that it virtually occupied the attention of that chamber will argue the quality of the

opposing arguments---truly in the highest tradition of one of the world's greatest deliberative institutions. Nor will many deny its significance at a time when reasoned discussion of national values and priorities appears threatened by the actions of those seeking to bypass deliberation and peaceful critical analysis.

On carefully reading and rereading the total record of the debate I felt that rearrangement of the materials on a topical basis would interfere with the reader's perception of the issues and arguments as they emerged. I felt chronological presentation exposed the rhythm emerging from the debate---the discussion of particular aspects of our foreign policy tended to lead as a logical consequence to other aspects. I felt it would have been ill-considered and presumptuous on my part to have substituted another approach for that which actually took place on the floor. Aside from a considerable reduction in the volume of debate, every effort has been made to keep editorial comment at a minimum in order that the essential qualities of authenticity and urgency be preserved.

The debate was marked by complex parliamentary maneuvering not really central to the issues deliberated. To have retained this material would have burdened and perhaps confused the reader. In addition, I deleted a number of proposed amendments to the Cooper-Church amendment to the Foreign Military Sales Act that were less significant than those I included. Wherever possible the original subheadings from the Record have been retained and I marked those which I inserted. I made every effort to present the debate as completely as possible within the brief compass necessary for classroom purposes.

My objective is to provide a volume supplemental to a wide range of texts in American government, public policy formulation, and United States foreign policy. I hope this book will be as useful as I intended. I accept full responsibility for errors of judgment and/or errors or omissions of fact.

E.P.D.

Los Angeles
October, 1970

Contents

PART I

Introduction

United States Senators have always prided themselves on the uniqueness of their legislative chamber and its traditions. Though less than one-quarter the size of the House of Representatives the Senate claims Constitutional power and enjoys prestige superior to that of the lower house. Few offices of state are as coveted as a Senate seat and few are as difficult to attain. Among second chambers of the world it has no equal in the Constitutional role it plays and the quality of debate is renown. Only since the second decade of this century have United States Senators been elected by the people of the several states but Senators still represent an equality of states rather than differences in numbers of people.

Despite a difficult birth at the Constitutional Convention of 1787, a birth made possible only by the great Connecticut Compromise, the Senate has loomed large in the formulation of the nation's public policy. Some truly great Presidents have led the nation but even of this select circle few have successfully challenged the awesome power of the Senate.

Yet, today the Senate exhibits a great unease. Reflective perhaps of the national mood it is questioning matters long unquestioned and raising issues holding little promise of simple or perfect answers. Prior to the twentieth century foreign affairs was a tangential rather than central concern of the Senate. At the beginning of the seventh decade of this century both the content and contours of the nation's foreign policy are high on the agenda of every Senator. The shift in emphasis is one consequence of two major wars declared by Congress and a number of Presidential military actions or ventures: Panama, Korea, the Formosan Strait, Lebanon, Cuba, the Dominican Republic, Vietnam and Cambodia.

Some of these Presidential ventures commiting American forces in foreign lands have been carefully managed with military action circumscribed by the specific and limited objectives sought. Korea and Vietnam, however, have failed to be confined to the pre-conceived boundaries sought by American power Presidential or otherwise. Both are compelling evidence that the nation may slide, suddenly as in Korea or by almost imperceptible degrees as in Vietnam, into major wars of long duration without the formal declaration of war foreseen by the Framers. The differences are partially legal but are also psychological, ethical and economic. From the formal declaration of war a long list of consequences may be anticipated for this is in accord with the "rules of the game" and the Constitutional foundation is well-laid. The undeclared war is another matter. In this situation the nation exists in an ill-defined state of non-peace--- neither declared war nor peace. In Vietnam the action has involved

1

American forces for nearly a decade. The price paid in high manpower
losses, internal domestic division and economic dislocation are already well documented and need not be recounted here.

     Disillusionment and frustration with Vietnam had already set
into a large portion of the body politic when President Richard Nixon
in early May 1970 ordered American forces to enter Cambodia. This
was a classic example of Presidential assertion of vast authority
under his Constitutional powers as Commander-in-chief. This action
was taken without Congressional consultation. The Senate, the
nation's premier chamber in foreign affairs, had no member who was
privy to the impending Presidential order. The evidence appears overwhelming that even key members of the President's Cabinet and White
House staff were equally uninformed or, at best, ill-informed.
Outside governmental circles the nation at large was caught by surprise. Despite a Presidential telecast as American forces were
crossing the border into Cambodia fears of a widening war throughout
Indochina were not easily allayed. Officials at all levels of government felt the impact of this new commitment of American air, land,
naval and riverine forces. Within a few days a large number of the
nation's Governors had arrived in Washington for a briefing on what
came to be termed "Nixon's gamble." Even local government officialdom
felt a direct stake in the turn of events. Indicative of the divided
and confused nature of a large segment of public opinion were the re-
actions of the Mayors of the largest cities on the Atlantic and
Pacific coasts. To New York's Mayor John Lindsay Vietnam was both
futile and immoral from the beginning and Cambodia, he declared, made
it more difficult to keep the city stable. To Mayor Samuel Yorty of
Los Angeles the decision to send American forces into Cambodia to find
and destroy enemy troops was praiseworthy and, he added, this was
"possibly the greatest decision that Mr. Nixon has ever made."*

     In every region of the nation the ethic of military escalation
was challenged by the ethic for escalation of domestic violence. The
militant peace movement which had become dormant in anticipation of
the President "winding-down" the war was channeling its activism into
other areas of concern. Feeling they "had been had" the activists
regarded the Cambodian venture as conflicting with frequent
Presidential exhortations of phased withdrawal from Vietnam. The
peak of domestic violence was reached with the death of four students
at Ohio's Kent State University.

     The Cambodian debate would merit wide attention if only because
it deals with the immediate questions of legality and strategic sound-
ness of Presidential policy. Yet, the debate goes far beyond this.
Its roots are in the past and, as the Congressional Record reveals,
in the dissatisfaction of Senators with themselves.

     As one follows the debate the impression increases that the
Senators are putting the Senate itself on trial---as an institution.
Is it doomed under contemporary conditions to be, in the words of one
member, "a Presidential echo rather than an independent voice?"
Few questions are more important for the future of the nation.

*Los Angeles Times (May 19, 1970).

The Cambodian venture---an offshoot of the Vietnam war---is the
storm center around which the debate swirls. It is so because it was,
in the eyes of many Senators, "the final straw that broke the camel's
back" in a history of Presidential aggrandizement in foreign affairs
at their expense. Perhaps it should be more accurately stated---at
the expense of the Constitutional check and balance system.

Cambodia emerged at that point in time when American commitments
throughout the world had grown "like Topsy" more often than not
through the device of Executive Agreements rather than treaties requiring the advice and consent of the Senate. The Cambodian venture
immediately raised questions of explicit or implicit commitments to
neighboring Laos and Thailand. Hovering in the background was the
possibility of a new war in the Middle East. The Senate reflected
genuine concern with the growth of Russian naval and air power in that
region and some Senators had begun to air suspicions that Vietnam was
misplaced as the nation's highest security priority. To these men
Europe was the key to America's world posture and Europe's future
would be determined by developments in the Mediterranean-Middle East-
Indian Ocean region.

Following the American incursion into Cambodia most Senators
sensed that the nation would best be served by a full-ranging and open
debate on the assumptions and alternatives to Presidential policy.
This was regarded as a healthy counter-balance to the extensive secret
closed-door hearings surrounding so much in technology-military-
security matters. In May 1970 the Senate Foreign Relations Committee
was in the process of reviewing a bill passed earlier by the House of
Representatives. This bill was to extend the Foreign Military Sales
Act of 1968. Through the 1968 Act the American government provided
arms to friendly nations. Rapid passage of the extension was a major
concern of President Nixon as it was a central feature of his "Guam
Doctrine" announced in July 1969. Under this doctrine the United
States would provide assistance to non-Communist Asian nations so
they could better defend themselves without the aid of American
manpower.

Cambodia was the issue that triggered a 9-5 vote in the Senate
Foreign Relations Committee to amend the Foreign Military Sales Act
as proposed by Senators John Sherman Cooper (R-Kentucky) and Frank
Church (D-Idaho). The so-called "Cooper-Church Amendment" was designed to draw Congressional purse-strings tight against a deepening
American commitment in Cambodia. Although the Cambodian debate in
the Senate was, technically speaking, on the Sales Act itself, it
soon became evident once debate was under way that the real vortex of
controversy was the Cooper-Church Amendment.

Few Americans are removed from the implications of the issues
raised during debate on the Cooper-Church Amendment. The final vote
on the Amendment was taken six weeks after the opening of debate.
Those six weeks are among the most important in the history of the
United States Senate.

PART II

Amendment of the Foreign Military Sales Act

(May 13, 1970)

Mr. MANSFIELD. [Page S7098.]* Mr. President, I ask unanimous consent that the Senate turn to the consideration of Calendar No. 868, H.R. 15628, I do this so that the bill will become the pending business.

The PRESIDING OFFICER (Mr. Cranston). The bill will be stated by title.

The Legislative Clerk. A bill (H.R. 15628) to amend the Foreign Military Sales Act.

The PRESIDING OFFICER. Is there objection to the present consideration of the bill?

There being no objection, the Senate proceeded to consider the bill, which had been reported from the Committee on Foreign Relations with amendments.

* * *

Mr. FULBRIGHT. [Page S7105.] . . . Mr. President, it is with both a sense of great reluctance and a feeling of guarded accomplishment that I present this bill to extend the foreign military sales program to the Senate.

My reluctance derives from the fact that I take no pride in asking my colleagues to approve the portion of this bill which contributes to the spread of conventional military hardware. On the other hand, there is a feeling of accomplishment because of the committee's adoption of a number of significant amendments, including the prohibition on further involvement in Cambodia and a number of restrictions on the military aid and sales programs.

The basic purpose of this bill is to authorize continuation of the military credit sales program for fiscal years 1970 and 1971.

*Numbers in brackets refer to original page numbers in the Congressional Record.

It would authorize credit sales of $300 million in military arms
and equipment for each of those years and would authorize the appropriation of $250 million each year to finance the sales. The
sales financed under this program are made primarily to less developed
countries. Credit sales to rich countries are generally financed
either through commercial channels or the Export-Import Bank.

But the credit sales program must be viewed in the context of the
total picture of U.S. arms exports. The Department of Defense estimates that in the current fiscal year the United States will sell
abroad a total of about $1.9 billion in arms and military equipment.
Of that, $300 million will be financed under authority of the Foreign
Military Sales Act. In addition to the sales volume, the United
States will supply $392 million in arms through the military grant
aid program and will have an additional $166 million in surplus arms
and equipment---valued at one-fourth of acquisition cost---to give
away. Thus, the United States will sell or give away nearly $2.5
billion in military materials this fiscal year.

I point out also that there are some $9 billion worth of surplus
arms and military equipment now available for the Department of
Defense to give away---even to Cambodia---without any congressional
limits. And the total is mounting rapidly as U.S. forces are withdrawn from Vietnam. In addition to the excess arms, the funds
available under the regular grant aid and sales program, the President
may, under section 506 of the Foreign Assistance Act, give other
nations up to $300 million of arms and equipment out of the Department
of Defense's stock if he considers it vital to our national security.
The sources of U.S. arms are many and the volume is vast. The credit
sales program authorized by this bill is only the tip of the iceberg.

All of these programs add up to the fact that the United States
is the world's largest producer and exporter of military equipment.
And in this global context, I call attention to the grim reminder
that for the period from 1964 to 1969 total military outlays around
the world amounted to over $1 trillion. According to the Arms Control
and Disarmament Agency, this sum when measured against available
economic resources exceeds the value of all goods and services pro-
duced in the United States in the past year; it is more than 2 years'
income for the world's developing countries in which 2-1/2 billion
people live; and it is equal to as much money as was spent by all
governments on all forms of public education and health care in the
6-year period.

Few would disagree that this is a pretty sad commentary on the
priorities set by governments around the world. But the future is
even more bleak. Drawing on a recent United Nation study, the
Christian Science Monitor graphically reported recently:

"If one silver dollar coin was dropped every second, it will take
126,000 years to exhaust the amount of money that will be spent on
world armaments in the next 10 years."

As a practical matter there is little that the committee can do
to change the outlook for that forecast. But it did act to try to
control the contribution the Pentagon planned to make toward making
the prediction a reality. It made a number of substantive changes
that may help to stem the flow of American weapons abroad. I would
like to describe briefly the most significant actions taken.

Nothing was more indicative of the Pentagon's blatant disregard for the intent of Congress than its giving away of some $140 million in surplus military equipment to Taiwan following Congress' refusal to appropriate $54.5 million in additional military aid above the amount authorized. As a result of this attempt to increase appropriations over the authorization level, and the Pentagon's attempt to make an end run around the Congress by using the surplus program, two amendments have been added to this bill to prevent such developments in the future.

The first, dealing with the excess property issue, restricts the Department of Defense's authority by imposing a $35 million ceiling on the amount of surplus military arms or equipment that may be given away in any fiscal year. A portion of the original cost of any surplus material given away above that amount would be deducted from the funds available for grant military aid.

The second, relating to appropriations, simply states that any appropriation above the amount authorized cannot be used and that any appropriation for which there is not an authorization cannot be expended. This amendment writes into law the principle, supported by the Senate in two votes last year, that the appropriation of funds which are not authorized is bad practice and, if carried to extremes, could seriously undermine the authority of all legislative committees.

In addition to these two amendments, the bill contains provisions which require: that recipients of military grant aid, including surplus equipment, pay in their local currency 50 percent of the value of the grants, the funds to be used to meet U.S. obligations in the country and to finance educational and cultural exchange programs; that the United States not approve requests by foreign countries to transfer military equipment, supplied under the grant or sales program, to any country to which the United States would not supply the arms directly; that the President be given explicit control over successive transfers of military equipment supplied under [Page S7106.] Government-financed programs; and that sales or grants of the International Fighter aircraft, except for those given to Vietnam or sold through commercial channels, be authorized under the regular military grant aid or sales programs.

Mr. President, the fact that the committee felt compelled to adopt these restrictions serves only to emphasize the failure of policies which have resulted in making the United States the world's leading arms merchant. This policy, which places such great reliance on arms as a means of solving problems of human and national relationships evidences a type of national illness.

It is the kind of illness that has spread deceptively and insidiously for many years and now permeates our entire body politic.

It is an illness that blinds both policy-makers and public to our Nation's basic traditions and values to produce a kind of "Doublespeak" where lives are saved by sending more men into combat; villages are destroyed in order to save them; and risks for peace are taken by buying more weapons of destruction.

It is the kind of illness that has drawn us into Vietnam; that has nurtured our adventure in Laos; and that has brought us to the brink of a far wider war throughout Indochina.

In short, it is the kind of illness that prostitutes and distorts. It is the kind of illness that must be cured if we are to ever achieve peace abroad or at home.

The Church-Cooper-Aiken-Mansfield amendment, to prevent any further U.S. involvement in Cambodia, is a small, but important step in the recovery process.

Last year, by a vote of 70 to 16, the Senate adopted the national commitments resolution expressing the sense of the Senate that "a national commitment by the United States results only from affirmative action taken by the executive and legislative branches of the U.S. Government by means of a treaty, statute, or concurrent resolution of both Houses of Congress specifically providing for such commitment." By its action of April 1970 in initiating hostilities within the territory of Cambodia without the consent or even the prior knowledge of Congress or any of its committees, the executive branch has shown disregard not only for the national commitments resolution but for the constitutional principles in which that resolution is rooted. In the wake of recent events, there is reason to reassert, with renewed conviction, a statement made in the Foreign Relations Committee's report of April 16, 1969, on the national commitments resolution:

"Our country has come far toward the concentration in its national executive of unchecked power over foreign relations, particularly over the disposition and use of the Armed Forces. So far has this process advenced that, in the committee's view, it is no longer accurate to characterize our Government, in matters of foreign relations, as one of separated powers checked and balanced against each other."

The notion that the authority to commit the United States to war is an Executive prerogative, or even a divided or uncertain one, is one which has grown up only in recent decades. It is the result primarily of a series of emergencies or alleged emergencies which have enhanced Executive power, fostered attitudes of urgency and anxiety, and given rise to a general disregard for constitutional procedure.

In fact, there was neither uncertainty nor ambiguity on the part of the framers of the Constitution as to their determination to vest the war power exclusively in the Congress. As Thomas Jefferson wrote in a letter to Madison in 1789:

"We have already given in example one effectual check to the Dog of war by transferring the power of letting him loose from the Executive to the Legislative body, from those who are to spend to those who are to pay."

As to the powers of the President as Commander in Chief, Alexander Hamilton, an advocate of strong executive power, wrote in Federalist No. 69:

"The President is to be commander in chief of the army and navy of the United States. In this respect his authority would be nominally the same with that of the King of Great Britain, but in

substance much inferior to it.   It would amount to nothing more than
the supreme command and direction of the military and naval forces,
as first General and admiral of the Confederacy, while that of the
British king extends to the declaring of war and to the raising and
regulating of fleets and armies---all which, by the Constitution under
consideration, would appertain to the legislature. "

The present administration's view of the President's power as
Commander in Chief is almost the polar opposite of Hamilton's.   In
its comments of March 10, 1969, on the then pending national commitments resolution, the Department of State made the following
assertion:

"As Commander in Chief, the President has the sole authority to
command our Armed Forces, whether they are within or outside the
United States.   And, although reasonable men may differ as to the
circumstances in which he should do so, the President has the constitutional power to send U.S. military forces abroad without specific
congressional approval. "

Like a number of its predecessors, the present administration is
basing its claim to war powers on either a greatly inflated concept
of the President's authority as Commander in Chief, or in some vague
doctrine of inherent powers of the Presidency, or both.   Another possibility is that the matter simply has not been given much thought.

Whatever the explanation may be, the fact remains that the
Executive is conducting a constitutionally unauthorized, Presidential
war in Indochina.   The commitment without the consent or knowledge of
Congress of thousands of American soldiers to fight in Cambodia---a
country which has formally renounced the offer of protection extended
to it as a protocol state under the SEATO Treaty, and to which, therefore, we are under no binding obligation whatever---evidences a conviction by the Executive that it is at liberty to ignore the national
commitments resolution and to take over both the war and treaty powers
of Congress when congressional authority in these areas becomes
inconvenient.

It is noteworthy that, in his address to the Nation of April 30
explaining his decision to send American troops to Cambodia, the
President did not think it necessary to explain what he believed to
be the legal ground on which he was acting, other than to refer to
his powers as Commander in Chief of the Armed Forces.   Equally noteworthy was the President's repeated assertion in his press conference
of May 8 that he---and he alone---as Commander in Chief was responsible for the conduct of the war and the safety of our troops.   This
sweeping assertion of the President's authority as Commander in Chief
amounts to the repudiation of those provisions of article I, section 8
of the Constitution, which empower Congress not only to "declare war"
but to "raise and support armies," "provide and maintain a Navy," and
"make rules for the Government and regulation of the land and naval
forces."   It is true, of course, that the present administration's
attitude in this area hardly differs from that of its predecessors---
except that preceding administrations took no special pride, as the
present administration does, in adherence to a "strict construction"
of the Constitution.

The Senate's adoption of the Church-Cooper-Aiken-Mansfield
amendment will be a significant step toward restoring the health of

our constitutional system of checks and balances. Both its purpose
and language are simple and straightforward. Its purpose is simply
to prevent involvement by the United States in a wider war in Asia
by insuring that our forces are withdrawn from Cambodia and that the
United States does not end up fighting a war in behalf of Cambodia.
I will not go into the several points of the amendment since the
sponsors of it will discuss its details in their presentations. . .

AN EXPLANATION OF THE COOPER-CHURCH AMENDMENT

   Mr. CHURCH. Mr. President . . . The United States is still stuck
fast in the longest war of its history in the former French properties
known as Indochina. Three Presidents, representing both political
parties, have been unwilling to put an end to the American involvement
in this Asian war.

   Throughout this protracted period, the Congress of the United
States has permitted each President to exercise blank-check powers.
In so doing, we have shrunk from the use of our own authority under
section 8 of article I of the Constitution, which vests in Congress
the purse strings, together with the power to declare war, to raise
and support armies, to provide and maintain a navy, and to make rules
for the government and regulation of the land and naval forces. Our
failure to make effective use [Page S7107.] of any of these powers,
while the war was passed from one President to another, is one for
which historians may judge us harshly.

   Within the past 2 weeks, another front has been opened in this
interminable war---again as the result of a Presidential decision
taken without so much as a bow to Congress. The dispatch of American
troops into Cambodia, though presently limited in scope, could easily
become the first step toward committing the United States to the defense of still another government in Southeast Asia. Sobering as this
specter should be, in light of our experience in Vietnam, it nonetheless presents Congress with a historic opportunity to draw the limits
on American intervention in Indochina. This is the purpose of the
amendment that Senator Cooper and I, joined by Senators Mansfield and
Aiken, urge the Senate to approve. If enacted into law, it would
draw the purse strings tight against a deepening American involvement
in Cambodia.

   There is a precedent for what we are asking the Senate to do. It
lies in the action taken last December when, you will recall, the
Senate adopted overwhelmingly a modification I proposed to an amendment
offered by Senators Cooper and Mansfield to the military appropriations bill for fiscal year 1970. It provided that "none of the funds
appropriated by this act shall be used to finance the introduction of
American ground combat troops into Laos or Thailand." There is reason
to believe that this amendment, which became law, had a restraining
effect on our newest venture, because the President is said to have
rejected recommendations that the current operation include Laos as
well as Cambodia. To have done otherwise, might well have placed the
President in the untenable position of breaking the law.

   We now seek to do for Cambodia what our earlier amendment did for
Laos. But since American forces have already entered Cambodia, the
amendment we propose would set limits on their intervention, prevent

them from remaining in Cambodia, and preclude any military entanglement on our part with the government of that country.

Unquestionably, Congress has the power to accomplish these
objectives. But this power, so little used in recent years, amounts
to so much idle talk, unless a majority proves willing to invoke it.
Our amendment is drafted in such manner as to invite, and offered in
the hope that it will attract, majority support.

Some have argued that it is useless for the Senate to legislate
limits, when the House of Representatives has already backed away
from them. I do not agree. Nor do I believe the Senate should be
put off on such a pretext. . .

The amendment itself is a realistic one. It is no exercise in
futility; it does not attempt to undo what has been done. Instead,
it is addressed to the immediate need of preventing the United States
from bogging down in Cambodia, and from committing itself to the defense of another Asian government on a new front.

It does this by: First, denying funds for the retention of
American forces in Cambodia; second, prohibiting funds for the instruction of Cambodian military forces or for hiring mercenaries to
fight for Cambodia; and, third, forbidding the use of any appropriation for conducting combat activity in the air above Cambodia in
support of Cambodian forces.

In sum, the amendment is directed against those very activities
which led to our entrapment in Vietnam. Its adoption would erect a
legal barrier against further penetration of American forces into the
jungles of Southeast Asia and help expedite the withdrawal of our
troops from Vietnam.

Mr. President, legislative action is needed now, not only to make
certain that the avowed perimeters of our attach upon Cambodian
sanctuaries are not exceeded, but also to bar the beginnings of an
escalating military assistance program to the new Cambodian regime.
We owe nothing to the generals who have seized power in Phnom Penh.
We have made them no promises. For once in our lives, we stand un-
fettered by any treaty obligations. We have no duty to furnish them
with arms, let alone to come to their defense.

Still, it takes no exercise of the imagination to forecast, now
that the Cambodian boundary has been breached and our gunboats ply
the Mekong, that pressures will soon develop for sending an American
military mission to Phnom Penh which, in turn, would generate a whole·
set of American obligations to the new Cambodian regime. This very
sequence of events led us ever deeper into the morass in Vietnam. We
must not travel down that tragic trail again.

This war has already stretched the generation gap so wide that
it threatens to pull the country apart. The new generation never saw
in Vietnam the demons that our generation perceived. Unlike American
Presidents, who were mesmerized by the "lessons" of World War II, our
brightest young people never believed that Ho Chi Minh was Adolf
Hitler in disguise, or that our failure to send in our own troops to
fight for the government we subsidized in Saigon would amount to
another "Munich." They knew that Vietnam really had nothing to do
with the security of the United States, the safety of the American

people, or the well-being of our society. And so they soon came to view the war as an unwarranted intrusion on our part in a Vietnamese struggle which we should never have made our affair.

It does no good to tell these young people that our "will and character are being tested," that we shall not be humiliated or accept our first defeat. They do not believe a mistaken war should be won. They believe it should be stopped. That, for them, is the path of honor.

Little wonder, then, that our generation has lost communication with young America. We move in two different worlds; we speak two different tongues. We would pass each other by, like two ships in the night, were it not for the collision course we oldsters have charted: we keep drafting them to fight our war. We persist in that course, even at the price of alienating millions of young Americans.

The deep disillusionment of college students in their country and its institutions has its roots in Vietnam. When the power of the State is used to force young men to fight a war they believe to be wrongful, under penalty of imprisonment if they refuse, the seeds of sedition are sown. We now reap the bitter harvest, manifested in the angry uprisings on campuses from coast to coast. Whenever the limb is shaken, all the leaves tremble. Once the moral authority of the Government is rejected on an issue so fundamental as an unacceptable war, every lesser institution of authority is placed in jeopardy. Every sacred principle, every traditional value, every settled policy becomes a target for ridicule and repudiation. Cauldrons of anarchy soon begin to boil.

So it has happened that our country is coming unstuck. The crisis in our land, the deepening divisions among our people, the festering, unattended problems at home, bear far more importantly upon the future of the Republic than anything we have now, or have ever had, at stake in Indochina. That is why the time has come for Congress to draw the line against an expanded American involvement in this widening war.

Too much blood has been lost, too much patience gone unrewarded, while the war continues to poison our society. If the executive branch will not take the initiative, then the Congress and the people must.

LIST OF COSPONSORS

Mr. President, when the amendment was originally offered, Senators Mansfield and Aiken joined Senator Cooper of Kentucky and myself in recommending it to the Committee on Foreign Relations. The committee adopted the amendment by a vote of 9 to 5 and affixed it to the Foreign Military Sales Act now pending before the Senate.

Since the committee took that action, many other Senators have asked to be listed as cosponsors of the amendment.

Mr. President, I ask unanimous consent that their names be affixed as cosponsors.

The full list of cosponsors is:

Senator Aiken of Vermont; Senator Bayh of Indiana; Senator Brooke of Massachusetts; Senator Case of New Jersey; Senator Church of Idaho; Senator Cooper of Kentucky; Senator Cranston of California; Senator Fulbright of Arkansas; Senator Goodell of New York; Senator Harris of Oklahoma; Senator Hart of Michigan; Senator Hatfield of Oregon; Senator Javits of New York; Senator Mansfield of Montana; Senator Mathias of Maryland; Senator Mondale of Minnesota; Senator Moss of Utah; Senator Pearson of Kansas; Senator Pell of Rhode Island; [Page S7108.] Senator Proxmire of Wisconsin; Senator Ribicoff of Connecticut; Senator Saxbe of Ohio; Senator Schweiker of Pennsylvania; Senator Symington of Missouri; Senator Tydings of Maryland; Senator Williams of New Jersey; Senator Young of Ohio; Senator McGovern of South Dakota; Senator Hughes of Iowa; and Senator Gravel of Alaska.

Mr. President, as of now, the total number of Senators sponsoring the amendment is 30.

The PRESIDING OFFICER. Without objection it is so ordered.

Mr. CHURCH. Mr. President, I also ask that a text of the amendment in its revised form, as reported from the Committee on Foreign Relations, be printed at this point in the Record.

There being no objection, the text was ordered to be printed in the Record as follows:

CHURCH-COOPER AMENDMENT

Sec. 7. The Foreign Military Sales Act is amended by adding at the end thereof the following new section:

"Sec. 47. Prohibition of assistance to Cambodia.---In order to avoid the involvement of the United States in a wider war in Indochina and to expedite the withdrawal of American forces from Vietnam, it is hereby provided that, unless specifically authorized by law hereafter enacted, no funds authorized or appropriated pursuant to this Act or any other law may be expended for the purpose of---

"(1) retaining United States forces in Cambodia;

"(2) paying the compensation or allowances of, or otherwise supporting, directly or indirectly, any United States personnel in Cambodia who furnish military instruction to Cambodian forces or engage in any combat activity in support of Cambodian forces;

"(3) entering into or carrying out any contract or agreement to provide military instruction in Cambodia, or to provide persons to engage in any combat activity in support of Cambodian forces; or

"(4) conducting any combat activity in the air above Cambodia in support of Cambodian forces."

[Page S7109.] . . . The purpose of this amendment is to set the outer limits of American penetration into Cambodia. We take the President of the United States at his word that the present operation is limited in scope, that it is confined to the capture of particular

border sanctuaries, and that, as soon as this objective is accomplished, American forces will be withdrawn.

The amendment simply says, in effect, that Congress undertakes
to set the outer limits of American involvement in Cambodia. As soon
as the bases are captured, as soon as the objectives of the operation
are achieved, then no further funds are available for retaining American forces in Cambodia. That is the first objective of the amendment.

The second objective is to lay down a legislative barrier against
the kind of escalating military assistance program which, once commenced, can easily lead this country into an entangling alliance with
the new regime in Phnom Penh.

We know from our experience in Vietnam that what commences as a
limited military aid program can readily expand into a much more extensive program; that small arms soon lead to more sophisticated
armaments; and that these weapons, in turn, lead to the necessity for
introducing American instructors and advisers who, once committed,
create pressures for the final commitment of American combat troops.
That was the sequence of events in Vietnam, and we must make certain
it does not become the sequence of events in Cambodia.

The adoption of this amendment would prevent this from happening.
If future developments were to lead the President to advocate a re-
newal of our attack upon Cambodian territory, or a more extensive
occupation of that country, then he would be obliged to come to Congress, make his case before us, and ask the Congress to lift its
prohibition against such an expanded war.

Now, Mr. President, we should have done this a long, long time
ago. For too long, we have abdicated away our authority to the
President, sitting on our hands hoping the American people would
look the other way, while this war has gone on and on, while casualties have mounted inconclusively, until today our involvement in
Vietnam has become the longest war of our history and one of the
costliest. Still there is no end in sight. The time has come for
the Senate to assume its responsibility under the Constitution,
drawing outer limits on this latest involvement, and insisting that
if the President intends in the future to expand still further our
participation in this war, he come back to the Congress, make his case
and ask Congress for the consent that the Constitution intended us
either to grant or to withhold.

I hope in the coming days of debate that we can clearly set forth
the constitutional issue involved here. I hope that we can encourage
the Senate to adopt this amendment as a proper assertion of congressional authority.

Last December, we took the first step, Mr. President, when the
Senate adopted overwhelmingly an amendment of mine, made a part of the
military appropriations bill for fiscal year 1970, that prohibited the
introduction of American ground combat forces into Laos or Thailand.
That represented the first instance, in the whole long course of this
war, that Congress had undertaken to use the purse strings to draw a
line. At the time, the President said it was in conformity with his
own policy. He did not raise questions about undermining his authority as Commander in Chief; he accepted the decision of Congress, as

consistent with its responsibility in determining how and where
public moneys shall be spent.

No different principle is posed by this amendment. If the
earlier amendment was acceptable to the President, it escapes me why
this amendment should not be, for each rests upon the right of Congress, under the Constitution, to control the spending of public
money, and each is pointed toward the necessity of establishing
limits to the American involvement in a wider Indochina war. I think
it is the second step, a necessary and logical step to take, in view
of the developments of the last 2 weeks, to reassure the American
people that Congress is alive and living in Washington, D.C.

So I hope, when the debate has been completed, that the Senate
will support the amendment. . . .

PART III

Undeclared War:
The Constitutional Issues

(May 13, 1970)

Mr. MCGOVERN. [Page S7117.] Mr. President, there are two profound issues involved in the amendments which have been proposed to limit U.S. activities in Southeast Asia.

The merits of whether it is politically, militarily, or morally sound for us to be entangled in that conflict will be debated at length, as they have been debated for many years. Most of us have strong opinions.

The other issue has received less attention, and for that reason alone it deserves a special focus. Regardless of how any Senator feels about the wisdom of our involvement, he has good reason for deep interest in the procedures through which it has come about, and particularly in the role Congress has or has not played. Concern has been expressed about a possible constitutional crisis over the war power. Is truth that crisis already exists, and the Vietnam war is the best possible illustration of that fact.

The complementary amendments introduced by Senators Church and Cooper, on Cambodia, and by Senators Hatfield, Goodell, Hughes, Cranston, myself, and other Senators on Vietnam, Cambodia, and Laos, are practical attempts to assert proper congressional involvement. In fact, they use the only vehicle---limitations on spending appropriated funds---that we have available to enforce our decisions on the use of American military power abroad. Moreover, it is a vehicle which the founders of our Republic believed should be vigorously employed. . .

THE OPENING SKIRMISH*

(May 14, 1970)

Mr. EASTLAND. [Page S7146.] Mr. President, I oppose the pending legislation for a number of very basic reasons.

*Asterisk indicates sub-heading provided by Editor: otherwise from the Congressional Record.

My opposition is based on the firm belief that this action comes at the wrong time and is directed toward the wrong President.

This President has already reduced---substantially---the number of Americans engaged in Vietnam and has announced another withdrawal of 150,000 of our GI's.

Further, the operation he ordered against areas under the complete control---for an extended period of time---of the Hanoi Communists is aimed directly at the achievement of the goal toward which we strive---the safe disengagement and removal of our fighting forces from Vietnam.

Any first-year student at West Point, Annapolis, or in an ROTC program---provided that some ROTC units survive the vicious attack that has been launched against this concept, which has done so much for our country---any of these students can state, with absolute certainty, that the denial of logistical support to an enemy is the first rule of warfare.

The capture---by American and South Vietnamese troops---of enormous amounts of weapons, ammunition, and other material will cripple Hanoi's capabilities over a wide operational front---furnish time for the orderly development of the Vietnamization program---and ---most important of all---contribute to the security of our own forces.

Mr. President, I ask unanimous consent to have printed in the Record a tentative list of the equipment which has been captured.

There being no objection, the list was ordered to be printed in the Record, as follows:

Military Update of Cambodian Operations, May 13, 1970

Latest cumulative data:

Individual weapons captured.	7,274
Crew-served weapons captured	1,012
Rice (tons).	2,390
Rice (man-months).	105,160
Rocket rounds captured	9,025
Mortar rounds captured	13,231
Small-arms ammunition captured. .	8,375,925
Land mines captured.	1,200
Bunkers destroyed.	3,294
Vehicles destroyed or captured	171

Note:---The above figures are tentative cumulative results as reported by Hq. MACV.

Mr. EASTLAND. Mr. President, this President has stated---publicly and repeatedly---his determination to bring our soldiers and sailors home at the earliest possible date. I am convinced that he is working very hard to attain this end, and I am equally convinced that his foremost concern---as the program moves ahead---is maximum support and safety for every man who wears our uniform and whom this Nation sent to Asia.

Therefore---I repeat---I shall vote against this legislation because it would do what the President is already doing. It comes before us in the wrong administration and at the wrong time in relation to the protection of American forces committed to combat in the region and with regard to the safe withdrawal of these forces. . .

[Page S7147.] These men---who have suffered to the limit of human endurance at the hands of their Communist captors---deserve what they have earned at the hands of the land they fought to defend.

We are solemnly obligated, Mr. President, legally, morally, and in the name of honor and decency, to stand by these men even as they stood by America.

We must not forget them, we cannot abandon them, our principles and our tradition forbid us to forsake them.

Mr. President, I have offered an amendment to the pending legislation, which would stay and enjoin any action under the terms of the legislation until the President of the United States has successfully arranged and obtained the release and safe return to their families and to their country of every American prisoner of war presently held by the Vietnamese Communists.

America---with President Nixon in the forefront---prays and strives for peace. Americans long for a cessation of fighting and dying---of separation and hardship.

This truly great Nation---with her record of unparalleled generosity to all mankind---would see Woodrow Wilson's dream become reality---"not a balance of power, but a community of power---not organized rivalries, but an organized common peace."

However, Mr. President, we must deal---not with noble dreams but with harsh facts created by the Communist masters in Hanoi, Peking, and Moscow.

I submit that President Nixon---confronted, as he is, with the cold calculations, callous aggression, and endless maneuvering of the latter-day oriental khans---is pursuing---with all his strength---our great goals of bringing peace to the Far East and bringing our troops back home. . .

Mr. PEARSON. Mr. President, in this morning's New York Times, there is an article published, under a Washington dateline, indicating that American and western intelligence sources report 100 Soviet pilots have been sent to the UAR, so that it is part of a military advisory force now numbering 8,000 to 10,000 men.

Mr. President, the widening conflict in Southeast Asia has obscured, for the most part, a dangerous escalation of force and intervention in the Middle East.

The Arab-Israel conflict and the cold war confrontation between the great powers represents the greatest danger to world peace because of the possible involvement of either Soviet or U.S. forces.

The participation of Soviet pilots as a part of the Egyptian defensive air command has not only had a serious effect on the balance of forces there, but could very well provide the spark which could ignite an ever consuming and ever widening war of global proportions.

Mr. President, while Mr. Nixon is being criticized for a move into Cambodia, it seems to me only fair to recall his restraint and caution in denying last March the Israeli request for additional phantoms and skyhawks. The President's decision to deny this request sought to reduce the dangers and the tensions in the Middle East. Furthermore, Mr. President, the administration's decision was made not only in the face of domestic and political pressure, but against the background of huge military aircraft purchases by the Arab Nations. These new inventory of military jets were not as dangerous as their numbers implied, we understood, because the Arab Nations, particularly the United Arab Republic, lacked trained pilots and competent personnel. Now that limitation has apparently been removed.

President Nixon has ordered a full review of the strategic balance in the Middle East. The State Department is asking Moscow for an explanation of its purpose and intent. But, in the meantime, the Congress should be prepared for the prospect that additional military aid to Israel is essential if a balance of force is to be maintained.

I suggest, Mr. President, that this Government should seek to provide this assistance if found to be necessary on an international and multilateral basis. Indeed the call from Israel was for international assistance.

Mr. President, the Soviet Union may not want war in the Middle East, but they also do not want peace. The Kremlin's policy is not aimed at returning peace and stability in that part of the world, but in establishing a strong Soviet sphere of influence in the Arab nations---particularly in the United Arab Republic. This policy which has led to direct Soviet intervention in the form of Soviet Mig pilots represents immense dangers. Nasser's threat to President Nixon on May 2; King Hussein's criticism of U.S. policy and his move toward the Soviet Union of May 4; and Prime Minister Meir's vow to fight the Russian pilots if necessary a day or so later are more than verbal eruptions, but are manifestations of a deteriorating condition, as we learn of repeated and stronger attacks across the Suez Canal and the Jordan River.

To repeat, Mr. President, serious as may be the problems in Southeast Asia, circumstances in the Middle East and the new developments there warrant our immediate and continued attention.

Mr. STENNIS. [Page S7175.] Mr. President, I address myself to the pending bill, particularly that part thereof known as the Church-Cooper amendment.

Referring to the area involved in Cambodia where we have crossed over the line to get at the sanctuaries, I requested the Department of Defense this morning to give me the actual figures, down to and including the latest available, with reference to just what had happened there since that part of the battle started, with reference to the capture of supplies, ammunition, and matters that go to make up military equipment, as well as the manpower situation.

About an hour ago the Secretary of Defense sent me this statement, which I shall read for the information of the Senate. I think it has a special place, too, in the Record.

Mr. President, in my opinion, during the few short days that this part of the battle has been going on, which is distinctly and essentially a part of the war in Vietnam, I think it has been relatively highly successful. I read this statement, a summary statement of the activities:

> On the basis of current reports of the amounts of enemy supplies and equipment located so far in Cambodia by South Vietnamese and American forces, the weapons alone are sufficient to equip about 20 enemy battalions. More than 7,000 rifles and 1,000 crew served weapons (e.g., mortars and machine guns) have been captured, along with more than 8 million rounds of small arms ammunition, which would have supplied these 20 battalions for upwards of a thousand battalion-size attacks.

Those are enormous figures. Continuing the statement:

> Food supplies located so far comprise almost five million pounds of rice, the basic food for Southeast Asia. This rice would have fed the entire enemy force in III and IV Corps in South Vietnam for 5 months.

We know that the III and IV Corps cover a very considerable area in South Vietnam. I wish that this had been given in terms of square miles, but that area is an important area, and a considerable area in square miles.

I quote again:

> Twenty-two thousand mortar and rocket rounds have been found. This amount of munitions would have supplied about 3,000 fire attacks in South Vietnam of the same intensity that the enemy has been conducting in recent weeks---about seven rounds per attack.

That refers to the small, quick, rapid mortar and rocket attacks that they have been very successful in. This would have taken care of 3,000 such attacks.

I continue the quotation:

> More than 5,400 enemy have been killed in Cambodia and about 1,400 have been detained. If earlier estimates of about 40,000 enemy troops in Cambodia are correct, this loss by the enemy means that about 17 percent of his Cambodian forces have been destroyed.

Losses by the enemy thus far in terms of men, munitions, and supplies will indeed have a significant
effect on his future operations.

That is the end of the statement.

Mr. President, that means that, almost within throwing distance
of the line between South Vietnam and Cambodia, and really a part of
the battlefield that our men are fighting on, and have been, all these
arms and munitions and battle supplies have been found which could
have been used and would have been used in the course of months.
Certainly they would have been used against our men and the troops of
South Vietnam.

Call it what we will about where the boundary line is, or what
strict construction of the Constitution of the United States requires,
this is a very significant thing, highly helpful to our position,
enabling the saving of a great number of lives of our men and those
of the allies. As a matter of fact, it is the first big thing that
has been done in a long time that really does substantially contribute to the bettering of our position there.

Yes, Mr. President, it is true I am a strict constructionist of
the Constitution. But the time has long since passed for making a
strict construction here, when we have been sending these men into
battle for months and years, and still are, right this minute---right
this minute---not as a part of an act of aggression, but as a part
of an action, now, of receding and trying to pull out.

It is under those conditions, and for those reasons---and because blood is being spilled, and lives lost, and will continue to be
as a result of the use of just such ammunition as we are destroying
here---that I say, let us not stay our hand now, and thus send the
enemy word that, "You will never be subjected to this again."

I hope we can pull out. I wish we could pull out tomorrow, out
of Cambodia, and stay out forever. But I know as long as we are
there, engaged in these battles, we ought not to be sending word to
the enemy, "We are going to leave you alone hereafter as far as this
area is concerned."

That is what we will be doing if we pass a law saying that our
Commander in Chief is prohibited from doing anything like this again,
regardless of the circumstances, unless he can get another law
passed.

There are a lot of things about this war that are not pleasing
to me. We have made plenty of mistakes. But I pray we will not make
this mistake. Not this one, sending such glad tidings to our adversaries, not only those in Hanoi, but those who are allied with
them---Peking, Moscow, and others---that we are going to tie a part
of our other hand behind us, and we are not going to proceed unless
another law can be passed.

Mr. President, I believe that when all these facts are exposed,
and this has sunken into the commonsense of the American people,
their verdict will be, "No; do not do it."

This is not a time to be stepping in [Page S7176.] here and stopping a procedure of battle that has every evidence of being highly profitable. There is no reason to promise now that we will never do it again unless we can get a law passed.

Mr. GRIFFIN. Mr. President, I wish to commend the distinguished Senator from Mississippi. Once again he has demonstrated that he is not only very learned and knowledgeable, but he is also a statesman as he rises at this point in the history of our country to say some things that ought to be said now on the floor of the Senate.

I am as concerned as any Senator about the prerogatives and the powers of the Congress, and particularly of the Senate.

But I do not understand the argument of some who support the amendment and variations thereof being talked about today. The Constitution says Congress shall have the power to declare war. Any Senator is perfectly within his rights if he wishes to introduce a resolution to declare war, or to argue the point that war ought to be declared or ought not to be declared, because the Constitution does say that Congress has the power to declare war.

It should be noted, however, that a declaration of war is a very broad policy declaration on the part of the Congress. On the other hand, the Constitution gives the President, as Commander in Chief of the Armed Forces, the responsibility for military decisions, strategy, tactics, and so forth. In Congress we cannot, and should not, attempt to make battlefield decisions, or to draw precise lines or to make decisions regarding the time or scope of a battle, nor should we try to direct the Commander in Chief specifically with regard to how battles should be conducted, or exactly where they should be conducted. Such decisions are beyond the Constitutional powers of Congress and it would not be in the interests of the United States for the Congress to attempt to make such decisions. I am very much concerned that the amendment before us gets into that territory and that area of decisionmaking---areas which are appropriately and properly left to the Commander in Chief.

As one Senator, I would not favor a declaration of war at this particular time, under these circumstances. At an earlier point I think that might have been a question properly to be put to the Senate. It is somewhat of a moot question now, because under the facts as they have developed, we are as a matter of fact engaged in a war with North Vietnam and the Vietcong.

We are not engaged in a war with Cambodia. We have not invaded Cambodia, as some of the critics say over and over again. We are not challenging the Government of Cambodia. We are not contesting the Armed Forces of Cambodia. In fact, we are not even on territory that the Government of Cambodia has occupied or controlled during recent years.

In Cambodia we are involved in hostilities with the same enemy and we are fighting him on territory and on geography that the enemy, and not the Government of Cambodia, has occupied and controlled during recent years.

As we consider these amendments resolutions, particularly the so-called Church-Cooper amendment, it is important to keep in mind

that one person is absolutely essential to the hope of negotiating a
peaceful settlement of this war, and one person is absolutely essential to the success of an orderly withdrawal of our troops. Of
course, that person is the President of the United States.

The credibility of the President of the United States is very
important. That the President of the United States should be believed; that others realize that he means what he says and says what
he means, is of utmost importance---not only in the United States,
but more important, as far as the enemy is concerned. Because if the
Senate should infer by the adoption of this amendment that we doubt,
or do not believe the President, then how can we expect the enemy to
believe what the President of the United States is saying?

Such an inference would not only be very damaging to the
prospects for peace, but it would also be very unfair, I submit, to
this President who has been cautious and very careful in his statements concerning the Vietnam war.

He has not made overly optimistic statements about our progress
in the war. He has made no promises that he has not felt firmly
convinced he could keep. On the basis of his record so far, surely
this President is entitled to some good faith support on the part of
Congress. He is entitled to the benefit of the doubt, particularly
because the credibility of the President of the United States is so
essential to the goals that we all want.

So, I believe the distinguished Senator from Mississippi is
performing a great service today when he points out the dangers that
are inherent in the amendment we are considering.

Even if we were to draft an amendment which was precisely tailor-
ed to the exact and actual intentions of the President, it seems to
me that it would be a mistake to adopt such an amendment. We would
be tying our own hands needlessly in a way that would serve the
enemy, and would make it more difficult to negotiate with the enemy.
I am sure the enemy would be delighted if we were to announce that
we are going to tie our own hands in this way.

So I hope that, as this debate goes on, that Senators and the
people will consider carefully what is at stake here, I hope and
trust that the Senate will not take any action which will have the
result of impeding the President in his efforts to withdraw our
troops on an orderly basis and to negotiate a settlement of this
conflict. . . .

THREE FOREIGN RELATIONS COMMITTEE AMENDMENTS*

The PRESIDING OFFICER. [Page S7177.] . . . The clerk will state
the first committee amendment.

The assistant legislative clerk read as follows:

On page 2, line 13, after the word "exceed," strike
out "$275,000,000 for the fiscal year 1970 and not to exceed

$272,500,000 for each of the fiscal years 1971 and 1972;"
and insert "$250,000,000 for each of the fiscal years
1970 and 1971."

The PRESIDING OFFICER. The question is on agreeing to the first
amendment. . . .

Mr. WILLIAMS of Delaware. Mr. President, I would hope that the
Senate would accept the amendment. It does reduce the amount from
$275 million to $250 million. It would restrict it to fiscal year
1970, which is about ended now and just for 1 year, 1971. This was
all approved, as I recall, pretty much unanimously by the committee,
and I would, therefore, certainly hope that the amendment would be
agreed to.

Mr. MANSFIELD. Mr. President, I would hope that the Senate
would follow the advice of the distinguished Senator from Delaware
because this is a reduction [Page S7178.]. It was approved unanimously in the committee. If we could have a voice vote, fine; otherwise, I will ask for the yeas and nays.

Mr. HANSEN. Mr. President, I ask for the yeas and nays. . . .

The result was announced---yeas 70, nays 3, as follows:

[No. 147 Leg.]

YEAS---70

Aiken	Fong	Muskie
Allen	Gore	Nelson
Allott	Griffin	Packwood
Anderson	Gurney	Pastore
Baker	Hansen	Pearson
Bellmon	Hartke	Pell
Bible	Hatfield	Percy
Boggs	Holland	Prouty
Burdick	Hollings	Proxmire
Byrd, Va.	Hruska	Randolph
Byrd, W. Va.	Hughes	Schweiker
Case	Inouye	Scott
Church	Jackson	Smith, Ill.
Cook	Javits	Sparkman
Cooper	Jordan, N. C.	Spong
Cotton	Jordan, Idaho	Stevens
Cranston	Magnuson	Symington
Curtis	Mansfield	Talmadge
Dole	McClellan	Tydings
Dominick	McGee	Williams, Del.
Eagleton	McGovern	Young, N. Dak.
Eastland	McIntyre	Young, Ohio
Ellender	Miller	
Fannin	Moss	

NAYS---3

Ervin   Thurmond   Tower

NOT VOTING---27

Bayh	Harris	Mundt
Bennett	Hart	Murphy
Brooke	Kennedy	Ribicoff
Cannon	Long	Russell
Dodd	Mathias	Saxbe
Fulbright	McCarthy	Smith, Maine
Goldwater	Metcalf	Stennis
Goodell	Mondale	Williams, N. J.
Gravel	Montoya	Yarborough

So the amendment on page 2, line 13, was agreed to.

The PRESIDING OFFICER. The clerk will state the next committee amendment.

The legislative clerk read as follows:

> On page 2, line 19, after the word "thereof," strike out "during the fiscal year 1970 shall not exceed $350,000,000 and during each of the fiscal years 1971 and 1972 shall not exceed $385,000,000," and insert "shall not exceed $300,000,000 for each of the fiscal years 1970 and 1971."

Mr. WILLIAMS of Delaware. Mr. President, this would reduce the amount of credit sales by $50 million. Again, as I recall, it was approved unanimously by the committee, and I hope the Senate will approve the amendment.

Upon request, I ask for the yeas and nays so that the conference will know the position of the Senate.

Mr. PASTORE. I ask for the yeas and nays, Mr. President.

The yeas and nays were ordered. . . . [Page S7179.]

The result was announced---yeas 64, nays 7, as follows:

[No. 148 Leg.]

YEAS---64

Aiken	Gurney	Packwood
Allen	Hansen	Pastore
Anderson	Hartke	Pearson
Baker	Hatfield	Pell
Bellmon	Holland	Percy
Bible	Hollings	Prouty
Boggs	Hruska	Proxmire

Burdick
Byrd, Va.
Byrd, W. Va.
Case
Church
Cook
Cooper
Cranston
Dole
Eagleton
Ellender
Fannin
Fong
Gore
Griffin

Hughes
Jackson
Javits
Jordan, N. C.
Jordan, Idaho
Magnuson
Mansfield
McClellan
McGee
McGovern
McIntyre
Miller
Moss
Muskie
Nelson

Randolph
Schweiker
Scott
Smith, Ill.
Sparkman
Spong
Stevens
Symington
Talmadge
Tydings
Williams, Del.
Young, N. Dak.
Young, Ohio

NAYS---7

Allott
Curtis
Eastland

Ervin
Smith, Maine
Thurmond

Tower

NOT VOTING---29

Bayh
Bennett
Brooke
Cannon
Cotton
Dodd
Dominick
Fulbright
Goldwater
Goodell

Gravel
Harris
Hart
Inouye
Kennedy
Long
Mathias
McCarthy
Metcalf
Mondale

Montoya
Mundt
Murphy
Ribicoff
Russell
Saxbe
Stennis
Williams, N. J.
Yarborough

So the second committee amendment, on page 2, beginning on line 19, was agreed to.

The PRESIDING OFFICER.   The clerk will report the final committee amendment.

The Legislative Clerk.   On page 4, line 21, insert the language down to and including line 21 on page 9.

The committee amendment is as follows:

Beginning on page 4, after line 20, insert as follows:

Sec. 7.   The Foreign Military Sales Act is further amended by adding at the end thereof the following new section:

Sec. 47.   Prohibition of Assistance to Cambodia.---In order to avoid the involvement of the United States in a wider war in Indochina and to expedite the withdrawal of American forces from Vietnam, it is hereby provided that,

unless specifically authorized by law hereafter enacted, no
funds authorized or appropriated pursuant to this Act or any
other law may be expended for the purpose of---

"(1) retaining United States forces in Cambodia;

"(2) paying the compensation or allowances of, or otherwise supporting, directly or indirectly, any United States
personnel in Cambodia who furnish military instruction to
Cambodian forces or engage in any combat activity in support
of Cambodian forces;

"(3) entering into or carrying out any contract or
agreement to provide military instruction in Cambodia, or
to provide persons to engage in any combat activity in support of Cambodian forces; or

"(4) conducting any combat activity in the air above
Cambodia in support of Cambodian forces."

Sec. 8.   Unless the sale, grant, loan, or transfer of
any International Fighter aircraft (1) has been authorized by
and made in accordance with the Foreign Military Sales Act or
the Foreign Assistance Act of 1961, or (2) is a regular commercial transaction (not financed by the United States) between a party other than the United States and a foreign
country, no such aircraft may be sold, granted, loaned, or
otherwise transferred to any foreign country (or agency thereof) other than South Vietnam.   For purposes of this section,
"International Fighter aircraft" means the fighter aircraft
developed pursuant to the authority contained in the proviso
of the second paragraph of section 101 of Public Law 91-121
(relating to military procurement for fiscal year 1970 and
other matters).

Sec. 9.   (a) Subject to the provisions of subsection
(b), the value of any excess defense article given to a foreign country or international organization during any fiscal
year shall be considered to be an expenditure made from funds
appropriated for that fiscal year to carry out the provisions
of part II of the Foreign Assistance Act of 1961, and at the
time of the delivery of that article a sum equal to the value
thereof shall be withdrawn from such funds and deposited in
the Treasury as miscellaneous receipts.

(b)   The provisions of subsection (a) shall apply during any fiscal year only to the extent that the aggregate
value of all such articles so given during that year exceeds
$35,000,000.

(c)   For purposes of this section "value" means not
less than 50 per centum of the amount the United States paid
at the time the excess defense articles were acquired by the
United States.

At the top of page 7, insert a new section, as follows:

Sec. 10. (a) No excess defense article may be given, and no grant of military assistance may be made, to a foreign country unless the country agrees---

(1) to deposit in a special account established by that country the following amounts of currency of that country:

(A) in the case of any excess defense article to be given to that country, an amount equal to 50 per centum of the fair value of the article, as determined by the Secretary of State, at the time the agreement to give the article to the country is made; and

(B) in the case of a grant of military assistance to be made to that country, and amount equal to 50 per centum of each such grant; and

(2) to make available to the United States Government, for use in paying obligations of the United States in that country and in financing international educational and cultural exchange activities in which that country participates under the programs authorized by the Mutual Educational and Cultural Exchange Act of 1961, such portion of the special account of that country as may be determined, from time to time, by the President to be necessary for any such use.

(b) Section 1415 of the Supplemental Appropriation Act, 1953 (31 U.S.C. 724), shall not be applicable to the provisions of this section.

On page 8, after line 2, insert a new section, as follows:

Sec. 11. (a) In considering a request for approval of any transfer of a defense article to another country under section 505 (a) (1) and (a) (4) of the Foreign Assistance Act of 1961, and section 3(a) (2) of the Foreign Military Sales Act, the President shall not give his consent to the transfer unless the United States itself would transfer the defense article under consideration to that country.

(b) The President shall not consent to the transfer by any foreign country or person to a third or subsequent country or person of any defense article given, loaned, or sold by the United States, or the sale of which is financed by the United States (through credit, guaranty, or otherwise), unless the foreign country or person which is to make the transfer first obtains from the country or person to which the transfer is to be made an agreement that such country or person will not give, sell, loan, or otherwise transfer such article to any other foreign country or person (1) without the consent of the President, and (2) without agreeing to obtain from such other foreign country an agreement not to give, sell, loan, or otherwise transfer such article without the consent of the President.

Sec. 12. (a) Notwithstanding any provision of law enacted before the date of enactment of this section, no
money appropriated for any purpose shall be available for
obligation or expenditure---

(1) unless the appropriation thereof has been previously authorized by law; or

(2) in excess of an amount previously prescribed by
law.

(b) To the extent that legislation enacted after the
making of an appropriation authorizes the obligation or
expenditure thereof, the limitation contained in subsection
(a) shall have no effect.

(c) The provisions of this section shall not be super-
seded except by a provision of law hereafter enacted which
specifically repeals or modifies the provisions of this
section.

Sec. 13. For purposes of sections 9, 10, and 11---

(1) "defense article" and "excess defense articles"
have the same meanings as given them in section 644 (d)
and (g), respectively, of the Foreign Assistance Act of
1961; and

(2) "foreign country" includes any department, agency,
or independent establishment of the foreign country.

Mr. GRIFFIN. Mr. President, the Chair said "the final committee
amendment." Is that correct?

The PRESIDING OFFICER. That is correct.

Mr. MANSFIELD. Mr. President, is the amendment now pending?

The PRESIDING OFFICER. The amendment is now pending.

The question is on agreeing to the amendment.

Mr. HOLLAND and Mr. HANSEN addressed the Chair.

The PRESIDING OFFICER. The Senator from Florida.

Mr. HOLLAND. Mr. President, I would like to address a question
to the Senator now handling the bill. I note that part of the amendment; namely, section 10, beginning at the top of page 7, and extending to the end of that section---indeed, extending to the bottom of
page 9, I think---relates in part to what is called "excess defense
article" and "excess defense articles."

I ask the handler of the bill if he can supply for the Record
a statement as to whether that term includes captured materiel, captured by our forces or coming into the possession of our forces,
[Page S7180.] from the raids of the sanctuaries, or otherwise. Before I conclude my question, I note that on page 9, beginning with

line 15, there is a provision which reads: "'defense article' and 'excess defense articles' have the same meanings as given them in sections 644 (d) and (g), respectively, of the Foreign Assistance Act of 1961"---which act we do not have before us.

I would like the Record to show, therefore, what is meant by the terms "excess defense article" and "excess defense articles" in this bill, as to whether or not that term covers captured material, arms and other captured material of use to armed forces.

Mr. CHURCH. First, Mr. President, I ask that the pertinent provisions of the law referred to in section 13 of the pending bill--- section 644 (d) and (g), respectively, of the Foreign Assistance Act of 1961---appear at this point in the Record.

There being no objection, the sections of the statute referred to were ordered to be printed in the Record, as follows:

Sec. 644. Definitions.---As used in this Act---

*   *   *   *   *

(d) "Defense article" includes:
(1) any weapon, weapons system, munition aircraft, vessel, boats, or other implement of war;

(2) any property, installation, commodity, material, equipment, supply, or goods used for the purposes of furnishing military assistance;

(3) any machinery, facility, tool, material, supply, or other item necessary for the manufacture, production, processing repair, servicing, storage, construction, transportation, operation, or use of any article listed in this subsection; or

(4) any component or part of any article listed in this subsection; but shall not include merchant vessels, or, as defined by the Atomic Energy Act of 1954, as amended (42 U.S.C. 2011), source material, byproduct material, special nuclear material, or atomic weapons.

*   *   *   *   *

(g) "Excess defense articles" mean the quantity of defense articles owned by the United States Government which is in excess of the mobilization reserve at the time such articles are dropped from inventory by the supplying agency for delivery to countries or international organizations as grant assistance under this Act.

Mr. HANSEN. Mr. President, will the Senator yield?

Mr. CHURCH. One minute, please. I would like to finish my statement.

Mr. HOLLAND. I have another question also.

Mr. CHURCH. I believe that these two provisions of the law should appear in the Record, so that they are available for everyone to read.

Mr. HOLLAND. Since they are not available now, will the distin- quished Senator state for the Record whether the provisions of the pending bill to which I have referred, "excess defense article" and "excess defense articles," include or exclude captured materiel and goods of military usefulness?

Mr. CHURCH. Although the committee did not raise that particular question, the two provisions of the law seem to be sufficiently in- clusive to embrace captured weapons.

However, the Senator raises a question for which I am not now prepared to give a precise answer. We shall endeavor to get that answer, and as soon as we have it, I will inform the Seantor, and place the answer in the Record.

Mr. HOLLAND. Mr. President, if the Senator will yield further, while I am not in a position to make any commitment as to my position on this amendment whatever at this time, I would hope, regardless of what that position may be, that the provision of this amendment is not so broad as to preclude our Armed Forces in the field from supplying to allies or those who are defending themselves in Cambodia or in Laos with guns, ammunition, and material of all kinds which have been captured from the North Vietnamese or the Vietcong.

Mr. CHURCH. I can reassure the Senator on that particular point. As he knows, a certain quantity of AK-47's which were captured from the North Vietnamese and the Vietcong in Vietnam have already been transferred to the new Cambodian Government.

The amendment does not prohibit the transfer of weapons of that kind to Cambodia. It addresses itself, rather, to a prohibition against American military advisers. The committee left out any ref- erence to such weapons because it was not the committee's intention to exclude the transfer of small arms to Cambodia. It was our inten- tion, rather, to prevent us from getting involved in an escalating type of military assistance program that would necessitate our sup- plying Cambodia with American military advisers and other military personnel. . . .

DOLE SUBSTITUTE FOR COOPER-CHURCH AMENDMENT*

[Page S7182.] The Senate continued with the consideration of the bill (H.R. 15628) to amend the Foreign Military Sales Act.

Mr. DOLE. Mr. President, will the Senator from Idaho yield?

Mr. CHURCH. I am happy to yield for questions.

Mr. DOLE. Mr. President, on Tuesday of this week, the junior Senator from Kansas submitted an amendment which I may offer as sub- stitute language for the so-called Church-Cooper amendment. At that time I said, and repeat today, that I applaud the sincere efforts,

of the Senator from Idaho, the Senator from Kentucky, and other sponsors of the Church-Cooper amendment; but I also share the concerns of
others in this Chamber regarding the right of any President to protect
American troops.

I am wondering whether the Senator from Idaho has had an opportunity to study the proposed amendment that I submitted on Tuesday.
It reads:

> In line with the expressed intention of the President
> of the United States, no funds authorized or appropriated
> pursuant to this Act or any other law shall be used to
> finance the introduction of American ground combat troops
> into Laos, Thailand, or Cambodia without the prior consent
> of the Congress, except to the extent that the introduction
> of such troops is required, as determined by the President
> and reported promptly to the Congress, to protect the lives
> of American troops remaining within South Vietnam.

This was commonly known in the other body as the Findley amendment. It was adopted by the other body and later dropped from the
Military Sales Act.

It occurs to me this language does, in essence, what the authors
of the Church-Cooper amendment intends to do or proposes to do. At
the same time, it does give the President that right, the right which
he might have in any event, to protect American troops remaining in
South Vietnam.

I take this opportunity to exchange my views with those of the
Senator from Idaho, if he has any comment to make.

Mr. CHURCH. I would say, first of all, to the Senator that the
substitute he proposes would, in my judgment, render the Cooper-Church
effort meaningless. If this language is adopted, the Senate will
merely be making an idle gesture. With all deference to the Senator,
the exception he recommends provides a loophole big enough to drive
the Pentagon through.

If we are to make a serious effort, within the constitutional
powers of Congress, to establish the outer perimeters on American penetration into Cambodia, it will be necessary, then, to adopt the language that the committee approved, or something very close to it.

The proposed subsitiute offered by the distinguished Senator from
Kansas is unacceptable. It would gut the amendment, rendering it
meaningless.

Mr. DOLE. Let me say to the Senator from Idaho that that is not
the intent of the Senator from Kansas. I am wondering, with reference
to the Senator's amendment, would he concede, notwithstanding the
language in the amendment, that the President has the constitutional
power and the constitutional right and obligation to take any action
he felt necessary to protect American troops.

Mr. CHURCH. I would say to the Senator that Senator Cooper and I have drafted our amendment in such a way as not to challenge the rights the President may have, under the Constitution, to act as Commander in Chief. We have also taken great pains to draft the amendment in such fashion as to assert powers that we believe are vested by the Constitution to the U.S. Congress. We have merely provided that the money appropriated by Congress shall not be available for the purpose of retaining American troops in Cambodia, or for the purpose of setting up an escalating military assistance program that could lead to an entangling alliance with the new Cambodian regime. These are the objectives of the amendment. They clearly fall within the power of Congress. They simply hold the President within the limits of his declared policy but, if he should decide later that these limits need to be exceeded, that the United States should extend its occupation of Cambodia, or enter into an obligation to come to the military assistance and defense of the Cambodian Government, then he would have to come back to Congress, present his case, and ask Congress to lift the limitations.

That kind of procedure reasserts the responsibilities the Constitution vests in Congress, powers which Congress should have been asserting down through the years.

With all deference to the distinguished Senator from Kansas, if we were to substitute his amendment in place of this amendment, we would merely be making an empty gesture.

Mr. DOLE. Mr. President, let me say and make it very clear that I share some of the reservations of the distinguished Senator from Idaho, and so stated at the outset publicly, that I hope our efforts in Cambodia were to protect American troops, and to keep the Vietnamization program on schedule, not an effort to shore up the Lon Nol government. Thus, I share the concern of the Senator from Idaho, the Senator from Kentucky, and others who have joined as cosponsors; but the point is that, notwithstanding the language in the Senator's amendment, or consistent with the language in the Senator's amendment, does the Senator from Idaho agree or disagree that the President, as Commander in Chief, notwithstanding the passage of the amendment and the enactment of the amendment as part of the Military Sales Act, would still have the power, under the Constitution, to go back into Cambodia or any country to protect American troops?

Mr. CHURCH. Whatever authority the President has under the Constitution, Congress cannot take from him. That is, however, only one side of the coin. The other side has to do with the authority of Congress, as vested in it by the Constitution. The Cooper-Church amendment is designed to assert that authority in such a way as to keep the present Cambodian operation within the limits declared by the President as his objective. It is idle for us to write language regarding the President's own constitutional authority. That is why we have avoided any reference to the President or to his responsibilities as Commander in Chief. We have confined our amendment to that authority which belongs to Congress---determining how and where public money can be spent.

Further, the Senator mentioned, in connection with his proposed amendment, that the Senate had earlier passed an amendment, which became law, limiting the expenditure of funds in regard to the introduction of American ground combat troops into either Laos or Thailand.

That amendment passed this body on December 15, 1969. It reads as follows:

In line with the expressed intention of the President of the United States, none of the funds appropriated by this act shall be used to finance the introduction of American ground combat troops into Laos or Thailand.

We did not then go on to say---

. . . except to the extent that the introduction of such troops is required, as determined by the President and reported promptly to the Congress, to protect the lives of American troops remaining within South Vietnam.

It was not thought necessary, then, to say that. It is not necessary now. Whatever power the President has under the Constitution we cannot take from him. But we can establish limits on the expenditure of public money, so that; if he wants to exceed those limits, he must then come back to Congress, present his case, and ask us to lift the limitations.

Mr. SYMINGTON.   Mr. President, will the Senator from Idaho yield?

Mr. DOLE.   Mr. President, will the Senator from Idaho yield further?
Mr. CHURCH.   I promised to yield to the Senator from Missouri. I shall then be happy to yield further to the Senator from Kansas.

Mr. SYMINGTON.   Mr. President, for personal reasons, it was not possible for me to be on the Senate floor on December 15 last. I am interested in an article from the newspapers on that day, which pointed out that the White House endorsed the amendment with respect to Laos and Thailand as being consistent with administration policy in Southeast Asia. The article quoted the minority leader as saying:

[Page S7183.] . . . After a White House meeting that President Nixon had told the Congressional Republican leaders that the prohibition, adopted yesterday by the Senate was "definitely in line with Administration policy."

Ronald L. Zeigler, the Presidential secretary, gave added emphasis to the Administration's acceptance of the Senate move by saying the White House regarded the prohibition as an "endorsement" rather than a "curbing" of Administration policy.

The amendment to the defense appropriations bill, adopted yesterday by a 73-17 vote, states: "In line with the expressed intention of the President of the United States, none of the funds appropriated by this act shall be used to finance the introduction of American ground combat troops into Laos or Thailand."

This wording, it was disclosed today, was approved by the White House in advance of adoption.

In the wake of the Senate action, the amendment, hastily drafted during a secret session on American

military involvement in Laos, was being subjected to
varying interpretations as to its significance and impact.

Senator Frank Church, Democrat of Idaho, the principal author of the amendment, described it as a "reassertion of Congressional prerogatives" in foreign policy, designed to make clear that the President could not
commit combat troops to Laos or Thailand without the
specific consent of Congress.

I have been in that part of the world many times, and do not see
any major difference between the terrain and problems of any of those
various countries; or differences with respect to what is or is not
the authority of the President, or of the Congress, with respect to
our relationships with said countries.

Does the Senator agree?

Mr. CHURCH. Mr. President, I agree wholeheartedly. As the Senator well knows, there lies within Laos as much of a threat to our
forces as lies within Cambodia. In Laos, the Communist supply lines
extend down the Ho Chi Minh trail. When we prohibited the use of any
funds in the military appropriations bill for fiscal year 1970 for the
purpose of introducing American ground combat troops in Laos, there
was no outcry from the White House that this was undermining presidential authority or conveying a message to the world that we were trying
to tie the President's hands. Yet, the same principles were involved
then as are involved now.

All of a sudden, we are told that a series of ominous developments will occur if the Senate rouses itself from its lengthy slumber
and begins to assert some of its constitutional authority.

Mr. SYMINGTON. Mr. President, I appreciate what the able Senator
says, because this latest venture seems comparable to the point of
similarity. It was in October that we found out, whereas the ground
war in Vietnam was being deescalated openly, the air war over Laos was
being heavily escalated in secret.

I am sure everyone wants to see hostilities out there lessened,
and the whole business terminated at earliest opportunity.

Mr. President, I worry about all this sudden apprehension over
the amendment now being offered by the able Senator from Idaho because of the parallel aspect of the amendment that everyone seemed
to agree on last December, only a few months ago.

I am especially worried because the people did not know what was
going on in Laos until we finally got our hearings out to the public
in April, many months after the testimony had been taken.

When it comes to Cambodia, no one in the Congress, to the best
of my knowledge---and I am on both of the committees primarily in-
volved---knew anything about it until well after our troops were in
combat in Cambodia.

I hope that any apprehension on the part of any Senator with respect to Cambodia---an apprehension that was conspicuously lacking with respect to Laos or Thailand last December---does not mean there will be more wars out there; or that we will have more combat instead of less.

I thank the Senator.

Mr. CHURCH. Mr. President, I thank the distinguished Senator from Missouri, I agree with him that the action we in the Senate took last December came following disclosures made in executive session dealing with the extent to which we had been committed in Laos, without our having even been informed.

Basic constitutional questions are at issue here. Are we going to permit our Government to slide relentlessly toward all power being concentrated in the hands of one Chief Executive?

Are we going to permit our Government to become a Caesardom, or are we going to reassert the authority that the Constitution placed in Congress?

That is the fundamental issue, I find it very hard to understand why objection is being raised, when the limitations we seek to impose are so reasonable, so modest, and so much in conformity with the President's own declared purposes.

And it also raises the same question that the Senator from Missouri posed here earlier. Is there something else the President has in mind? Are we going still further, or returning to Cambodia again and again?

If that is the case, then all the more reason for setting the outer limits and for requiring the President to come here and seek our advice and consent concerning any move that would involve us still deeper in the morass of Southeast Asia.

Mr. SYMINGTON. Mr. President, I heard the Vice President of the Government of South Vietnam on the television this morning. The net effect of what he had to say was that he did not have any intentions of stopping at any particular line in Cambodia.

It seems to me this is another illustration of why the limitation on what we supply, as presented in this amendment, is so important. General Ky is going right ahead in Cambodia, based on what it was said he asserted this morning.

I wish that the statement made by our distinguished Ambassador to South Vietnam in executive session before the Foreign Relations Committee only this morning, and in reply to my bringing this interview up could be printed in the Record at this point. Of course, it cannot be. But I must say the whole Indochina operation is becoming increasingly disturbing.

I have never taken the floor before to criticize in this way the conduct of this war by this Administration; but I just do not want to see our people again in the position where they think we are doing one thing, only to find out later we were actually doing another.

I am puzzled about current policy of the United States, all over
the world. Only a few days ago---I believe earlier this week---I went
to a meeting in the House Office Building attended by many distinquished Members of the Congress.

Among those who talked in very strong fashion in support of now
supplying badly needed planes to the State of Israel were the distinquished minority leader of the Senate, the Senator from Pennsylvania
(Mr. SCOTT), and the distinguished minority leader of the House of
Representatives, Representative Ford.

They assured the group gathered at this luncheon of their full
support of Israel when it came to selling them the planes in question;
good, because this is the only country that could sell them these
modern planes, except for France and the Soviet Union.

I heard this morning also that 168 young Americans were killed
last week in Southeast Asia. That is many more than have been killed
for many weeks, as a result of these new offensives in Cambodia.

In effect for justification for our being in the Far East we are
told the wars in Indochina are important to the security of the United
States. We must defend this country against Communist satellites in
that part of the world.

If it is important for us to defend the United States and all
other countries of the free world against Communist satellites in the
Far East, why is it not to our own interest, especially when we are
the only country willing and able to do so, to sell airplanes to the
one country that without any American military, the only country I
know of so fighting without our assistance, is fighting Communist
satellites in the Middle East?

This is one of those peculiar twists in the foreign policy of the
United States that is not entirely clear to me.

Mr. President, let me commend the able Senator from Idaho. I
listened for many hours to him and our colleague on the other side of
the aisle, the senior Senator from Kentucky, when they drafted this
amendment. I am glad to support it especially in that I note the able
majority leader and the ranking Republican, not only of the Foreign
Relations Committee, but of the Senate, are now also cosponsors.

Whereas I have full respect for the authority under the Constitution of the President of the United States, I have equal pride,
under the advise-and-consent clause of the Constitution, for the
prerogatives and rights of the Congress of the United States, of
which I am a Member.

I thank my able friend.

Mr. CHURCH. Mr. President, I very much thank the Senator for his
spendid contribution to the debate.

I remember, apropos of the Senate's [Page S7184.] action last
December in limiting the use of public money for the purpose of introducing American ground combat troops into Laos, that we took that
action after we finally learned the facts. Things have come to a
sorry pass in this country when neither the American people nor the

Congress is even told that our country is being involved overtly in combat in a foreign country.

Mr. DOLE. Mr. President, will the Senator yield?

Mr. CHURCH. I shall yield to the Senator in just a moment.

What was true with respect to Laos is also true of Cambodia. We tried to find out what was planned for Cambodia. Twice the Secretary of State came to meet with the Committee on Foreign Relations, once on April 2 and again on April 27. At neither time were we told, nor was it hinted to us, that the President intended to order American troops into Cambodia.

Mr. SYMINGTON. Mr. President, will the Senator yield?

Mr. CHURCH. I yield.

Mr. SYMINGTON. Would the Senator have included Cambodia in his resolution last December if he had had the remotest conception that we would be attaching Cambodia at this time?

Mr. CHURCH. If anyone had suggested that Cambodia was on the list, there is no question in my mind that Cambodia would have been added to Laos and Thailand. I am sorry it was not. Perhaps if we had added it then, we would not be faced with this serious crisis now.

Mr. President, I yield to the Senator from Kansas.

Mr. DOLE. I take issue with the word "attack" used by the distinquished Senator from Missouri. I also remind him that another great Missourian, former President Truman, went into Korea without the consent of Congress.

Let me say to the Senator from Idaho that I supported and voted for the resolution on Laos and Thailand. The Senator knows the language of my substitute is almost identical with the language drafted with great care by the Senator from Idaho and others, except it has one additional provision.

Does the Senator believe the President, whoever he may be, has a right, notwithstanding whatever Congress might do, to protect American troops?

Mr. CHURCH. As I said before and will say again, whatever right the President has, is vested in him by the Constitution.

It is not within the legislative power of Congress to deny him that right. That is not what we are trying to do here. We are trying to assert the rights we have under the Constitution.

Mr. DOLE. I concur in that.

Mr. CHURCH. If the Senator would stop where we stopped in December and suggest, in line with what we have already done, that in the case of Cambodia, we adopt a similar amendment which would read:

In line with the expressed intention of the President of the

United States, no funds authorized or appropriated shall
be used to finance the introduction of American ground
combat troops into Laos, Thailand, or Cambodia without the
prior consent of the Congress---

Then I would consider it as a substitute. It is the final language that undoes the limitation.

The final proviso reads, "except to the extent that the introduction of such troops is required, as determined by the President and
reported promptly to the Congress, to protect the lives of American
troops remaining within South Vietnam."

Mr. DOLE. Mr. President, will the Senator yield?

Mr. CHURCH. I shall yield to the Senator in a moment.

It is our responsibility here to set limits with respect to the
spending of public money. We cannot undertake to define the President's power, but we can undertake to set limits on the expenditure
of public funds. If the President feels those limits should be exceeded, let him come here and make his case.

Mr. DOLE. I appreciate the Senator's expertise. The Senator is
an expert in this area and I wish to ask this question. In the event
the Cooper-Church proposal passed, as in the case of the amendment
last December, which was by a vote of 73 to 17, as I recall, does the
Senator believe that takes away any right of the President or gives
him more rights than he had under the Constitution? In the Senator's
opinion would it mean that he had a right to protect American troops,
if it meant crossing a border into Laos or Thailand? What is the
Senator's best judgment?

Mr. CHURCH. My best judgment is that he did not send troops into
Laos, which it was recommended that he do, because he recognized that
Congress had established limits in the law with respect to Laos and
Thailand. In other words, if we assert our authority, we can establish
limitations which the President will respect. If he feels the need,
he will come here and present his case. That was the role Congress
was authorized to fulfill in regard to war and peace until we abdicated our authority, placing most of it in the President's hands. We
do very little nowadays except vote the money, while leaving it to the
President to decide who, where, and when we shall fight.

We have reached the point, however, where we must reassert our
constitutional powers. We must now recognize that Congress must re-
cover its authority in those areas that mean the most to the country,
such as war and peace, and ultimately, the life and death of this
Republic.

Mr. DOLE. Does the Senator from Idaho agree or disagree that a
President, whether it be President Nixon or some other President, has
the right under the Constitution to protect American forces? Does
the Senator agree that he has this right, or does the Senator believe
he does not have this right? Perhaps we can work out some accommodation on the language if we can agree.

Mr. CHURCH. I repeat to the Senator what I have said before,
because it is the only way I know to say it. I do not believe the
power lies with the Senate or the House of Representatives, or both
bodies of Congress, to define the President's authority under the
Constitution. That would be an act of futility.

On the other hand, we can move affirmatively within the bounds of our own powers, and that is what this amendment is designed to do. But if you "fudge" it up, then it is an empty gesture, and the Senate becomes nothing more than a fudge factory.

Mr. DOLE. I would like to ask the Senator what happens if we agree to the amendment and then the President finds it necessary to move troops across a boundary line? Is he then faced with another confrontation with Congress because we would not make clear what the President's rights might be in that case?

Mr. CHURCH. There is no doubt in my mind that if ever the safety of American troops is involved, then the President can make his case and the Congress will quickly move to do whatever is necessary to support the President in his efforts to safeguard American troops. There is no problem along these lines. That is a decision which should be shared between the President and the Congress, as the Constitution intended. It is not a decision which lies exclusively in the power of one man. The President can always come up here and present his case. If we draw no limits, then it is open to him to act alone, which he has been doing, and which his recent predecessors have been doing. In fact, it is this process which has gotten us stuck so fast in a bottomless bog in Southeast Asia.

Mr. DOLE. In the face of imminent danger to American troops, the Senator says the President must come to Congress and request the authority from Congress to give protection to these American troops?

Mr. CHURCH. I have said, and I do not think it is necessary to say it again---

Mr. DOLE. I feel it is necessary and beyond that vital.

Mr. CHURCH. That if the President should act under his authority, as vested in him by the Constitution of the United States, this authority cannot be diminished or withheld from him by Congress; but we also have authority that we can assert, and that is the objective of the Church-Cooper Amendment.

Mr. GORE. Mr. President, will the Senator yield?

Mr. CHURCH. I yield.

Mr. GORE. I have listened with a great deal of interest to this colloquy, which deals with a fundamental constitutional question. I would like briefly and impromptu to express some views.

The genius of our system is that we have coordinate, coequal branches of government, with checks and balances one upon the others and the others upon the one. The warmaking powers are vested in the legislative and the executive. A war cannot be waged except with the support of both.

By the rationale advanced, by my distinguished and able friend the junior Senator from Kansas, the President would have the authority to launch an attack upon China tomorrow, or tonight, or at this moment, without the approval of Congress. China is a sanctuary, indeed [Page 7185.] the greatest sanctuary of the war, to the enemy in Southeast Asia. It supplies rice, ammunition, the supplies, equip-

ment, and materiel of all sorts. So by that reasoning, by that rationale, without the approval of the elected representatives of the
people, the Congress, indeed, even without any consultation with them,
the President could say, it is in the interest of saving American
lives, the lives of those who are now in Vietnam, to bomb, to attack,
to eradicate the sanctuary in Red China.

    Would not that be just as logical, just as constitutional, as
what we have just heard?

    Mr. CHURCH. I must concede that it would. The Senator's ar-
gument underscores the fact that the authors of our Constitution
never envisioned that a President, on his own decision, would send
American troops to a war in a distant, foreign country.

    The whole purpose of placing the war power in the hands of Con-
gress was to make certain that such a fateful decision would be formulated by the representatives of all the people, including the
President, and not by the Chief Executive alone. Why, the framers
of the Constitution would turn in their graves if they knew how the
shared responsibility, which they provided in that document, has
eroded away.

    Mr. GORE. Mr. President, will the Senator yield?

    Mr. CHURCH. I am happy to yield.

    Mr. GORE. This seems to the senior Senator from Tennessee a
strange interpretation for one who is a self-proclaimed strict constructionist. I must say that I was struck by the lack of logic, by
the lack of reasoning, by the absence of principle, when the President said to a group of Representatives and Senators, at which conference I was sitting beside the distinguished senior Senator from
Idaho, that he would not go farther than 35 kilometers without the
approval of Congress. I thought that strange. A President who,
without the approval or even consultation with Congress, had ordered
an invasion of a sovereign country by thousands of American troops
was yet telling representatives of the people that he would not invade farther than 20 miles without the approval of Congress.

    What is the difference in principle between 20 miles and 30
miles, or the whole country?

    Mr. CHURCH. It escapes me.

    Mr. GORE. The tragic mistake was ordering the invasion, the
crossing of the boundary of a small neutral country. When the reaction in the country and in the world was adverse then to placate
the Congress he promises about 50 of us that he will not invade
farther than 20 or 21 miles without the approval of Congress and
that all U.S. troops would be withdrawn from Cambodia by June 30,
1970. But now that the Congress wishes by this resolution to take
his promise at face value, a lobbying effort is undertaken and the
propaganda minions are unloosed to accuse those of us who wish to be
strict constructionists of the Constitution where war or peace and
the lives of American boys are concerned of being unpatriotic. Deplorable, perfectly deplorable.

    Mr. CHURCH. I thank the Senator from Tennessee for his comments.

Mr. PELL. Mr. President, will the Senator yield?

Mr. CHURCH. I yield to the Senator from Rhode Island.

Mr. PELL. Along the line of the previous questions and points,
when the partriotism of those of us who support this amendment, who
believe our present policies wrong, is questioned by the two largest
veterans' organizations, I think it is of interest to note that 82
percent of the sponsors of the amendment under discussion are veterans, as opposed to 71 percent in this body as a whole. I think it
is an interesting statistic.

Now I would like to ask the Senator, who, as a lawyer, is more
educated in the law than I am, and is also versed in international
law, what is the difference between the sanctuaries in Thailand from
which our bombers move and the sanctuaries in Cambodia from which
the North Vietnamese move.

Mr. CHURCH. The difference is that the Thai sanctuaries are
ours and the Cambodian sanctuaries are theirs.

[Laughter in the galleries.]

Mr. BYRD of West Virginia. Mr. President, may we have order in
the galleries?

The PRESIDING OFFICER. The galleries will be in order.

Mr. PELL. I thank the Senator for that correct reply.

What would be the difference in international law if, just as we,
the big brother of South Vietnam, have moved into Cambodia to extirpate North Vietnam's sanctuaries, let us say China, as big brother
of North Vietnam, offered to extirpate our sanctuaries in Thailand.
So far North Vietnam has intelligently resisted the blandishments
of China, but suppose one day she succombed. Would there be any difference in international law?

Mr. CHURCH. I say to the Senator that the sequence of possibilities he suggests exposes the weakness of the decision that the
President has made to strike against the Cambodian sanctuaries.
After all, all of Indochina behind the enemy lines constitutes the
enemy's sanctuary, and, as the Senator has observed, we have our
sanctuaries, too, in Thailand, in the sea around the Indochina
peninsula---dominated entirely by American naval forces---and even,
in a sense, in the air above the battleground, which is also dominated by American air forces.

If this war becomes a pursuit of sanctuaries, then, if past
experience is any guide, our thrusts will be met by enemy counter-
thrusts, and the danger, of course, is that this will force a
spreading of the war, perhaps beyond our imaginations.

Mr. PELL. I would like to ask another question of the Senator
in the field of law, where I need perhaps to be educated a little
more.

It has seemed to me that in the last few days that a new di-
mension has been added to the Cambodian invasion, or involvement,

or incursion, or whatever we wish to call it, in that we are now not only involved on the land and in the air, but we are also involved on the sea. We in the Committee on Foreign Relations took some note of that fact, and actually strengthened the amendment of the Senator from Idaho to cover the sea forces on the river. But at that time events were moving so fast that we did not realize that what seems to be a blockade would be extended at sea.

As I understand it, now there is what is called a protective patrol, which, from my memory of service in World War II, means a blockade around Cambodia and South Vietnam up to the DMZ line.

In other words, we are treating Cambodia more sternly, when it comes to a naval blockade or whatever we call it, than we are Hanoi and Haiphong, which seems odd.

I was wondering if the Senator's recollection is the same as mine, that a blockade usually means war, is considered as an act of war or can be considered as an act leading to war.

Mr. CHURCH. The Senator is correct.

Mr. PELL. And, in order to be legal, does it not have to be effective, in other words total?

Mr. CHURCH. I would not attempt to pass judgment upon the legality of a blockade. The actual effectiveness of a blockade depends upon its totality.

Mr. PELL. All of these questions on which I am being educated bear out the necessity for the passage of the amendment under discussion, and I further affirm my delight and pride in being one of the cosponsors.

Mr. CHURCH. I thank the Senator very much for his generous comment.

Mr. HOLLINGS. Mr. President, will the distinguished Senator yield?

Mr. CHURCH. I am happy to yield.

Mr. HOLLINGS. Would the distinguished Senator pass on the legality as to the effective date? Is the intent, since it is an appropriations act, not until July 1? Is that the intent?

Mr. CHURCH. No; the amendment is written in such a way that it would take effect upon its enactment into law; that is, it would take effect immediately after signed into law by the President.

Mr. HOLLINGS. So, then, in that provision, for example, on page 5 at lines 4 and 5, "it is hereby provided that, unless specifically authorized by law hereafter enacted, no funds authorized or appropriated pursuant to this Act or any other law," since the moneys presently being expended for the military activity that we now have in course in Cambodia are being expended under "any other law," it would, immediately upon signature, cut off funds for the present military activity in Cambodia at this time, or prior to July 1?

Mr. CHURCH. I would like to clarify that for the distinguished Senator.

Mr. HOLLINGS. Yes.

Mr. CHURCH. The amendment goes into effect upon enactment, but the amendment provides that no funds shall be appropriated, or no appropriated funds shall be used, for certain purposes. So the effect of the amendment has to be considered in the light of those purposes.

[Page S7186.] The first purpose is against retaining American forces in Cambodia. If it were to happen that this amendment could be affixed to this bill, could go to conference, could survive conference, and then go to the President for his signature before the current operations are finished---

Mr. HOLLINGS. Right.

Mr. CHURCH. The language of the bill would still be such as to permit the President to complete the present operation.

The amendment prohibits American forces from being retained, in Cambodia. The President has said he does not intend to retain American forces in Cambodia. He has assured the country that they will be coming out within the next few weeks, and that he will withdraw all American forces from Cambodia, in any case, on or before July 1 of this year.

So the amendment is drafted to permit him to proceed with the present engagement within the confines of his own declared policy. It would, however, prohibit him from changing that policy and retaining American forces in Cambodia, without first obtaining congressional consent.

Mr. HOLLINGS. But on page 5, that number, which is "retaining," is succeeded by No. (2), which says "paying the compensation or allowances of, or otherwise supporting, directly or indirectly, any U.S. personnel in Cambodia."

Mr. CHURCH. As instructors. This is the second objective of the amendment, which is to prohibit the use of funds for sending American military advisers and instructors into Cambodia in support of Cambodian forces. According to the President, there are none there now.

The President has stated, moreover, that the only military assistance he has thus far approved has been the transfer of small arms to Cambodia. Our purpose is to prevent that modest military assistance program, which involves no American personnel, from escalating into the transfer of sophisticated weapons, requiring American instructors and American advisers. This would move us into Cambodia as we moved into Vietnam, first with a modest military assistance program, then with military instructors, advisers, and personnel, and finally with combat troops.

Mr. HOLLINGS. Obviously, from the Senator's answer, he understands it clearly. But in this use of terminology, where some say we are "withdrawing" and others say we are "invading," we cannot tell which direction we are headed. Would the Senator object to a July 1 effective date, since he says all this is going to end by July 1 and

since this is an appropriation act for the next fiscal year, and that
is what the Senator intends and the President intends? Would that be
all right?

    Mr. CHURCH. I certainly would give it serious consideration. I
would want to discuss it with other sponsors and cosponsors of the
amendment.

    This particular point came up in committee hearings. I want to
tell the Senator the reasons that we decided not to put the actual
date into the amendment so that he will understand why it was that a
specific date was not included.

    The first reason was that it might be construed as an approval
of the action, which concerned some members of the committee very
gravely.

    Second, it was felt that a dateline, though it is the President's
own declared dateline, might be held up as a manacle to the President
which would prevent him necessary latitude of a week or two if developments in the field made that desirable.

    We wanted to give him all the flexibility he should reasonably
have, while still taking him at his word, that we decided not to
insert the date.

    However, an argument can be made on the other side of that pro-
position; and I know the argument, I respect it, and I say to the
Senator that any suggestion along that line would be one that we
would seriously reflect upon.

    Mr. CHURCH. Mr. President, I know that the Senator from Kansas
wishes the floor, and I will not detain him much longer!

    I do think it is interesting, however, in view of the questions
he posed earlier, to remember that in 1846 President Polk sent American forces into disputed territory in Texas which precipitated the
clash that began the Mexican War.

    Abraham Lincoln was then a Congressman from Illinois, and he
took strong exception to the Presidential decision that led to our
involvement in the Mexican War. He wrote some memorable words concerning the Constitution and the intended limits on Presidential
discretion in the matter of war. I should like to read those words
to the Senate. Abraham Lincoln wrote:

        Allow the President to invade a neighboring nation
    whenever he shall deem it necessary to repel an invasion,
    and you allow him to do so whenever he may choose to say
    he deems it necessary for such purpose---and you allow
    him to make war at pleasure. Study to see if you can
    fix any limit to his power in this respect, after you
    have given him so much as you propose.

        The provision of the Constitution giving the war-
    making power to Congress, was dictated, as I understand
    it, by the following reasons. Kings have always been
    involving and impoverishing their people in wars, pre-
    tending generally, if not always, that the good of the

people was the object. This, our convention undertook
to be the most oppressive of all kingly oppressions; and
they resolved to frame the Constitution that no one man
should hold the power of bringing this oppression upon us.

I yield the floor.

Mr. DOLE. Mr. President, I am aware of that quotation by Lincoln,
and I am aware that he lost the next election. I am not certain it
was because of his position on that issue.

Mr. CHURCH. Mr. President, will the Senator yield?

Mr. DOLE. I yield.

Mr. CHURCH. I think it was. I think he did, indeed, lose the
next election because he stood on a constitutional principle that he
felt was more important.

Mr. DOLE. Mr. President, let me remind the Senator from Idaho,
as I stated on Tuesday---and again today---that I approve in part, of
his efforts. I know of his sincerity and that of the senior Senator
from Kentucky.

Everyone, with the exception of some 17 members, supported the
Senator from Idaho's amendment on December 15 of last year with reference to Laos and Thailand. I have quickly reviewed the debate on
that amendment, and find no reference at all to protection of American troops. Of course, there was no reference to Cambodia because
at that time Sihanouk was still in power, and it is understandable
why we did not concern ourselves with that country at that time.

I can also understand why we did not address ourselves at that
time to the very vital question---and perhaps the overriding question
---in my mind and that of other Senators, and that is the protection of
American troops and what right the President may have in respect
thereto. We all recognize, and say publicly---that we should not be
involved in another Vietnam, whether it be in Laos, Thailand, Cambodia, or wherever. But I remind my colleagues that President Nixon
has kept the faith. He has kept his promises with reference to South
Vietnam. He has announced troop withdrawals, and he has carried out
each troop withdrawal on schedule---in fact, in some cases ahead of
schedule.

It appears that in our efforts to circumscribe the powers of the
President, we are saying to the President, in this instance, "Even
though you say you will disengage from Cambodia on July 1, even though
you are reducing the war in Vietnam, even though you have deescalated
the bombing, even though you have reduced the number of troops by
115,000 and have announced another reduction of 150,000 since January
20, 1969, you are not to be trusted." So it is incumbent upon us, in
the U.S. Senate and in the U.S. House of Representatives, not to lit-
erally handcuff the President of the United States.

We can always rely on the Constitution. I trust we always may
have that right. It seems, however, that we should have some position on the vital question: Do we or do we not believe that the

President of the United States, when American troops are threatened
with imminent danger, has the right to move to protect them?

The language of my substitute, which I may offer as a substitute
for the so-called Cooper-Church amendment, is identical for the most
part to the language drafted by the senior Senator from Idaho last
December. It contains just one proviso and one exception:

"Except to the extent that the introduction of such troops is
required as determined by the President and reported promptly to Congress to protect the lives of American troops remaining within South
Vietnam."

Let me make it very clear that I share the concern expressed by
the distinguished Senator from Idaho and do not want to become involved in a war in Cambodia. I would reject being in Cambodia to
shore up the Lon Nol government. I do believe, however, we must give
this President, or any President, the right to protect American troops
who may remain in South Vietnam.

Therefore, the junior Senator from Kansas feels that either
through some substitute language or some provision added to the so-
called Cooper-Church amendment, it should be made clear that [Page
S7187.] this Congress recognizes that right of the President. I say
to my friend from Idaho that it appears that by him not commenting
directly on the question, I assume that one may see it either way---
either the President has that right or the President does not have
that right.

It also appears we are in general agreement as are most Members
of this body concerning some of the basic purposes of the Cooper-
Church amendment. But there are some---I count myself in that group
---who want to make certain that the President of the United States,
the Commander in Chief by the Constitution and the Chief Executive
Officer by the Constitution, has that right when he determines it is
necessary to protect the lives of American troops remaining within
South Vietnam.

Extreme arguments can be made that perhaps the largest sanctuary
is Red China or that there may be other sanctuaries in Laos or Thailand, and that this language could be used to undo what Congress feels
it should do.

But if this issue is seriously considered, then what is really
the question and what is being said to the American people is that
this Congress lacks faith in the credibility of this President. But
I would say again that the President of the United States, since
January 20, 1969, has kept faith with the American people with reference to South Vietnam. He has kept his promise on troop withdrawals.
The level of troop reduction is now 115,000 below the level when he
took office. He has announced an additional troop reduction of
150,000, and that will be carried out on schedule.

The purpose of my exchange with the Senator from Idaho is to
determine whether there may be some common ground or some area where
not only the President can be accommodated, but also the consensus
of Congress.

I recognize the power of Congress under the Constitution to

declare war and the power of Congress to appropriate money. I am
aware of the 2-year prohibition and know the purpose of that prohibition and agree with it.

Mr. President, the junior Senator from Kansas also recognizes
that this issue has been raised ever since the time of George Wash-
ington---in almost every administration since then. Thus it seems,
and I would hope that in the debate on the pending amendment perhaps
some broad agreement can be reached. I would, therefore, again ask
the Senator from Idaho, in all sincerity and with great respect,
whether he believes, knowing the Constitution as he does, and knowing
the rights and powers of the Congress and the President as he does,
whether he believes that, in the event of danger to American troops
and the need to protect the lives of those troops, does the President
have that right?

Would the distinguished Senator from Idaho comment on that?

Mr. CHURCH. I would be very happy to comment. Is the Senator
going to continue his remarks?

Mr. DOLE. Yes.

Mr. CHURCH. We are, then, going back again over the old ground---

Mr. DOLE. Let me say ahead of that---

Mr. CHURCH. I can answer the Senator. I will answer the Senator.
The President of the United States, acting as Commander in Chief, has,
in the past, and will in the future, take action he feels necessary
to protect American troops in the field. We could not deny him his
powers under the Constitution to do that, if we tried. But, we are
not trying to do that with this amendment.

It is wrong to characterize this amendment as handcuffing the
President of the United States.

It is wrong to cast it in the light of not trusting the President
of the United States.

There was reason that the Constitution vested certain responsibilities in Congress when it came to war and when it came to control
of purse strings. Our Founding Fathers thought that that authority
could better be exercised by many men rather than only by one man.

All this amendment attempts to do is to impose certain limits
upon the use of public money, which is the prerogative of Congress.
The amendment looks to two objectives; namely, one prohibits use of
money to retain American forces in Cambodia---which the President
says he does not intend to do; and, second, it prohibits the use of
money to get us entangled in a new military alliance with the Cambodian regime in Phnom Penh.

Congress has that right. If the President later thinks that
these restrictions on the use of public money should be lifted, then
he can come here and make his case and we can decide.

But the insistence that, somehow, the exercise of the powers
which were vested by the Constitution in Congress is an affront to

the President of the United States, seems to me to be the most demeaning of all possible arguments that could be made where the integrity of Congress is concerned.

That is why I say to the Senator---and I have answered him several times over regarding it---that I think it is as plain as it can
be, that we intend neither to handcuff the President nor to interfere
with his right to act within his responsibilities under the Constitution, nor do we intend to raise questions concerning the sincerity
of his purposes.

We simply undertake to impose, on our own responsibility, certain
limits as to the use of public money. I think the time has come for
us to do that.

If, indeed, the President should decide at a later date to plunge
this country even more deeply into Southeast Asia, then I think he
should come to Congress and ask for our consent.

That would be, I think, the result of this amendment. And I
think it would be a healthy result for the institutions of this Republic.

Mr. DOLE. Mr. President, I thank the senior Senator from Idaho.
Again, I believe there can be some area of accommodation here. I am
certain that the Senator from Idaho is aware of the broad support
that was enjoyed by him, on both sides of the aisle, last December
for his amendment with reference to Laos and Thailand.

Therefore, if that language was adequate in December of 1969,
it should be adequate in May of 1970.

It also occurs to me, there could be that same broad support
simply by restating the Laos and Thailand amendment to read:

> In line with the expressed intention of the President
> of the United States, no funds which shall hereafter be
> authorized or appropriated pursuant to this act, or any
> other law, shall be used to finance the introduction of
> American ground troops into Cambodia without prior con-
> sent of Congress.

Or, perhaps some other language, just to make certain we protect
the rights of those there at the present time. Because, as stated
earlier, I supported the Senate amendment last December. I recognize
the rights of Congress and its responsibilities under the Constitution. I would hope that, during the course of this debate, some
agreement with reference to the pending amendment, or some substitute
language therefore can be reached.

But, I repeat, whatever we may feel in this Chamber, I believe
the American people would interpret action by the Senate, if the
pending amendment were to be adopted, as a direct slap at the President of the United States for taking the action he deemed was necessary on April 30, to accomplish two things, to protect the lives
of American troops and to keep the Vietnamization program on schedule.

Mr. President, it will be some months before we know whether the President's judgment was correct.

It will be several months before we know whether American lives were saved, and whether casualties were, in fact, reduced.

It will be several months before we will know whether, because of the action in Cambodia, the Vietnamization program can be kept on schedule.

Thus, whatever the intention may be---and I question no one's motives---but whatever the intentions may have been at the time, it appears clearly now that this amendment confronts the President of the United States, who has said time and again that on July 1, or before, all American troops will be withdrawn from Cambodia, and appears to question his judgment and his word as Commander in Chief.

I appreciate the response by the senior Senator from Idaho, and would assume from his response that he might agree, in the event of danger to American troops, that the Commander in Chief could use such powers he has under the Constitution, to do what he thinks appropriate to protect the lives of American troops, or other Americans for that matter.

Accordingly, I say to my distinguished colleague from Idaho, per-haps some accommodation can be made, to demonstrate to the American people that Congress wants to share the responsibility, that it has an obligation to share the responsibility, but in doing so, it will not take an indirect slap at the Commander in Chief, whoever he may be.

Mr. CHURCH. Mr. President, I have just one final word this afternoon. I believe that the discussion has made it clear that the central issue involved here has to do with the constitutional powers of the Congress and the President in the matter of a foreign war. . . .

GORE AMENDMENT TO COOPER-CHURCH AMENDMENT*

Mr. GORE. [Page S7188.] Mr. President, I submit an amendment which I send to the desk and ask that it be printed and lie at the desk.

The PRESIDING OFFICER. The amendment will be received and printed, and will lie on the table.

Mr. GORE. Mr. President, this amendment proposes to strike from lines 5 and 6 page 1 of the pending amendment the words "expedite the withdrawal of American forces from . . ." and insert in lieu thereof the following words: "facilitate a negotiated peace in. . . ."

The section presently reads as follows:

In order to avoid the involvement of the United States in a wider war in Indochina and to expedite the withdrawal of American forces from Vietnam, it is hereby provided. . . .

As I would amend it, it would read as follows:

In order to avoid the involvement of the United States
in a wider war in Indochina and to facilitate a negotiated
peace in Vietnam, it is hereby provided. . . .

What I seek to do by this amendment is to draw a clear distinction between a negotiated peace, on the one hand, and the policy of
"Vietnamization," so called, which we have had since June of last
year and which has not brought an end to the war and during the existence of which this country has suffered more than 50,000 casualties on the other hand. . . .

THE PRESIDENT AS COMMANDER-IN-CHIEF*

Mr. THURMOND. Mr. President, adoption of the amendment being debated here today would prevent the President of the United States
from taking future actions he might deem necessary to insure the safety of our 400,000 troops remaining in Vietnam.

Furthermore, tying the President's hands in the proper exercise
of his role as Commander in Chief of our committed military forces,
would certainly hamper the chances for success of the Vietnamization
program.

In this connection it could delay the return home of some 150,000
more U.S. troops scheduled to come out of Vietnam by next spring. The
President has promised faithfully to carry out this withdrawal but if
we restrict him he may be unable to follow through.

Many argue President Nixon had no right to attack the Communist
sanctuaries in Cambodia. It is my contention he had an obligation to
do so. In taking this action he will undoubtedly reduce our casual-
ities over the next year and also insure continued success of the
Vietnamization program.

This limited action in Cambodia is within the range of power of
the President as Commander in Chief of our Armed Forces. He was exe-
cuting a constitutional prerogative, clearly supported by history.
His power under article 2 of the Constitution as Commander in Chief
is broad and sweeping. Many Presidents have committed American forces
to combat in foreign countries without a declaration of war by the
Congress. These operations, for the most part, did not involve an
act of war by the United States against the country involved but were
measures to protect American interests, personnel or troops. Most of
these operations met with the approval of the governments whose territory was involved. And further, the vast majority of these operations
were limited in nature and scope, as is our present involvement in
Cambodia.

Our fighting men have moved into foreign territory many times.
In recent history President Truman sent U.S. forces into Korea and
we fought there for several years without a declaration of war.

President Eisenhower sent American forces into Lebanon and President Johnson sent them into the Dominican Republic and South Vietnam.

Generally accepted rules of international law support the President in the Cambodian operation. As a matter of international law when a neutral country like Cambodia cannot maintain its neutrality, and when the result threatens the lives of U.S. forces nearby, then the right of self-defense is clearly recognized.

The Cambodian operation is a limited military operation and it has been extremely successful. Can anyone in this Chamber deny that this action will, in the long run, reduce American and allied casualties in South Vietnam?

It seems to me the reults of the operation to date should amply answer that question. As of today the Pentagon reported the following information:

Enemy killed	5,404
Detainees.	1,431
Individual weapons captured.	7,540
Crew-served weapons captured	1,071
Rice (tons).	2,499
Rice (man months).	109,956

"Man months" means the number of men who could live on that rice for a month.

Rockets (each) captured	9,405
Mortars (each) captured	13,384
Small arms ammunition captured . . .	8,474,425
Land and personnel mines captured. . . .	1,384
Bunkers destroyed	3,318
Vehicles destroyed or captured	178

In the face of these figures, how can critics of the President dispute the fact this operation was needed, was successful, and will save American lives as well as shorten this war?

Mr. President, while the general thrust of this amendment argues for U.S. detachment from Cambodia, its provisions go much further. A brief examination of the amendment clearly supports this fact.

[Page S7189.] In paragraph 1 the amendment prohibits "the retaining of United States ground forces in Cambodia." This simply would prevent the use of American forces in Cambodia for any purpose at any time. It is unwise to tell the Commander in Chief and the military leaders in the field that the enemy operating from across the street can come over and attack you, but you cannot cross the street to his side in self-defense. There is no clear line defining this border and the present Cambodian Government is opposed to the use of their territory by North Vietnam as a military base to launch attacks against a friendly neighbor. President Nixon has described the Cambodian operation as limited in scope, and he predicts withdrawal of all our forces by July 1.

The President also stated any further operations into Cambodia to destroy the Communist sanctuaries there will be conducted by the South Vietnamese. However, suppose a South Vietnamese force of several thousand should make a raid into the sanctuary areas of Cambodia and should be trapped and threatened with annihilation. This amendment would tie the hands of the President and the military leaders in such a situation to the extent they would be unable to launch a rescue operation should it be required.

Further, who is to say that the present Cambodian Government will not collapse and thereby open Cambodia to unrestricted use by the North Vietnamese? In such an event should we prevent the President from striking massive buildups of enemy troops who are poised to thrust into South Vietnam and kill American soldiers remaining there? I will not be a party to such a restriction.

In paragraph 2 of the amendment the United States is prohibited from "paying compensation or allowances of, or otherwise supporting, directly or indirectly, any person in Cambodia who, first, furnishes military instruction to Cambodian forces; or second, engages in any combat activity in support of Cambodian forces."

Mr. President, the committee report on the Military Sales Act to which this amendment is affixed, states the purpose of this paragraph is to prohibit involvement of the United States in support of the Cambodians through the use of advisers or military instruction.

The President has already made it clear that such action is not presently necessary or desired. Furthermore, the Cambodian Government has not requested such support. Nevertheless, if the safety of our remaining forces in Vietnam would be enhanced by such action it seems unwise to me for the United States to telegraph to the world it would not undertake any steps in sanctuaries which threaten our fighting men in South Vietnam.

Paragraph 3 of the Cooper-Church amendment prohibits the United States from "entering into or carrying out any contract or agreement to provide military instruction in Cambodia, or persons to engage in any combat activity in support of Cambodian forces."

This paragraph could bring into question the legality of our support to the South Vietnamese Government should they decide their national security would be strengthened by providing military instruction or support to the Cambodians. These two countries are fighting the same enemy, the North Vietnamese, so why should the South Vietnamese be denied the right to work with their allies against a common enemy?

The Foreign Relations Committee report on this paragraph states its purpose is to "prohibit the United States from doing indirectly what cannot be done directly," such as paying for the services of "mercenaries or others who, without this provision, could be brought in to aid the Cambodian forces."

Mr. President, I submit we are supporting the South Vietnamese, and if their security is threatened by North Vietnamese forces in Cambodia, why should we withdraw our aid if they find it necessary to strike the enemy sanctuaries there as is presently being done? Such an action by the South Vietnamese would surely aid the Cambodians, and this paragraph apparently would prevent any forces supported by the United States from aiding the Cambodians.

If the South Vietnamese deem it necessary to their own security to work with the Cambodian forces in defeating a common enemy, why should the United States stand in their way? That is what the whole Vietnamization program is about---allowing the people of these threatened and invaded countries to fight their own wars as best they can.

Finally, paragraph 4 raises another serious question. As stated in the amendment, it would prohibit "supporting any combat activity in the air above Cambodia by U.S. air forces except the interdiction of enemy supplies or personnel using Cambodian territory for attack against or access into South Vietnam."

In connection with this paragraph I raise this question: Who is to say where the North Vietnamese weapons of war are headed and for what use? Are these supply movements against the South Vietnamese or the Cambodians?

Mr. President, if we pass this amendment it will undermine the President in carrying out his constitutional duty to do his utmost to provide for the protection of our fighting men. Its passage would wreck any chance we might have left to obtain a just solution in South Vietnam by peaceful negotiations.

Finally, passage of this amendment would be met by jubilation in Hanoi, Moscow, Peking, and other Communist capitals throughout the world, as it would signal the waving of a white flag to the forces of tyranny and oppression.

Surely the Members of this body must realize that passage of this amendment would tie the hands of the President and Commander in Chief in many crucial areas which might not even be visualized in this debate. Its passage could deny him options which at some later time might be critical to the safety of our remaining forces in South Vietnam.

The Senate might be interested in knowing that during the War between the States President Lincoln's conduct of the war did not always meet with favor from the Congress. As a result the Congress established a committee in January 1862, known as the Committee on the Conduct of the War.

This committee told President Lincoln how to manage the war, and there was considerable political meddling in military affairs. In his book titled "Lincoln or Lee," author William Dodd wrote the committee "hounded the President" on the conduct of the war despite the great burdens on the President at that time.

Mr. President, we should avoid any such parallel in these modern times. The people of this country elected President Richard Nixon Commander in Chief in 1968. In 1972 they will have an opportunity to approve or disapprove of his conduct while in office. It would be nothing less than tragic if the legislative branch tries to take upon itself the dictating of military decisions clearly within the purview of the President.

Let us not make the U.S. Senate a war room from which we dictate tactics and strategy to a Commander in Chief who has pledged to Vietnamize this war. He has kept every pledge made concerning Vietnam. Some 150,000 of our troops have been successfully withdrawn and another 150,000 will be out by next spring.

The previous administration kept saying the war would end soon. President Nixon has made no such pledge, but he has pledged to gradually reduce our involvement. He does not desire an expansion of the war. He favors the opposite. It would be a tragic mistake to tie his hands and proclaim to the enemy that which he has been unable to win on the battlefield may now be won in the United States. . . .

(May 15, 1970)

Mr. STENNIS. [Page S7236.] Mr. President. . . .

We are now attempting to legislate with respect to a battle which is actually being fought now---today---near the Cambodian-South Vietnamese border. By the assurances which have been given us by our highest officials, from the President on down, we know that the present action is limited in scope, limited in purpose, limited in geography, limited in size, and limited in time. I submit to all Senators that, under the circumstances, there is no precedent in all history for Congress to outline, limit, or define the perimeter of a battlefield here in the halls of the Congress. I believe this is the first time it has ever been undertaken. That is exactly what we will be trying to do, in this Chamber, to form the perimeter of a battlefield, where the battle is already in progress and men are dying today---I repeat, today.

If we are going to do that, we should draw every one of those men out immediately, not only from Cambodia but also from Vietnam. We cannot have it both ways at once. That is clear to me.

I believe that as this sinks into the minds of the American people, concerned as they are and vexed as they are about this war, their thoughts will be, "Do not stay the hands of our Commander in Chief. If we are going to stay there at all, do not put bonds on him; instead come out altogether."

I know of no one in this body who wants to increase the hazards to our young men in Vietnam and Cambodia. Of course not. It is a matter of judgment. I am glad that we have a President who had the courage to act on the facts as he saw them.

If we adopt this amendment, it would be unthinkable and an affront to reason and to the President.

Mr. President, I am not thinking in terms of President Nixon. I am thinking in terms of a constitutional American Commander in Chief, a constitutional Chief Executive who has been chosen by the people and who is known throughout the world as our Commander in Chief, who know that he is the only American who can carry out that role. We cannot put in a substitute for Mr. Nixon just because we do not like his judgment.

Mr. COOPER. Mr. President, will the Senator from Mississippi yield at that point, or would he prefer to finish his remarks first?

The PRESIDING OFFICER.   (Mr. Eagleton).   Does the Senator yield?

Mr. STENNIS.   My remarks are not long.   I should like to finish them, and then I will be happy to yield to the Senator from Kentucky.

I want to make it clear that I think Congress has the power---I am not arguing that Congress does not have the power---to withhold an appropriation.   We can just vote nay on an appropriation.

My position is that when a man is Commander in Chief, as long as he is exercising a judgment that is within reason---that would not apply in a case of a man that happened to be insane---as Commander in Chief, he is the only one that we have to make decisions.   We have no one else.   It is a matter of either or nothing, as I see it, in backing him up in these unusual and extraordinary conditions.

I know fairly well about the present President's feelings of responsibility in this war as a whole.   I do not think it is necessary to say this, but I will say it anyway.   If I did not feel that the President is absolutely, down-to-earth honest in trying to use his best judgment, based on the best advice he can find, and that he is dedicated in this matter regardless of politics---it was a long chance that he took politically---and if I was not satisfied with those things, then I would be driven to some other conclusion and believe that something else had to be done.

I am impressed with his attitude in the matter.   I am impressed with his judgment.   And I give some value to his experience in handling these difficult questions and decisions.

I say that not to build up the President.   He does not need any building up.   It is something that I decided ought to be said to the American people.   They are being told a lot of things about this situation, some of which are misleading.

As I say, I am glad that he had the will to move against these sanctuaries.   Under these facts, I concur in his judgment. . . .

I find it difficult to believe that we really want to convert the Senate of the United States into a war room and to try to direct battle, prescribe tactics, control strategy, draw boundaries, and otherwise to usurp the responsibilities and the prerogatives of the President and our military leaders.   This is not a proper function of the Congress; and it should not be.   And I do not believe that it ever will be.

We can be certain if we pass this amendment and advertise to the world that, as far as American troops are concerned, the Vietcong and the Northvietnamese can reoccupy and roam the sanctuaries of Cambodia at will and without fear of attack, there will be unrestrained jubilation in Moscow, Peking, Hanoi, and every other Communist capital in the world.

Mr. FULBRIGHT.   Mr. President, will the Senator yield?

Mr. STENNIS.   Mr. President, I have requested that I be permitted to finish my prepared remarks.

Mr. FULBRIGHT.   I am sorry.

Mr. STENNIS. Mr. President, we can also be sure that the negotiating power of the President of the United States, as far as his
ability to bring this war to an end by negotiation will be reduced to
nothing---absolutely nothing.

I heard the astronauts describe how the gages went down to zero
when they had the explosion. The astronauts realized what that meant
concerning their chances of getting back or surviving. And I think
that the passage of the pending amendment will restrict the power
of the President as a negotiator to that same level---zero. . . .

[Page S7237.] Going back to the constitutional question involved,
I do not know of any sound, legal basis or any real and valid precedent for that which is being proposed here. Under article 2 of the
Constitution the President is made Commander in Chief of the Armed
Forces. As early as Fleming v. Page, 50 U.S. 602, 614 (1850), the
U.S. Supreme Court held that the responsibility of the President under
article 2 is "to direct the movement of the naval and military forces
placed by law at his command and to employ them in the manner he may
deem most effectual."

As the President indicated in his speech on April 30, the activity in Cambodia is designed to clean out major North Vietnam and
Vietcong occupied sanctuaries which for many years have served as
bases for attack on American and South Vietnamese forces in South
Vietnam. The President indicated that this exercise of this responsibility as Commander in Chief of the Armed Forces, was considered necessary to defend the security of American men, which, in turn, was
essential to accomplish his basic purpose of assuring the continuing
success of the withdrawal program, to end the war in Vietnam, to reduce American casualties, and to win a just peace. It seems to me
that we would be taking a rather rash and reckless step to enact an
ironclad statute which would absolutely deny him the funds to do what
he thinks is necessary along these lines.

The broad and sweeping powers of the President as Commander in
Chief have not always demanded a declaration of war by the Congress.
There are many instances where this was not done. We fought an undeclared war with France in our early days; we fought an undeclared
war with the Barbary pirates in the early days; Marines have landed
on foreign shores many times; we went into Korea under President
Truman's directions; under President Eisenhower we landed in Lebanon;
and there are many other instances which could be cited where similar
actions were taken without a declaration of war. There is a great
deal of precedent to support the Commander in Chief in taking the
action President Nixon took in making the thrust into Cambodia.

As far as I can ascertain, the nearest thing to a precedent
along these lines was the adoption of the amendment to the defense
appropriation bill last year---which now appears as section 643---
providing that---

In line with the expressed intention of the President
of the United States, none of the funds appropriated by
this Act shall be used to finance the introduction of
American ground troops into Laos or Thailand.

Aside from the fact that this is far less restrictive than the proposed amendment, at that time the American troops were not on the mission which the statute was designed to prevent and were not engaged in the prohibited combat. Incidentally, I opposed that amendment and voted against it. But there was no one being sent into battle, no battle was going on, men were not called upon to die in those battles, and that is the big distinction, as a practical matter, from the conditions today.

While the Cooper-Church amendment and its general thrust is somewhat similar to the President's expressed intention concerning our limited role in Cambodia and the completion of our operations by July 1, there are certain elements of it which raise serious questions and which could affect adversely the President's policy on Vietnamization and the steady withdrawal of American combat forces from Vietnam. Therefore, I think that it would be wise to look at the provisions of the amendment.

Before I leave that point, I wish to say with respect to the subject of declarations of war: I remember standing within a few feet of where I am now standing when word came that President Truman had sent our Armed Forces into Korea. I realized very clearly then that act, within itself, even though I supported the concept of the United Nations, was a terrific precedent and that it might plague us. But I also noted that, for many years after I came here, the idea of the issuance of a declaration of war by Congress was laughed at and scoffed at as being old-fashioned and out of the times; why, it was ridiculous. Some of you remember that. I can give names and I can almost give dates, if you want me to.

Most of the thought behind all of these alliances that we signed up for, whereby we tried to underwrite everything all over the world, was based partly on the idea that declarations of war were old-fashioned and out of date. There is very much concern about it now. I am glad there is. I hope we can bridge that gap as a general proposition, but now it is too late with respect to South Vietnam. We stood here and sent all of those men over there to fight and now we talk about a declaration of war, and some say, "We ought to declare war." We are now on the way out. It is too late in this war. We are on the way out; we are withdrawing. We are trying to cover our withdrawal and make it safe for ourselves and our allies. . . .

I think that it is very important that we stop and consider carefully what we are now asked to do. There is a serious question here of the separation of powers, and a serious question of whether or not it is either prudent, necessary, or wise to place such limits and restrictions on our military operations along the South Vietnamese-Cambodian border. The prohibitions we are asked to legislate may very well be of great aid and assistance to the enemy and could well result in added American casualties.

At the very least the adoption of this amendment will telegraph our plans to the enemy and let him know that, as far as American troops are concerned, he can operate in the Cambodian sanctuary areas with immunity. In addition, it will put the President in a legal straitjacket with respect to military operations directed against enemy forces in such sanctuaries and would tie his hands to an extent which to me is unthinkable. . . .

[Page S7238.] I return now briefly to the constitutional question involved. I think it is essential that the President be able to issue orders to military units, and to take [Page S7239.] necessary steps to bar any hostile move against American bases or against our own troops stationed either at home or abroad. I think his position as Commander in Chief of the Armed Forces necessarily gives him the power to take such action and I think that the Senate and the Congress would be ill advised to attempt to deprive him of it, especially under these circumstances.

It appears to me that this amendment invades areas of responsibility which are and properly should be reserved by the Constitution to the President alone. As Commander in Chief the President has the primary responsibility for directing the operations of the armed services, either within our country or outside of it. Reasonable men may very well disagree about the wisdom of his actions, but it would appear both from the Constitution and from historical precedents that the President has the power to send U.S. military forces abroad when he deems it to be in the national interest. As John Marshall noted when a Member of the Congress in 1799:

> The President is the sole organ of the Nation in its external relation and the sole representative with foreign nations.

I think that is a significant point, not just from the military standpoint, but that he is the sole organ---the sole organ of the Nation, both as Executive and as Commander in Chief. When we close his mouth or cut off his power, there is no substitute that we can put in his place. Who is going to be a substitute? Are we, the Congress, going to be the substitute?

Even leaving aside such pertinent matters as the Tonkin Gulf resolution and the SEATO pact, I think there is a sound legal basis for what the President has done. His power as Commander in Chief under article 2 of the Constitution, as already cited, is broad and sweeping. Historically, it has not always required a declaration of war by the Congress, as I have illustrated.

Therefore, Mr. President, I believe that we would commit a grievous error, especially now, if we enact into cold, hard law this proposed limitation on the powers of the Commander in Chief while our fighting men are still in battle. From my position and from my understanding of the problem I must warn the American people against being stampeded, against coming to quick conclusions, against going over the brink in support of this resolution, prompted by the desire we all share, including its sponsors, to bring the war in Vietnam to an end just as soon as possible. We have a serious and difficult problem in South Vietnam but we should not allow this to cause us to go over the brink and cut and run without stopping to reason. We must and should take time to give this grave question serious and complete second thoughts. . . .

Mr. COOPER. Mr. President, will the Senator yield?

Mr. STENNIS. Mr. President, I had said I would yield to the Senator from Kentucky. At this point I yield to him.

Mr. COOPER. . . . I say with all deference to the distinguished chairman of the Armed Services Committee that during his speech---and I know it has been a very honest speech, because it comes from an honest man---I do not believe he has delineated precisely the effect of this amendment, first, as it affects the constitutional powers of Congress and the President and, second, as to its policy implications.

I think I can tell the Senator the intended purpose of the amend- ment, the intention of the sponsors of the amendment, and they are the Senator from Idaho (Mr. CHURCH), the Senator from Montana (Mr. MANSFIELD), the Senator from Vermont (Mr. AIKEN), as well as myself. We are concerned about the situation in Southeast Asia and also we are appreciative of the President's intentions and constitutional powers. We have worked to prepare an amendment which is applicable to the circumstances in Southeast Asia, and to the constitutional powers of both the President and the Congress.

There are two purposes of this amendment. The first purpose is expressed in subsections (2), (3), and (4). The purpose is to pro- hibit all U.S. forces from becoming involved in a war in Cambodia, for Cambodia, for any government in Cambodia, for any Cambodian military forces.

What is the constitutional basis to support the first purpose? We have tried in this amendment to assert the powers of the Congress. We do not attempt to construe the powers of the President, except in one respect, our purposes to prohibit funds for a war for Cambodia, for its forces, for any government, and as I have said, it does pro- hibit the support of any U.S. forces on the soil of Cambodia, in support of Cambodia, and Cambodian forces without the approval of the Congress.

Further, subsection (3) provides that we shall not employ, through contract or agreement, the citizens or nationals of another country to fight in Cambodia, for Cambodia, or their forces; because if that were done, and even though our forces were not in Cambodia, the United States would be committed to their support, and inevitably, I believe, we would be drawn into a war for their support, as we have been drawn over 20 years to the support of South Vietnam.

The Senator stated---and many have stated their comments on this amendment, that we are inhibiting the constitutional powers of the President to protect the lives of American soldiers. Of course, this argument has great appeal. It has appeal to me. The President of the United States, as Commander in Chief, does have large wartime powers. But I do not believe this power can be employed to enter a new war in another country---for Cambodia---particularly when there is no obligation, no treaty obligation, no obligation under the SEATO Treaty, which Cambodia denounced. Certainly, we have no obli- gation to engage in the self-defense of Cambodia. And it would be extreme to enter a larger, expanded war in Cambodia upon the basis of the protection of our forces.

[Page S7240.] The President has great powers as Commander in Chief in wartime to protect our Armed Forces. With respect to this power, this amendment would not limit, except in one respect, and I want to be frank about the exception. It would say to the President, "We respect your power to defend our forces and to protect their lives, but you cannot use that power to enter into another war in another country without the consent of Congress."

The President has said with respect to all these issues that it is his intention to carry out the purpose of section 1, which would prohibit the retention of U.S. forces in Cambodia. He has said at the White House that the outer limit was 7 weeks or July 1, and nearly 2 weeks have passed. I respect his statement, and I believe that he intends to do what he has said. He said, also, that he did not intend that the United States should become engaged in a war for Cambodia, and I respect that statement.

But there are forces and events outside the control of the President of the United States, and certainly of Congress, which---against the best intentions---could make it impossible to carry out those intentions if we remain in Cambodia. I hope this will not happen. I hope the purpose of the President is realized. But we have the duty to do what we can to see that forces beyond the President's control may not happen. If there should be a change in the government in Cambodia, would we support the new government? If Sihanouk is placed in northern Cambodia and is recognized by the U.S.S.R. as he has now been recognized by Communist China, should we support the present government or a successor government and become engaged in a civil war? If the North Vietnamese and the Vietcong move larger concentrations of forces, flanking the sanctuaries, does it then follow that we would stay, to fight in the area, and defeat the express purpose of the President to move out in a fixed time limit?

I say with great respect to the Senator---and the Senator knows how I feel about him---that many of his arguments gave me the impression that likelihood of being involved in Cambodia would occur. The Senator asked: If we clean out the sanctuaries and they are established again, what will we do? The most effective way to protect the sanctuaries after they have been cleaned out would be to stay in or near the sanctuaries; but a new flank, and new sanctuaries to the west would be established. The logic is that in the worst of events, we could be compelled to stay in a country to which we have no obligation at all. . . .

This stalemate has occurred in other situations in our history, and when it comes, the power of each branch is unclear. As the great writers have said, the best that can be done is to try to respect each other, to reach some accommodation. And this our amendment would do.

Without trying to delineate his powers, we are saying to him, "Mr. President, with great respect for you, if this amendment becomes law, you cannot use the authorized and appropriated funds of the United States to become involved in a larger and wider war in Cambodia." It shows our respect for him. It also shows our respect for our obligations and duties as Senators. I have supported the President's program of Vietnamization. It represents a change from the policies of the past and represents what I consider to be an irreversible policy to bring our forces home. . . .

Mr. WILLIAMS of Delaware. Now, Mr. President, in discussing the pending amendment, as the Senator from Kentucky pointed out, it is effective immediately upon enactment. Thus, we are assuming, if we vote on the amendment today, that we are willing for it to be put into effect today. Reading the amendment, I believe the interpretation has been generally accepted to mean just that.

The amendment provides---

. . . no funds authorized or appropriated pursuant to this
Act or any other law may be expended for the purpose of:

> (1) retaining United States ground forces in Cambodia.

> (2) paying the compensation or allowances of, or other-
wise supporting, directly or indirectly, any person in Cambodia who (a) furnishes military instruction to Cambodian
forces; or (b) engages in any combat activity in support of
Cambodian forces. . . .

I believe, therefore, that the effect of the amendment would be
that the moment it was enacted---and we are voting on it in good faith,
figuring it to be passed by the House and signed by the President---we
would be saying that American troops and personnel who were drafted
into the Army, who did not ask to be assigned to Vietnam, who did not
ask to have to march into Cambodia, who went there under orders---they
certainly would be subject to court-martial if they would not go---but
we say here the moment this amendment is passed, "You draw no further
pay. You draw no further military pay. Your family allowances are
likewise stopped until you are withdrawn and competely out of Cambodia."

Mr. President, I believe that is rather harsh treatment. I think
we have the cart before the horse when we figure to hold as hostages,
these men who are defending the principles of the American Government
abroad. I do not believe that by any line of reasoning we can justify
such action.

Yet I say that as one who wants to bring this war to an end as
quickly as possible and as much as anyone else does.

I believe that as long as one American boy is assigned anywhere
in the world and wears the American uniform the full resources of his
country should be back of him until he is brought safely home.

I do not believe that 5,000 miles away, in the security of the
Capitol, drawing our pay daily, we can say to these men, "You are not
going to get paid until you get out of Cambodia."

I raise another question. This stops the "allowances as well as
making them ineligible for any pay during the time they are on Cambodian soil. . . ."

In my opinion if there are those in the Senate who feel that the
good faith of this country could best be demonstrated to our own citizens as well as to nations abroad that we are going to withdraw our
troops from Cambodia as the President has promised, by a monetary
factor, then instead of placing the salaries and family allowances of
our servicemen as hostage why not place our own salaries in escrow?
Why do we not, as Members of Congress, simply say that we will lay
our salaries on the line and draw no pay until we get our American
troops out of Cambodia? . . .

Mr. COOPER. [Page S7241.] Mr. President, the logic of the Senator's argument is that Congress should never do anything.

Mr. WILLIAMS of Delaware. No.

Mr. COOPER. I would like to finish, with all deference. The
only certain constitutional power that Congress has over a war is
through its power of the purse strings. That is all.

It can pass resolutions. We can through sense of the Senate resolutions and sense of the House resolutions express our positions
to the Executive. But if he thinks we are incorrect, he does not
have to follow our suggestions. The purse is our power.

Mr. President, the Constitution did not give the Congress the
power lightly. The Constitutional Convention made a distinction between the King of England and the President of the United States. The
King of England had the power both to declare war and to raise armed
forces for war.

The Constitution gave to Congress the power to raise and support
an army and navy.

The logic of the argument the Senator makes is that we can never
use this constitutional power, because he says the soldiers will not
be paid and their wives, their widows and children, will not receive
allowances.

That decision would be a matter for the President.

If the Congress passes this amendment, it will then be a matter
for the President to decide whether it shall be followed. If by some
mischance, there was a period of time when this was not observed or
any other factor intervened to affect the rights of our servicemen,
that matter could be corrected. We respect our servicemen. I know
that Congress and the President of the United States would see that
such a situation would not remain.

We are trying to deal with the large question of avoiding another
war. That far overshadows these objections.

Mr. WILLIAMS of Delaware. Mr. President, I respect the position
of the Senator from Kentucky. And I do not advance this in a critical
manner, but that is the mathematical effect of his amendment. . . .

I think this point should be clear.

I agree that the power of the purse is in the hands of Congress,
and perhaps directing that power in certain directions would have influence on the Government.

Rather than using the power of the purse to withhold pay from the
boys in Vietnam and Cambodia who are there through no fault of their
own, let us put our own salaries on the line and put them on the line
as a demonstration of our good faith. We should not put their pay on
the line.

I think it would be most unfortunate for the families of the
servicemen to feel that they are being cut off from all benefits under
any circumstances regardless of how short this period may be.

I question the effect of such action on the morale of our troops.
If we could do this today for troops in Cambodia we could do it tomorrow in Vietnam. Does anyone dare suggest we stop the pay of all
military personnel in Southeast Asia? . . .

Mr. FULBRIGHT. Mr. President, . . . I think this is the most
irrelevant argument that one could make. I cannot imagine why anyone
would make such an argument. I have never heard the Senator from
Delaware, in the 20 years I have been in the Senate, make an argument
with no more substance than that. The Senator from Delaware knows
the [Page S7242.] provision would not go into effect until the President signed the bill. That would not be today, tomorrow, or next
week. The Senator knows that as well as anyone. . . .

Mr. President, to make the Record clear I am quoting the President's words in his press conference. I do not think there is the
slightest doubt he said this.

The action actually is going faster than we had anticipated. The middle of next week,---

This was last week---

. . . the first units, American units, will come out. The
end of next week, the second group of American units will
come out. The great majority of all American units will
be out by the second week of June, and all Americans of all
kinds, including advisers, will be out of Vietnam (the
President meant Cambodia) by the end of June.

That is what he said. . . .

If I may say, under the conditions which prevail and, in view of
the President's statement, it would not have the effect of restricting
pay while the battle is going on. This measure prohibits use of funds
to retain them there. This is an effort to carry into effect, into
law, the words of the President.

He said that not only in his press conference but also to the
Representatives and the Senators who were invited to meet with him.
This statement was obviously designed by the President to reconcile
the Congress and the public to this move, which he took without any
consultation with the Senate. It was an effort to bring about acceptance of something that was already done.

It seems to me that it is not only our right but it is our duty
to take him at his word and to put this promise in language that is
unmistakable in intent. The Senator from Kentucky and the Senator
from Idaho were extremely careful to restrict this to Cambodia, as
the Senator knows. I and others would like to see the same approach
taken with respect to getting out of Vietnam. But for reasons that
are too complex to go into now, this was a minimum step, taking the
President at his word.

Unless you do not believe the President, I do not see how one
could say that this could interfere with combat operations because

the President said they would all be out of Cambodia and back in Vietnam soon. If you do not believe the President, that is an additional
reason why you should support this amendment. If you really have a
suspicion that he does not mean what he says, then by all means every
Senator should support it; to do otherwise would betray our fundamental
duty. . . .

    Mr. McGEE. [Page S7246.] It seems to me that now is the time for
a long pause in taking an important step such as this, because of what
we have been through. But we have had a chance to learn from the past
5 or 6 years. I dare say that none of us---hopefully---is immune from
the lessons of recent years---especially the senior Senator from
Wyoming.

    I can recall well how, in the first critical test of our role as
leaders of the world in the 1950's, those of us in the liberal community were groping for some middle ground in exercising our responsibility between the "massive retaliation" that John Foster Dulles was
talking about on the one hand, which meant nuclear weapons, and "Fortress America" on the other.

    It was then that we felt crowded into a position of at least
weighing the dimensions of a limited, undeclared war. Our belief was
that in the nuclear age we did not dare take the risk of a declared
war unless it was total war, "The" war, whatever that means. Hopefully, that will never occur.

    To fend off the holocaust of nuclear warfare on the one hand and
the ridiculousness of such a policy as "Fortress America" on the other,
we thought it was better to learn from World War II, from the experiences with Japan, which began to nibble at Manchuria and then to dominate Asia, which involved us in war as a result of Pearl Harbor; from
the experiences with Hitler, who nibbled away at the Versailles Treaty
until he occupied the Rhineland in violation of that treaty, and involved us all in world war at such terrible cost. So it is understandable that our generation sought some alternative. That alternative was a limited war without a declaration.

    That is what I think poses the problem now with us today.

    Under the Constitution of the United States, our Founding Fathers
never envisaged such an exigency as that, and understandably so.
They envisaged a declaration of war in what would be today an old-
fashioned war. There are a great many gray areas in question as to
the role of the Senate which derive from the circumstance of an undeclared war.

    I must confess, as a student of the problem, that I am not sure
to this day whether we, as a free society, can wage an undeclared war.

    We are spending a great deal of time on this subject here today.
We are caught up in where we are, for better or for worse. I think
it would behoove us all to devote more of our energies, and all the
foresight that we can mobilize to figure out how we best should conduct the role of the Senate in this nuclear age in its relationships
with the President of the United States. . . .

    The problem that this becomes is one of definitions. Whatever
else, however we got in there, whether it is right or wrong in each

man's conscience, it would appear to me to be that the fact is: We are there. We are in combat. We have been in combat, at great cost and blood, for a long time. We cannot repeal all of that. Therefore, the question has to be, in the light of an undeclared war which is underway: What is the responsible role of the Senate?

I submit, Mr. President, that that role is not one of trying to tie the President's hands, to try to shackle his initiative, to try to curb his options, even as he is in the midst of trying to withdraw with responsibility. To me, that is the ultimate of foolishness, if not national irresponsibility.

I just think that the time of the Senate must be addressed to the potentials of the future. I do not think it should be addressed to the catastrophes of the past. It is too late for that.

Therefore, let us not hobble the President at this moment. . . .

Thus, I would say, if we only could resolve in this body not to risk, jeopardize, or give away an opportunity for the President to slow down and disengage from this miserable conflict in Southeast Asia in some responsible way, we could be addressing ourselves instead, to what do we do in the nuclear age, the next time we are faced with this test. We will be faced with it. It will not go away, because we have resolved ourselves as to Cambodia and Laos, or whatever else. It will be here again. It may be here right now---in the Middle East, say. It may come in Burma. It may come somewhere else. We have no choice about those things. We cannot predetermine them. But, we are here in this world today. We are in the position which makes a difference as to how the world will go. I would hope, Mr. President, that we would, indeed, marshall more of our intellectual resources, of our capabilities in colloquy, of our honest search for the answers down the road ahead, rather than shackling the blame on the road behind in terms of what the Senate, under our constitutional system, should do.

I have no doubt that in terms of this war, that, had it been successfully concluded in a year or 18 months, Members of this body would have been bragging about how the Senate of the United States approved the Gulf of Tonkin resolution and participated in that decision, and they would be seeking the credit for that resolution; but, because of the mystery of the Orient, because of the vagaries of the new kinds of conflict that guerrilla warfare has raised in the East, and because of all the other pressures and the timetables in the world crowding in on us, it did not go as Republicans and Democrats would have preferred. It turned out to be much more complicated and much larger than partisan politics, even larger than Presidents of the United States, or the American people as a whole.

For that reason, I would express my desperate wish that we not take a step here that will, in fact, jeopardize the leadership role of the President of the United States as Commander in Chief in the midst of a conflict, when we should be readdressing ourselves to his proper role in cooperation with the Senate in all future such decisionmaking processes in the kind of world in which we live. . . .

[Page S7248.] The amendment, in effect, states that U.S. war power resides in the Congress, that the power of the purse may legitimately be extended in such a way as to shape the course of a war in which we are already deeply involved.

I oppose this position. I believe the framers of the Constitution meant it when they said that the President shall be the Commander in Chief of the Army and Navy of the United States. I believe
they meant it when they said that the Congress shall declare war, not
make war. The language is clear.

However cloudy the issues may be surrounding an undeclared war
in the nuclear age, the fact is that for several years we have been
engaged in armed combat.

The authority to respond with speed and dispatch in foreign
affairs when military force is required and regress after it has already been committed, should vest in the Office of the President. He
is elected by all the people. He commands our military power. He
has unique access to classified information. He has, and ought to
have, the constitutional power to send U.S. military forces abroad
when he deems such action to be in the national interest. Thus, the
burden of the pending decision in this body is less that of the war
in Southeast Asia, than it is one of political science; of responsible
self-government.

My studies show political scientists agreed that, early in our
history, if we had not seen the need for centralized control, the new
Nation would have been split apart by rancorous factionalism.

The leaders of the Thirteen Colonies repelled by the arbitrary
authority of the English king and his colonial governors, launched
the Nation upon its new life without a chief executive. Events demonstrated the urgent need for central control when the new nation
proved unable to deal with the chaotic overlapping of state jurisdictions resulting from the Articles of Confederation. National authority has been given the President ever since, with only weak Presidents shrinking from its use.

And so I find the present the wrong time to establish as congressional policy interpretations of the Constitution which 200 years
of history do not substantiate.

Never in our history has it been a function of the Senate to
advise and consent on operational military decisions made by the Commander in Chief.

Never in our history have we conducted a war by committee.

And on many different occasions prior to World War II, U.S.
Presidents have ordered undeclared acts of war.

The Congress is the greatest deliberative body in the world, but
as a military leadership group, notoriously unable to arrive at rapid
decisions, it could become a multiheaded monster if it attempted to
second-guess the conduct of a war. . . .

[Page S7249.] Today, only wishful thinking can lead to the notion that an assertion of Congressional war power will resolve the
problem of our involvement in Southeast Asia. I think we must recognize that our trouble there stems not from divided authority to
conduct the war, but from the fact that so far we have failed to
achieve our objectives.

In considering these grave questions, we must start from where we are. We cannot amend history. We cannot repeal it. We cannot, in good conscience, pin the rap on the past, charging the President with usurpation of power because our efforts have resulted in an apparently unwinnable war. No power has been usurped. On the contrary, historic precedent has been followed.

The Congress passed the Tonkin Gulf resolution in good faith, agreeing then on the course of action proposed by the President. And now, we do not enhance our stature if we blame the system, the division of powers, or Presidential deception for our tragic lack of success; and so concluding, tie the hands of the Commander in Chief as he tries to deal with one of the most difficult military situations in our history.

I ask the Senate to reject the amendment but I thank its sponsors for reminding us that we must now shape a meaningful role for the Senate in determining the future direction of our foreign policy. As decrying the past is fruitless, so looking ahead can enhance the Senate's part in determining where we go from here. We must anticipate the next crisis; we must begin to address ourselves to restructuring the function of Congress in foreign affairs. Surely we can learn from the past; surely we must apply its lessons to the months ahead before it is too late.

Perhaps we should seek a sharper delineation of war power. Perhaps the future will require changes and redefinitions. I would be more than willing to explore all possibilities.

Clearly, we must address ourselves well in advance of crises to the broad outlines and directions of American policy. If we do this, we will have acted far more constructively and influentially than we would be curtailing the President's authority in the midst of crisis and after the fact. . . .

Mr. CHURCH. I have listened with great interest to the debate during its final phases.

I must state frankly that I have been left to wonder what amendment is being discussed.

The arguments I have heard bear little relationship to the pending amendment as Senator COOPER and I drafted it. I believe it might be well to reconsider just what it is that this amendment does. In order to put an amendment of this kind in its proper perspective, often it is best to think about the things it does not do.

It does not raise questions about the credibility of the President of the United States. It accepts the President at his word. How that could possibly raise doubts in this body, in this country, and throughout the world is hard for me to understand. . . .

Warmaking was supposed to be a shared responsibility. The framers of the Constitution did not conceive the Presidency to be an autocracy. They never intended that one man, as President, should have all the power to decide where, when, and under what circumstances the United States would fight. They never intended that he alone should pass upon the vital questions of war and peace which would involve the life or death of this Republic. No, indeed. The framers

of the Constitution and Presidents for nearly two centuries, in adherence to the provisions of the Constitution, have recognized that
Congress has its role to play, as well as the President, when it comes
to the matter of war. . . .

Mr. PELL. [Page S7251.] I wonder if the Senator is as struck as
I am with the fact that under our system of government it is rather
hard, sometimes, for the people of our country to make their will
known, if the President is in opposition.

Under a parliamentary democracy, we have the vote of confidence,
and upon a failure in it, the representatives go back to the people.
Even in the Soviet Union, certainly the opposite of a democracy, a
committee form of government exists where, if there is a consensus
within the committee that the head of government is going too far in
an incorrect direction, he is quietly nudged aside, as we have seen
happen to Mr. Khrushchev and his predecessors. But with our system,
there is very great difficulty in the majority will expressing itself
except at 4-year intervals.

[Page S7252.] We also have the question of what is the majority
will. How do you weigh the intensity of feeling?

We have at this time, it seems to me, a very dangerous situation
developing within the country, developing with great intensity of
feeling---one might call it decibels, if such a term could be used
relating to emotion---decibels of emotion of high intensity and high
anguish on the part of many young people who believe they are not being heard, that there is no dialog or communication, and who want to
see some action taken.

At the same time, I think there is a majority opinion in the Nation that somewhat apathetically believes these decisions are best
left to the President alone---the old idea of "father knows best."

This is a situation that can lead to real confrontation and real
violence, unless some means are found of permitting the high decibel
emotions of our younger people also to vent.

To my mind, the adoption of this amendment, which I am so glad
to be supporting, would be a very real step in the direction of letting
those who feel that their emotions or their views are being expressed
but are not being heard, believe that they are being heard. . . .

Mr. CHURCH. I agree with the Senator, I want to get back to the
original point he made, that public confidence in our political institutions is at stake here. During previous years, the direction of
protest, demonstration, and antiwar effort was pointed at the White
House. When 250,000 young Americans came to the Capitol last November, hardly any of them came up to Capitol Hill. They all turned
their backs on the Capitol and went down and faced the White House.
They recognized that we had permitted enormous powers to be concentrated in the President's hands, and unless they could convince the
President, they had no chance. Congress was irrelevant.

That was the pattern of the protest until the distinguished Senator from Kentucky (Mr. COOPER) and I went to the press galleries a
couple of weeks ago and suggested that the time had come for Congress
to begin to use some of its power, so long overlooked, for the purpose

of establishing the outer limits to American participation in this widening war. Ever since, for the first time, attention has been directed at Congress. Indeed, Congress has been rediscovered. The issue is whether we can summon up the resolution to use the powers which were meant to be not only lodged in Congress, but also exercised by Congress.

If we fail to do that, on a proposal so modest as the one now pending, which merely takes the President at his word and says, "No further, without coming back and making your case and securing congressional consent," then what are our young people going to think about Congress? Are they going to think that it is alive at all, or dormant?

Mr. PELL. If I may interject, I do not believe they have a very high opinion of Congress now.

Mr. CHURCH. If they do not have a high opinion of Congress now, it is because we have given little cause for them to feel that way. But, if, on this occasion, we can arouse ourselves from our lazy slumber, begin to assume our responsibilities to the American people under the Constitution, then I think that respect for Congress will rise again, and nothing could be healthier for the well-being of the institutions of this Republic.

Perhaps, in the long run, this revival [Page S7253.] will be more important than the actual limiting effect of the amendment itself.

Mr. PELL. If the Senator will yield to me for one last comment, it would also make apparent to the younger people that they can work within the system. Yet, what so many of them are concerned with is they cannot see any signs of success from working within the system. They do not realize that some of their efforts can be counterproductive. But they are beginning to realize that violence, the kind which occurred at the University of Maryland yesterday, is counterproductive, that it turns middle America further "of," rather than further "on."

Another very interesting change in tactics, not in strategy, is the increasing realization of our young people that beards---which I have always rather envied but never had the courage to grow---long hair and weird costumes turn people more "off" than "on."

We find that perhaps, in part, because they see signs of possible success in this amendment, the young people are getting cut-rate haircuts now and are going around canvassing neighborhoods in support of the adoption of this amendment. We must remember that these young people, 30 years from now, will be the leaders in this country---not those who are sitting on their hands and doing nothing now---but this group will work within the system or will be pushed outside, and the leaders of this group, will have more conviction that they can work within the system.

Mr. CHURCH. I agree again with the distinguished Senator from Rhode Island. If we want to take the war protests off the streets, if we want to stop the violence, if we want to still the spirit of revolution on campuses north, south, east, and west, the way to do it is to demonstrate that here in the Halls of Congress representative government still lives.

Mr. BYRD of West Virginia. If the able Senator will yield at
that point, let me say that I may vote for the Cooper-Church amendment but not on that pretext.

Mr. CHURCH. The Senator's support for the amendment, if he so
decides to vote for it, is very welcome indeed. But with regard to
the argument I made as being a pretext, even though the Senator may---

Mr. BYRD of West Virginia. Let me say, if the distinguished
Senator will yield, that I have not made up my mind as to whether I
shall vote for or against the amendment. But, if I decide to vote
for the amendment, it will never be because of threats of demonstrations, or violence in the streets, or on the campuses. If it is to
be adopted on that basis, then I will not vote for it.

Mr. CHURCH. May I say, with respect to the Senator's statement,
that I believe he misunderstands the point I made.

Mr. BYRD of West Virginia. I may have. I hope that I have. . . .

Mr. CHURCH. It was certainly not because Congress is bending to
any such threats, but because the place to settle this question is in
the Halls of Congress, not in the streets. . . .

THE ECONOMIC CONSEQUENCES OF CAMBODIA

(May 18, 1970)

Mr. PROXMIRE. [Page S7320] Mr. President, the Cambodian intervention has raised many questions involving congressional responsibility for spending, budgeting, and in many other vital respects. Today I intend to discuss these significant economic implications.

It is now clear that the forecast of a budget surplus of $1.3
billion for fiscal year 1971 will not occur. This small estimated
fiscal year 1971 surplus has disappeared even before fiscal year 1971
has begun.

While no new official budget figures have been given, the decline
in corporate profits will bring a major fall off in receipts. And
several of the gimmicks and jerry-built estimates on which the $1.3
billion surplus was based, have now been exposed for all to see. One
example alone will suffice. The President's wholly unrealistic budget
request for a postponement until January 1971 of the postal and civil
service pay raises due on July 1, 1970, has been replaced by a pay
increase which added $1.2 billion to fiscal year 1970 outlays and will
add additional amounts to the 1971 estimates of expenditures.

We should face the facts. Instead of a $1.3 billion surplus for
fiscal year 1971, we now face both an increase in expenditures---pay
increases, interest payments, farm price supports---and a decrease in
receipts---from corporate profits, offshore oil leases, a delayed
postal rate increase---which have turned around the fiscal year 1971
estimate from a slight surplus to a deficit of several billions.
While the details have yet to be made public, this basic truth has
been admitted by the administration and by the Secretary of the

Treasury. Unofficial estimates are that the deficit from these
causes alone will run as high as $5 billion.

The figures released Friday by the Department of Commerce indicate that we are now in a recession as reportedly defined by the
National Bureau of Economic Research. The gross national product has
now declined for two successive quarters.

The first quarter figure has now been revised downward by some
$2.6 billion from the preliminary estimates. It now stands at $959.6
billion. In constant 1958 dollars it fell from $730.6 billion in the
third quarter of 1969 to $724.3 billion in the first quarter of 1970.
This is very disheartening economic news.

The figures for corporate profits show a sharp decline in the
first quarter of 1970. The figures released Friday show a seasonally
adjusted annual rate of $85 billion for the first quarter of 1970.
This is $6-1/4 billion less than in the fourth quarter of 1969 and
more than $10 billion below the record high profits attained in the
first two quarters of 1969.

But there is more fiscal bad news. We must face up to the economic consequences of Cambodia. There will be additional increases
in spending because of war.

[Page S7321.] Unfortunately, administration spokesmen, including
the Secretary of the Treasury and the Director of the Bureau of the
Budget, stubbornly and foolishly refuse to admit it. They persist in
stating that the military operations in Cambodia are not expected to
add to total defense spending in 1970 or 1971. Such a judgment was
made by the Secretary as late as May 9 in his speech at Hot Springs.
But that is merely putting their heads in the sand.

The President's actions in Cambodia will raise the cost of the
war. Military expenditures in Southeast Asia will rise. Whatever
views we as individual Americans may hold about the President's action
in launching the Cambodian expedition, we can be sure that as night
follows day the costs of the war will go up. We must face that
fact. . . .

The question then becomes, What can we do about it? How can we
prevent inflation from continuing, restore confidence in the business
community, and provide for our starved domestic needs at the same time
that military and other costs rise and receipts go down? . . .

In the present circumstances there is only one way to meet these
problems. That way is to cut spending. Unfortunately, the Secretary
did not specify where we might impose rigid economics.

But there is one place and only one place where big spending can
be cut. That is the $75 billion defense budget proposed for next
year.

It is therefore incumbent upon us to make big cuts in the regular
military budget in order to offset the certain increase in the cost
of the Vietnam war and the decrease in revenues from the slump. Unless that is done, we are bound to have a new round of price increases,
a huge unbalanced budget, and a new economic crisis.

Let me develop the arguments both as to why the costs of the war will increase and why cutting the regular fiscal year 1971 military budget is the only feasible way to meet the new and serious problem of the budget deficit and the escalation in the costs of the Vietnam war.

On April 30, the President of the United States ordered American troops into Cambodia. Here is the indication and the documentation that this Cambodian adventure is going to cost money in a substantial amount. Reports are that some 20,000 American and 20,000 South Vietnamese troops are involved in military operations into North Vietnamese-Vietcong sanctuaries along the South Vietnamese-Cambodian border.

Some solace for those of us who oppose this action has come from the President in his promise that he will limit the penetration of troops into Cambodia to 19 to 21 miles and that he will withdraw the American troops entirely from Cambodia by July 1. In addition, he has justified the Cambodian operation, in part, on grounds that it will make it possible to carry out his pledge to remove an additional 15,000 American troops from Vietnam by next spring.

We all hope that events will make it possible for the President to adhere to these limits and that the Cambodian expedition will become, in fact, a means to advance the date when our troops can leave Vietnam entirely.

But, in the meantime, the thrust into Cambodia, the troops and ammunition involved, the planes, tanks, and supporting helicopters, and the supplies needed to support them are bound to cost money and to raise the costs of the war.

In addition to the ground troops sent into Cambodia, at least four new major bombing missions over North Vietnam have taken place since April 30. Fifty to 100 planes flew 240 miles deep into North Vietnam during each of them.

Furthermore, in any military expedition of this kind, every commander will insist upon adequate reserves of ammunition, troops, planes, tanks, and supplies. There are, therefore, not only built-up costs involved in this endeavor, but reserve and replacement costs as well.

An increase in the costs of the war is also indicated by the casualty figures. The weekly casualty report released May 14 showed the highest American casualties in 8 months and the highest South Vietnamese casualties in 27 months.

While American troops were only indirectly involved and were very careful to avoid exceeding the 19-mile limit, the cost of the forays up the Mekong River by a flotilla of ships was obviously borne to some considerable degree by the United States.

Finally, we propose to support the South Vietnamese troops even after we leave Cambodia and withdraw further troops from Vietnam. And there is as yet no guarantee that the South Vietnamese and even the United States will not be involved in further forays, incursions, and expeditions. At least, the administration is arguing that we should not tie their hands, in arguing against the pending amendments.

All of this will cost money. In my judgment, tens of millions of additional funds are at stake. Unless some unusually fortuitous events take place, we should not be surprised if the additional costs [Page S7322.] of the Cambodian expedition and the stepup in fighting in Vietnam are several billions more than has been budgeted.

And if the Cambodian operation ties down our troops for a period longer than anticipated, or if it leads to an escalation of the war, then the costs will go up even more.

With the shift in the 1971 budget from precarious surplus to an admitted and growing and substantial deficit in the context of a situation where we have already failed to stop inflation and where prices are continuing to rise, the one thing that could really put a strain on the economy at this time is a rapid increase in spending as a result of the Vietnam-Cambodian War.

The huge inflation brought about by the escalation in the Vietnam war in the fiscal year 1966-67 period has not yet been brought under control. The pesimism engendered by the failure of the administration's anti-inflationary policies---if indeed they have carried out any meaningful anti-inflationary policies---has rocked the financial community and sent the stock market into a tailspin.

But already the administration appears to be living in a dream world. The assurances of the Secretary of the Treasury, Mr. Kennedy, at Hot Springs, that the economic and budgetary impact of the escalation in Cambodia would be negligible, are impossible to accept.

This is where many of us came in. The same thing was said when the Vietnam war was escalated. In fiscal year 1966, new obligational authority for Vietnam was $14 billion more than the estimate in the budget. In fiscal year 1967, new obligation authority for Vietnam was $12 billion in excess of the budget figure.

And the same thing happened to spending. Vietnam spending in fiscal year 1967 rose from a $10 billion estimate in the budget to $20 billion before the year was out.

As a result, when the bills became due we incurred an $8 billion deficit in fiscal year 1967 and a $25.2 billion deficit in fiscal year 1968. The inflation from which we are still suffering, was induced by the failure to act at that time and because too many officials viewed the world through rose-colored glasses.

At that time, just as we are hearing now, we received assurances from the President and his advisers that the economic and budgetary impacts of the Vietnam war would be much smaller than they were.

There is an old Chinese saying which admirably describes the danger we face of once again underestimating the economic consequences of the Indochinese war. "Fool me once, shame on you. Fool me twice, shame on me."

It cost us a $25 billion deficit and massive inflation to learn our lesson once. Let us not make the same mistake twice.

In situations of this kind, certain elementary steps can be taken. They are familiar to every businessman, economist, and Budget

and Treasury official. If this were merely a classroom exercise one
might recommend taking any one or a combination or all of the following actions. They are, first, decrease the money supply and tighten
monetary policy; second, increase taxes to decrease spending in the
private sector and pay for the increased cost of the war in the public
sector; third, resort to guidelines and persuasion and forms of credit restrictions in an effort to keep prices and wages and credit in
line; and fourth, reduce spending in order to compensate for the increased spending for the war.

Those are the classic classroom things to do. But the problem
we face now is that not all of them are available to us.

Because of past policies, administration reluctance, preconceived
predilections, and public opposition to the war, the options are now
limited---and I mean very limited.

In the present circumstances, there is only one clear course of
action. That is to cut the regular military budget and to cut it hard
in order to pay for the increased costs of Cambodian expedition, balance the budget, prevent runaway inflation, release funds for housing
and construction in the private sector, and restore confidence to the
business and economic community.

That this is so is clear from a statement of the facts. . . .

CUTTING MILITARY EXPENDITURES ONLY REASONABLE ALTERNATIVE

[Page S7323] In the face of new inflationary pressures which will
inevitably flow from the prospective budget deficit and the action in
Cambodia, it is both impossible and undesirable to tighten money, because money is now already too tight and interest rates are excessive.
This would merely wreak more havoc on housing and raise unemployment.
It is neither desirable nor possible to raise taxes, because taxes are
now at an intolerable level, are unjust in their application, and the
vast opposition to the war itself would prevent any increase to pay
for expenditures which a very large and intense minority believes to
be bad policy or immoral. The President and his advisers have stead-
fastly refused to use other more gentle forms of persuasion, such as
credit controls, or guidelines. There is, therefore, only one policy
left by which the new inflationary pressures can be offset.

That policy is to cut expenditures. And the only area of expenditures which can be cut and cut decisively in a big and significant
way are those for the on-going, regular, military budget.

Where these cuts can be made has been detailed time and again.
The Congressional Quarterly, in a survey of Defense Department officials,
set forth $10 billion in cuts which could be made without cutting back
on military muscle.

Robert Benson, formerly in the Office of the Comptroller of the
Defense Department, indicated where almost $10 billion could be cut,
also without affecting the basic strength or security of the country.

We have held detailed hearings into procurement, and especially
the procurement of weapons systems where billions upon billions of

dollars in overruns exist. The General Accounting Office indicated to my subcommittee last December that the overrun on 38 weapons systems alone was $20 billion. Savings can and must be made here.

I think that sufficiently detailed areas where military spending can be cut have been pointed out in the past so that one need not repeat them here.

The military budget is the only logical place for major cuts in spending. The Pentagon is asking for $71 billion next year. The additional funds for national defense for military assistance, military construction, and atomic energy raise that figure to almost $75 billion.

Of the Federal budget of $200 billion, almost half of it is what the Budget Bureau calls "uncontrollable." That means about $100 billion is composed of social security payments, interest on the national debt, veterans payments, or expenditures such as CCC payments which cannot be cut except by changing the laws of the land.

Of the $100 billion in "controllable" items---what we can cut---$75 billion is for national defense. If there is to be any major cutting of the Federal budget it must be made here.

The logic of the situation calls for cutting the military budget. It is only by cutting back on the military budget that we can stop inflation, stimulate housing, restore some sense of confidence in the business community, and meet even a modicum of the priorities and needs of the civilian economy of the country.

[Page S7324.] Even before the escalation of the war in Cambodia, the military budget was out of control. The military received a disproportionate share of the resources of the country.

Now they will want even more.

But the military budget already contains areas of excesses and unnecessary expenditures. To continue the wastefulness is wrong. To escalate military expenditures is unconscionable.

If the military is intent on additional forays into the jungles and swamps of Asia, let them pay for it out of their existing budget. They must not receive budgetary rewards for their military excesses.

A cut in the military budget is the only means by which we can reduce the budget deficit and pay for the additional expenditures which the Cambodian expedition will generate.

The military excesses are already so great that large cuts can be made without endangering the effectiveness of our forces or the lives of our soldiers. In fact, the fighting strength of this country could be enhanced by stopping the gold plating, increasing the ratio of combat to supply troops, and reforming the entire system of military procurement and supply.

We should cut the military budget. It is no longer just a desirable end. It is now a necessity.

Mr. PERCY. Mr. President, will the Senator yield for a comment?

Mr. PROXMIRE. Mr. President, I would be very happy to yield to the distinguished Senator from Illinois.

Mr. PERCY. Mr. President, I have been concerned about the economy and our present economic problems. However, I cannot really imagine that in a trillion dollar economy, the Cambodian incursions have put a strain on the economy.

The implication of the Senator from Wisconsin is that this incursion is leading to a broadening of the war and involves a great deal more in expenditures. I cannot see that at all. I think the implication is very strong that this is a very short-term situation.

I take the President at face value when he says that we will be out of there by June 30.

I cannot imagine that the expense involved will have a material effect upon the economy if the business community and financial interests recognize that the President will stick to his word. And I do not doubt that for a moment.

So, I do not look upon this as having a materially adverse effect upon the economy. I hope that business leaders and financial leaders will not use this as a reason for saying that the outlook in the future is bleak.

We have some real problems to face. But I do not believe they are caused, other than psychologically, by the incursion into Cambodia. . . .

Mr. CHURCH. Mr. President, I do not suppose that anyone speaks with greater authority than the senior Senator from Wisconsin when it comes to Government finances. I think he has made a worthy contribution this afternoon by pointing up the impact of this continuing war on the finances of the Government.

President Nixon had no more cherished objective than to balance the budget. And as this war has poisoned the hopes and aspirations of his predecessors before him, so it now poisons the best laid plans of President Nixon.

The war is causing great economic distress in the United States. It is the single most important cause for the inflation which still remains unbridled.

It is the central cause for the failure to which the Senator alludes, Nixon's failure to balance his budget.

It is the cause for the special war taxes that have been laid upon the people, and it doubtlessly accounts for the precipitous slide in the stock market that has so disturbed the entire financial community.

Now, I think from the standpoint of the economy alone, from the fact we have spent over $100 billion on this pointless war, it honestly can be said that never in the history of our country has so much been spent for so little. . . .

CONGRESS AND WAR: PAST AND PRESENT*

Mr. ERVIN.   Mr. President I rise to voice my opposition to the so-called Church-Cooper amendment.

Mr. President, one of America's greatest constitutional authorities and historians, Edward S. Corwin, had the following to say at page 259 of his illuminating book, entitled, The President: Office and Powers, 1787-1957:

> Actually Congress has never adopted any legislation that would seriously cramp the style of a president attempting to break the resistance of an enemy or seeking to assure the safety of the national forces.

I believe that the Church-Cooper amendment constitutes a recommendation by its proponents that Congress adopt for the first time in the history of our Nation legislation which would seriously cramp the style of the President in attempting to break the resistance of an enemy or seeking to insure the safety of the national forces. . . .

The Cooper-Church proposal and certain other proposals which have been introduced in the Senate attempt to do the impossible, that is, to repeal history and the consequences of history.   The Creator of this universe made it impossible for a nation or for an individual to repeal past mistakes.   I certainly wish it were possible for me to repeal the mistakes I have made in the past.   I can assure the Senate that if I had this power, I would have one of the most unblemished records ever possessed by any man since the angels sang together for glory at the creation.

All that a nation can do and all that an individual can do in reference to past mistakes is to take the wisest action under existing circumstances to minimize to the highest possible degree the consequences of those mistakes. . . .

[Page S7332.] Section 8 of article I of the Constitution declares that Congress shall have the power to declare war.   Section 10 of article I of the Constitution contains a provision that no State shall, without the consent of Congress, engage in war unless actually invaded or "in such imminent danger as will not admit of delay."   Section 4 of article IV of the Constitution provides that the United States shall guarantee to every State in this Union a republican form of government and shall protect each of them against invasions.

Mr. President, the provisions of the Constitution which I have just read make these things clear.   First, Congress and Congress alone has the power to declare a national or foreign war; and second, that the United States or even a State may engage in war without waiting for the consent of Congress when the United States or the State so acting is invaded or threatened with imminent invasion.

It seems to me that these propositons are made extremely plain by the words of the Constitution itself.   The question which arises in respect of the war powers of the United States is this: Who is to direct the tactical operations of the military forces of the United

States **when** a war is being fought? As I analyze the Church-Cooper amendment it asserts, in effect, that the Congress has some power to **direct** the actual operations in war of American troops in the theater of operations.

Mr. President, I submit that the Founding Fathers were not foolish enough to place the command of American troops engaged in **combat** operation in a Congress of the United States which is now composed of 100 Senators and 435 Representatives. I cannot imagine anything that would more nearly resemble bedlam than to have a council of war composed of 100 Senators and 435 Representatives to determine where the **enemy is to be attack**ed or how the defeat of the enemy is going to be undertaken, or how to protect American forces from destruction by an armed enemy.

We have had some historic filibusters in the Senate but the longest of those filibusters would, by comparison, constitute just a few laconic remarks if we were to undertake to have a war council composed of 535 different men with different notions. The Founding Fathers were wiser than that, so they put a provision in the Constitution to determine that the Commander in Chief of the Armed Forces of the United States was not to be the Members of the Senate and the Members of the House of Representatives, and it was not to be the Members of the Senate and the Members of the House of Representatives, **acting in conjunction or in opposition to the President.**

To make this plain, the Constitution of the United States declares, in section 2 of article II, that---

> The President shall be Commander-in-Chief of the Army
> and Navy of the United States, and of the Militia of the
> several states, when called into the actual service of the
> United States.

To be sure, no President or no power on earth can declare war, that is, put the United States in a national or foreign war, except the Congress of the United States; but after the Congress of the United States declares war, the President of the United States becomes the Commander in Chief of the Armed Forces of the United States and has the power to direct the action and practical operations of those forces in the theater where war is being waged.

This power is usually exercised by the President by way of delegation to military trained men. It may be noted, however, that on certain occasions President Washington undertook to direct the forces of the United States himself, as in the case of the Whisky Rebellion, and that President Lincoln on several occasions during the War Between the States undertook to direct, to a more or less limited degree, the actual operations of the Union forces.

I have high admiration and deep affection for those who are proponents of the Church-Cooper amendment, but I cannot escape the abiding conviction that this amendment, if adopted, would represent an attempt upon the part of the Congress of the United States to usurp and exercise, in part at least, the constitutional powers of the President of the United States as the Commander in Chief of our Army and Navy.

The Supreme Court declared, in an early case, Fleming v. Page, 9 Howard (U.S.) 603, that as the Commander in Chief, the President is authorized to direct the movement of the naval and military forces placed by law at his command, to employ them in the manner he may deem most effectual to harness, conquer, and subdue the enemy. It goes without saying that the President has the right to employ military forces in the manner he deems most effectual to protect them from destruction by an armed enemy.

The President, of course, has the advantage of the intelligence received by him from the intelligence sources on the scene in South Vietnam. He also has the advantage of the advice of men who have spent their lives studying military matters, and who for that reason are quite competent to give advice and assist in reaching conclusions as to what actual tactical operations should be undertaken at a specific time and at a specific place.

If the Church-Cooper amendment should be adopted by Congress, it would forbid the President from acting as Commander in Chief and it would forbid every military man acting under his command from putting a foot within the borders of Cambodia after the enactment of the amendment, even though such action was necessary to protect the American forces from annihilation. The amendment would also constitute the granting of an assurance by Congress that the North Vietnamese and the Vietcong can use the borders of Cambodia, even against the will of the people of Cambodia, to their hearts' content as sanctuaries for operations against American and South Vietnamese troops and the people of South Vietnam, and that the United States, as far as Congress can prescribe, will not do anything to molest them in such activities, even though such activities would threaten the destruction of American soldiers serving under the flag of our country in that far off corner of the earth to which they have been sent by the President, with the consent of Congress.

Mr. President, when I first rose to speak, I mentioned a book by one of our most distinguished constitutional lawyers and constitutional historians, Edwin S. Corwin, entitled The President: Office and Powers, 1787-1957. On page 228 of this book, he quoted a statement made on this subject by Alexander Hamilton in Federalist No. 69. I will not trespass upon the time of the Senate to read Alexander Hamilton's entire statement, but I should like to state to the Senate the interpretation placed on that statement by Professor Corwin. Professor Corwin makes this statement on page 228 of his book: "Rendered freely, this appears"---that is, Alexander Hamilton's statement---

to mean that in any war in which the United States becomes involved---one presumably declared by Congress---the President will be top general and top admiral of the forces provided by Congress, so that no one can be [Page S7333.] over him or be authorized to give him orders in the direction of the said forces; but otherwise he will have no powers that any military or naval commander not also President might not have.

In the succeeding pages of this book Professor Corwin proceeds to demonstrate that Alexander Hamilton was something of a piker when he said that the President will have no powers that any high military or naval commander not also President might not have.

The succeeding pages of Mr. Corwin's book demonstrate the great extent to which the powers of the President as Commander in Chief of the military forces of this Nation in time of war have been expanded. I would suggest to some of our friends, who are not willing to accord the President the power to direct the actual operation of troops in combat, to read Professor Corwin's book and see how the powers of the President as Commander in Chief have been expanded by interpretations placed upon this provision in the Constitution by the Supreme Court in subsequent days and particularly during the First and Second World Wars.

There is nothing obscure in reading Chief Justice Marshall's so well declared statement in the case of Gibson against Ogden:

> We should take it for granted, in seeking to interpret the constitution, that the framers of the Constitution used words just as ordinary men do to express their intentions.

Mr. President (Mr. FANNIN), let us see what words the framers used in setting out the congressional power to declare war. They said, "Congress shall have the power to declare war."

Now there is no obscure meaning in the word "war." There is no obscure meaning in the word "declare."

Anyone can pick up a dictionary and find that the word "war" means---"A state of open, armed conflict carried on between nations, states, or parties."

He will also find that the word "declare" means---"To state officially or formally, to state with emphasis or authority."

It also means---"To affirm."

Now, Mr. President, I maintain that the Gulf of Tonkin resolution, which is technically known as the Southeast Asia resolution, constitutes a declaration of war in a constitutional sense.

What does that resolution say?

It asserts in its preamble---

> Whereas naval units of the Communist regime in Viet Nam, in violation of the principles of the Charter of the United Nations and of international law, have deliberately and repeatedly attacked United States naval vessels lawfully present in international waters, and have thereby created a serious threat to international peace. . . .

That is one of the assertions in the preamble, a preamble passed by both Senate and House with only two dissenting votes.

The next assertion is that---

Whereas these attacks are part of a deliberate and systematic campaign of aggression that the Communist regime in North Viet Nam has been waging against its neighbors and the nations joined with them in collective defense of their freedom. . . .

Thus, here in the preamble of the Southeast Asia resolution, the Congress of the United States declares two significant facts. First, that the naval vessels of the United States have been deliberately and repeatedly attacked by North Vietnamese naval forces; and, second, that the attacks are a part of a deliberate and systematic campaign of aggression that North Vietnam is waging against South Vietnam.

Then, after the account of those recitations and those facts, it states:

Resolved by the Senate and House of Representatives of the United States of America in Congress assembled, That the Congress approves and supports the determination of the President, as Commander-in-Chief, to take all necessary measures to repel any armed attack against the forces of the United States and to prevent further aggression.

Mr. President, there is no other way that has ever been devised by the mind of man to repel an armed attack except by force. Thus, Congress expressly stated in the first paragraph, following the preamble to the Southeast Asia resolution, that the President was empowered to take all the necessary measures to repel any armed attack against the forces of the United States and to prevent further aggression. Now, "aggression" as mentioned in the resolution means the aggression of North Vietnam upon its neighbors and the nations joined with them in collective defense of their freedom.

Section 2 of the resolution states in effect that---

Consonant with the Constitution of the United States and the Charter of the United Nations and in accordance with its obligations under the Southeast Asia Collective Defense Treaty, the United States is, therefore, prepared, as the President determines, to take all necessary steps, including the use of armed force, to assist any member or protocol state of the Southeast Asia Collective Defense Treaty requesting assistance in defense of its freedom.

Mr. President, that is strikingly in harmony with the declaration that the United States made when it went to war with Spain in 1898.

On April 20, 1898, after the sinking of the battleship Maine in the harbor of Havana, the Congress of the United States passed the following resolution, which every one who has studied the subject admits to being a declaration of war. It is strikingly similar to the Southeast Asia resolution and even contains the same assertion made in the closing paragraph of the Southeast Asia resolution, that the United States has no territorial ambitions:

Whereas the abhorrent conditions which have existed
for more than three years in the island of Cuba, so near
our own borders, have shocked the moral sense of the people
of the United States, have been a disgrace to Christian
civilization, culminating, as they have, in the destruction
of a United States battleship, with two hundred and sixty-
six of its officers and crew, while on a friendly visit in
the harbor of Habana, and can not longer be endured, as has
been set forth by the President of the United States in his
message to Congress of April 11, 1898, upon which the action
of the Congress was invited: Therefore,

Resolved by the Senate and House of Representatives of
the United States of America in Congress assembled, First. That
the people of the island of Cuba are, and of right ought to be,
free and independent.

Second. That it is the duty of the United States to
demand, and the Government of the United States does hereby
demand, that the Government of Spain at once relinquish its
authority and government in the island of Cuba and withdraw
its land and naval forces from Cuba and Cuban waters.

Third. That the President of the United States be, and
he hereby is, directed and empowered to use the entire land
and naval forces of the United States, and to call into the
actual service of the United States the militia of the several States, to such extent as may be necessary to carry
these resolutions into effect.

Fourth. That the United States hereby disclaims any
disposition or intention to exercise sovereignty, jurisdiction, or control over said island except for the paci-
fication thereof, and asserts its determination when that
is accomplished to leave the government and control of the
island to its people.

Let us see what it takes to declare war. A very learned scholar,
W. Taylor Reveley, III, wrote an interesting article which appeared
in the Virginia Law Journal for November, 1969, entitled, "Presidential War-Making: Constitutional Power or Usurpation."

I read this statement from pages 1283 and 1284:

It seems reasonably clear from proposals made and rejected at the Constitutional Convention, from debates there,
subsequent statements by the Framers and from practice in
early years that the Drafters intended decisions regarding
the initiation of force abroad to be made not by the President alone, not by the Senate alone, nor by the President
and the Senate, but by the entire Congress subject to the
signature or veto of the President.

Mr. President, in other words Mr. Reveley says in substance that
the Congress declares war when it authorized the initiation of the

use of the military force of the United States in lands lying outside of the United States. He then adds, on page 1289 and following:

> Congressional authorization need not be by formal declaration of war. . . .

In other words, the Congress does not have to pass a resolution saying: "Congress hereby declares war."

Mr. Reveley adds further in the Virginia Law Journal:

> "[N]either in the language of the Constitution, the intent of the framers, the available historical and judicial precedents nor the purposes behind the clause" is there a requirement for such formality, particularly under present circumstances when most wars are deliberately limited in scope and purpose. A joint resolution, signed by the President, is the most tenable method of authorizing the use of force today. To be meaningful, the resolution should be passed only after Congress is aware of the basic elements of the situation, and has had reasonable time to consider their implications. The resolution should not, as a rule, be a blank check leaving the place, purpose and duration of hostilities to the President's sole discretion. To be realistic, however, the resolution must leave the Executive wide discretion to respond to changing circumstances. If the legislators wish to delegate full responsibility to the President, it appears [Page S7334.] that such action would be within the constitutional pale so long as Congress delegates with full awareness of the authority granted.

I am certain that when Congress passed the Gulf of Tonkin joint resolution, it was aware of what authority it was granting to the President of the United States. This is made exceedingly clear by a statement which one of the opponents of the resolution made on the floor of the Senate.

Former Senator Wayne Morse made this statement:

> We are, in effect, giving the President of the United States warmaking powers in the absence of a declaration of war. I believe that to be an historic mistake.

Former Senator Morse stated that by passing the Gulf of Tonkin joint resolution Congress was giving to the President warmaking powers. I agree with that statement of former Senator Morse to that extent. But I disagree with the statement that Congress was doing it without a declaration of war, because I contend that the Gulf of Tonkin joint resolution is clearly a declaration of war.

Let us now examine another facet of this situation. When the resolution was under consideration in the Senate, the Senator from

Kentucky (Mr. COOPER) put this question to the distinguished Senator
from Arkansas (Mr. FULBRIGHT), the floor manager of the Gulf of Tonkin
joint resolution:

> Mr. Cooper. Does the Senator consider that in enacting
> this resolution we are satisfying that requirement of Article
> IV of the Southeast Asia Collective Defense Treaty? In other
> words, are we now giving the President advance authority to
> take whatever action he may deem necessary respecting South
> Vietnam and its defense, or with respect to the defense of
> any other country included in the treaty?
>
> Mr. Fulbright. I think that is correct.
>
> Mr. Cooper. Then looking ahead, if the President de-
> cided it was necessary to use such force as could lead into
> war we will give that authority by this resolution?
>
> Mr. Fulbright. That is the way I would interpret it.

Mr. FULBRIGHT added:

> If a situation later developed in which we thought
> approval should be withdrawn it could be withdrawn by con-
> current resolution.

Mr. President, there are two interesting cases in which the Supreme Court passed on the question of what is a declaration of war.
The earliest of these cases is entitled Bas against Tingy, 4 Dallas,
page 36. The question involved the rescue of an American vessel and
the right to certain compensation. The amount of compensation de-
pended upon whether the rescue was from an enemy. The question arose
in this case as to whether or not this American vessel, which had
rescued another vessel from the French---who were then giving us a
good deal of trouble by seizing vessels on the high seas---was entitled to a high rate of compensation because the rescue occurred in
time of war. The Supreme Court unanimously decided that the rescuing
ship was entitled to the higher compensation because the rescue occurred during a war between the United States and France.

Now, Congress had never passed any act or any resolution declaring
war against France in so many terms, but it had passed laws governing
that Americans could seize vessels operated by the French, something
in the nature of letters of marque and reprisal. In that case Judge
Chase said:

> What, then, is the nature of the contest subsisting
> between America and France? In my judgment, it is a
> limited, partial war; Congress has not declared war, in
> general terms; but congress has authorized hostilities on
> the high seas, by certain persons, in certain cases.
> There is no authority given to commit hostilities on land;
> to capture unarmed French vessels, nor even to capture
> French armed vessels, lying in a French port; and the

authority is not given indiscriminately to every citizen
of America, against every citizen of France, but only to
citizens appointed by commissions, or exposed to immediate
outrage and violence. So far it is, unquestionably, a
partial war; but, nevertheless, it is a public war, on
account of the public authority from which it emanates.

This statement appears on page 43 and clearly recognizes that
where Congress authorized certain Americans to carry on hostilities
against French vessels that Congress had declared war within the
purview of the section of the Constitution vesting the Congress the
power to declare war.

Another case is Marks v. United States, 161 U.S. 297. I will
read the opinion of Justice Brewer on page 301:

As war cannot lawfully be commenced on the part of the
United States without an Act of Congress, such an Act is,
of course, a formal official notice to all the world, and
equivalent to the most solemn declaration.

Now, manifestly when Congress passed the Southeast Asian resolution, it solemnly declared, in effect, that our naval vessels were
being attacked by North Vietnam, that this attack was part and parcel
of the aggression which North Vietnam was inflicting upon South Vietnam, that pursuant to the Constitution, the Charter of the United
Nations, and our obligations under the SEATO Treaty, Congress was
authorizing the President to take all necessary measures, including
the use of armed forces to repel attacks on our ships, to repel aggression on South Vietnam and the other nations covered by the SEATO
Treaty. When Congress declared these things, it was certainly declaring that a state of war existed. Congress was declaring that it
consented for the President to initiate hostilities and the use of our
Armed Forces in South Vietnam and Southeast Asia. Nothing could be
plainer than that.

A study of this very question was made and is set forth in the
Notes in the Harvard Law Review for June, 1968, entitled "Congress,
the President, and the Power to Commit Forces to Combat." This is a
long article and deals with the war powers of Congress and the President. I wish to read a statement from page 1804, in which the writer
of the Notes makes this declaration:

The second section, however, proclaims that "the United
States is . . . prepared, as the President determines, to
take all necessary steps, including the use of armed force,
to assist any member or protocol state of the Southeast Asia
Collective Defense Treaty requesting assistance in defense
of its freedom." This rather comprehensive language certainly supports the interpretation given it by the administration that it is a functional equivalent of a declaration
of war and as such the President my conduct the war as he
sees it.

I do not see how anything can be plainer than the fact that when Congress adopted the Tonkin Gulf resolution, or the Southeast Asia resolution, as it is sometimes called, it declared war on North Vietnam and authorized the President of the United States to use our Armed Forces to protect the Armed Forces of the United States, and to repel aggression from North Vietnam.

Mr. President, I digress here for a moment to note that a plausible case can be made for the proposition that when Hanoi declared, in 1960, that it would . . . "liberate South Vietnam from the ruling yoke of United States imperialists and their henchmen" Hanoi declared war upon the United States and upon its forces then stationed in South Vietnam.

This brings us to the question whether or not President Nixon exceeded his constitutional and legal powers when he ordered our Armed Forces in Vietnam to join the South Vietnamese in wiping out the sanctuaries which the North Vietnamese and the Vietcong had established on the borders of Cambodia fronting on South Vietnam.

During his remarks which will follow my speech, the distinguished Senator from California (Mr. MURPHY) portrays in eloquent language the purpose of this action and the results thus far obtained by this action.

Charges have been made that this was the initiation of a new war. I controvert that charge. This is just the same war with the same enemy. For 5 years the North Vietnamese have been using these sanctuaries along the border of South Vietnam. They have been sallying forth and making attacks, destroying American lives and destroying the lives of South Vietnamese troops and the lives of South Vietnamese civilians, and then running back to the sanctuaries where the United States had been giving them total exemption from the hot pursuit doctrine which prevails in wars.

Cambodia is a neutral country, or has attempted to be a neutral country, but it has been compelled to permit the North Vietnamese and the Vietcong to use these sanctuaries as a base of military operations against U.S. forces and South Vietnamese forces for 5 years.

In my honest judgment, President Nixon, as the Commander in Chief of the American military forces in Vietnam, and as the individual charged above all others with responsibility for protecting the American forces, as far as possible, against unnecessary deaths and wounds had a perfect, legal right---a perfect constitutional right---to put American troops into action to wipe out these sanctuaries of our enemy in Cambodia along the border of South Vietnam.

Also, President Nixon had a right to do this under international law. International law places upon every neutral country the duty to protect its neutrality, that is, to deny the use of its territory by a belligerent nation as a base for its [Page S7335.] military operations. If a neutral country is unable to enforce its own neutrality, then, under international law, a belligerent which is being injured by the use of the territory of the neutral nation by an opposing belligerent has a right to enter such territory and take such steps as are reasonably designed to put an end to this unlawful use of the territory of the neutralist nation by the opposing belligerent nation. This is what the United States has done in going into Cambodia.

During previous years, I have received many requests from fine and well-meaning persons that I rise upon the Senate floor and denounce our presence and conduct in South Vietnam as illegal and outrageous.

Even if I were sure that these persons had complete possession of all the truth on the subject, I would be reluctant to do this for one reason and incapable of doing it for another.

While I am always ready to participate in efforts to persuade our National Government to pursue wise policies or abandon foolish ones, I am ever reluctant to denounce my country in respect to its contests with foreign foes. This is true because I was nurtured on the brand of patriotism which prompted Senator <u>CRITTENDEN</u> to make this statement while the Mexican War was raging:

> I hope to find my country in the right; however, I will stand by her, right or wrong.

My incapability to stand upon the Senate floor and denounce the United States for its presence and conduct in South Vietnam arises out of this consideration: My action in so doing would lend aid and comfort to Ho Chi Minh and his Vietcong because it would tend to engender in them the belief that America's will to fight is weak and that they will be masters of South Vietnam if they prolong the war and slay more Americans.

I think that the Church-Cooper amendment is unconstitutional, in that it attempts to have Congress usurp and exercise some of the powers to direct the military forces in the theater of operations which belong, under the Constitution, to the President of the United States.

But apart from any question of constitutionality and any question of legality, I would say that we should remember what St. Paul said in I Corinthians chapter 10, verse 23:

> All things are lawful for me, but all things are not expedient: all things are lawful for me, but all things edify not.

My dictionary informs me that the word "edify" means "to instruct or enlighten so as to encourage moral and spiritual improvement."

I do not think it would encourage moral or spiritual improvement, and therefore it would not edify, for the Congress of the United States to pass a resolution which would tend to destroy the last hope we have of achieving a just and lasting peace in South Vietnam by negotiations now being carried on in Paris between the

representatives of the United States and the representatives of the
South Vietnamese Government with the representatives of North Vietnam
and the Vietcong or the National Liberation Front.

The passage of a resolution of this character would say that if
they just continue, the United States, in effect, has lost the will
to carry on, and that they can take over everything there after we
depart, which will be speedily. That is the inference they will draw
from it.

I think it would not be edifying for the Congress of the United
States to say that American troops cannot put a foot across the borders of Cambodia to destroy sanctuaries of the enemy, but that the
enemy, as far as Congress is concerned, can use those areas as sanctuaries from which to make sudden surprise attacks upon American
soldiers.

I think that the country is in no mood to seek a military victory
in South Vietnam, and for that reason it should undertake to withdraw
in a sound and sensible manner---in a manner which would make that
area we have been trying to protect as safe as possible from our enemy, in a way which would contribute to future peace and security.

I remember, between the First and the Second World Wars, when
Hitler and Mussolini came to power in Germany and Italy. They began
to rattle their sabers, Americans did not want to be involved in another world war, as they had been involved in the First World War;
so they decided that they would contrive some way to make certain
that we would not be involved in another world war if Hitler and
Mussolini saw fit to plunge the world into darkness again. So Cong-
gress passed the Neutrality Act. It passed that act with good motives; it passed it with the desire to keep America out of any new
world war.

The Neutrality Act declared that we would be neutral, that we
would not assist any nation, even though it was fighting for its
ultimate liberty, and that we would not even furnish any supplies to
help a nation fighting for its liberty against Hitler or Mussolini
with our material of war unless that nation came here, in its own
ships, and paid us cash on the barrelhead for those materials.

That act was passed with good motives. It was passed to keep us
from becoming involved in another world war. But it was exactly what
Hitler and Mussolini were looking for, that is, having the assurance
from Congress that Europe could go hang so far as the United States
was concerned. After passage of that act, Hitler and Mussolini realized that they could extinguish the liberties of the peoples of
Europe, and they need not fear the intervention of the United States.

Hitler and Mussolini went to war, and the declarations of the
Neutrality Act, which were passed in good faith, with the noble purpose of keeping us out of war, were the things which prompted Hitler
and Mussolini to plunge the world into the Second World War; and it
contributed, by so doing, to the deaths, the untimely deaths, of
millions of helpless men, women, and children.

What will happen if Congress passes resolutions such as the
Cooper-Church amendment and tells the enemy, "You can use the sanctuaries to kill our boys," but our boys cannot invade the sanctuaries

to protect their own lives? If we pass such resolutions, regardless of whether there has been any peace agreement and regardless of what the conditions are, we will be attempting to repeal history, in an effort to repeal past mistakes. It cannot be done, I said at the beginning of my argument that the Creator of the universe made it impossible for either a nation or an individual to repeal its mistakes or the consequences of its mistakes. I think that is undoubtedly true. As the Persian poet said:

> The Moving Finger writes; and, having writ,
> Moves on: nor all your Piety nor Wit
>   Shall lure it back to cancel half a Line,
> Nor all your Tears wash out a Word of it.

We cannot wash out our involvement in the war. We cannot escape the mistakes of history. We must try to minimize those mistakes.

One of the worst mistakes we could make would be to withdraw from Vietnam without getting a peace treaty or without having the South Vietnamese troops trained to the point that we could reasonably hope that they could defend their own country.

I am in favor of trying to settle this war by negotiation. I am in favor of withdrawing from Vietnam if we can do so in a safe and sound manner. If we cannot come to an agreement by negotiation, then let us train the South Vietnamese troops in order that they might be able to defend their own country. Let us not precipitately flee from South Vietnam because we may save our hides at this moment. It will not contribute to the future peace or the future safety of our country. Instead of doing that, it will be sowing the seeds of future wars of this character. . . .

Mr. MURPHY. First of all, I should like to associate myself with the very learned and well-prepared remarks of the Senator with reference to the constitutional conditions with which we are here confronted. I think the distinguished Senator has clarified a great deal of the contrived confusion that has been rampant in the country.

It is of great concern to this Senator that amid the intense objections to the President's decision---which was taken, as my distinquished colleague points out, on the basis of all the intelligence, all the information, and all the knowledge of the experts---we hear very little about the success of this operation.

I have looked as carefully as I can to find the information which I know is available. I have listened to the reports. I hope that my distinguished colleague will permit me, at this point, to suggest that so far, rather than extending or expanding the war, this military operation, this expedition into Cambodia, has in my opinion done more to shorten the war than any other one thing that has happened in 6 years.

I will explain why. In the first place, as of this morning, we had captured 3,305 tons of rice. That is enough to provide manmonths of food for 145,420 North Vietnamese soldiers. We have captured 15,763 rockets. We have captured mortar rounds. These are the ones

that are extremely troublesome, where they can sneak in at night, set
it down, fire five or six rounds, move off with it, and be gone before dawn. This is the one that lately has been hitting hospitals
and schools indiscriminately, as part of the system of atrocity that
has been used by the North Vietnamese in order to frighten [Page S7337.]
the South Vietnamese into subjugation. Mortar rounds captured, 38,879.

Small arms ammunition captured, 11,502,740. Let us say that one
bullet out of 50 hits an American soldier. I think this alone is
worth the trip.

I should like to point out that, in keeping with the President's
promise, the first group of the ARVN troops, the South Vietnamese who
had gone into the southernmost perimeter, had completed their mission,
and were moving out as of 3 days ago. I do not understand why we do
not hear about this.

Land mines: These are the scourge of the troops. The mines
are hidden in the bushes, in the jungle, in the swamps, triggered in
all sorts of ways.

They have captured 1,865, almost 2,000, that will not go off and
injure and maim Americans and South Vietnamese.

Bunkers destroyed: These are heavily constructed, permanent type
bunkers, from which the North Vietnamese had been conducting their
entire operation in this area. Bunkers destroyed, as of this morning,
4,651.

This, without question, has been even a greater success than envisioned by those who pleaded, as my distinguished colleague has
pointed out, that it was necessary and the immediacy forced it to be
done at the moment.

The President's program, based on the weather in that area, will
gain us 8 to 9 months in the continuation of the Vietnamization program, so that the good people of South Vietnam will have an opportunity to be trained, armed, and supplied so that they can carry on
their own job, which they are perfectly willing to do, once they are
given the chance.

The enemy killed in this operation, because of the surprise, because of the logistics, the way it was planned, number 6,945. Pris-
oners taken, 1,576. Individual weapons captured, over 9,000. This
goes on endlessly.

Without question, this is the most successful operation. Those
who say, "Well, we don't believe that the President means it when he
says they are going to go in, clean up this area, and get out," have
no reason to doubt it, no reason whatever. He has promised, and he
has kept his word thus far. . . .

Mr. JORDAN of North Carolina. [Page S7339.] It has been
brought out here on the floor of the Senate today---this was the Friday casualty list---that our forces have killed 6,495 of the enemy,
that we have captured 1,576 enemy soldiers, and we are getting a lot
of information from them.

In addition, they have captured individual weapons, 9,109, and that includes machineguns and all types of guns used that would have been used to kill our own boys, not theirs.

Mr. ERVIN. I rejoice in the figures that we have captured, approximately 8-1/2 million rounds of small arms ammunition, including ammunition for large-caliber machineguns. A lot of men can be killed with 8-1/2 million rounds of ammunition. I thank the good Lord, as a result of this incursion into Cambodia, that these 8-1/2 million rounds of ammunition will not be used to kill American boys.

Mr. JORDAN of North Carolina. The information I have up to today is that they have captured 11,502,740 rounds of ammunition.

Mr. ERVIN. I knew it was higher than the figure I gave. My figure was based on May 13.

Mr. JORDAN of North Carolina. In addition to that, no army can survive very long without something to eat. Our forces have captured 3,305 tons of rice, which would support the large detachment of soldiers for, I understand, 4 months that they have over there. There is no question about it, this maneuver has done irreparable damage to their forces.

The question I should like to ask the Senator now is---I think I know what his answer will be---but in his opinion, all the damage we have done over there and the supplies and material captured and taken away there, and the other things which have been done in this partic- ular engagement, in the Senator's opinion, will this not shorten the war and bring our boys home quicker?

Mr. ERVIN. I would think so. According to all the information I have from the military who are familiar with the situation, it will certainly prevent the North Vietnamese from mounting a substantial offensive from that area until after the monsoon rains next November. That will give us that much more additional time to train the South Vietnamese. . . .

PUBLIC OPINION AND THE VIETNAM WAR*

(May 19, 1970)

Mr. GORE. [Page S7462.] Mr. President. . . .

It takes fortitude to admit a mistake but, as the Confucian maxim goes, the man who makes a mistake and fails to correct it has made a second mistake. Some weeks ago, in testimony before the Sen- ate Veteran's Affairs Subcommittee, a former Air Cavalry captain who lost both legs and his right arm when he picked up a live grenade at Kje Sanh, came close to summing up our entire country's dilemma in these words:

> To the devastating psychological effect of getting
> maimed, paralyzed, or in some way unable to re-enter
> American life as you left it, is the added psychological

weight that it may not have been worth it: that the war
may have been a cruel hoax, an American tragedy that left
a small minority of Young American males holding the bag.

There is much to be proud of in the debate we have held among ourselves in the Senate and in the debate the American people have engaged
in between themselves. It is a mark of the strength and resiliency of
American democracy that we do not fear to air our differences in the
open. The leaders of the Soviet Union would never dare to permit a
public debate like the Vietnam debate in America; they lack the necessary confidence in themselves and in their society. I believe, with
Justice Holmes---

    That the ultimate good desired is better reached by free
    trade in ideas---that the best test of truth in the power of
    the thought is to get itself accepted in the competition of
    the market.

True, a Senator's words uttered here in this Chamber may be quoted
in Hanoi, but shall this prevent us from speaking the truth to our own
people and among ourselves? Shall we permit the possibility of being
quoted to subvert our system? Shall we forsake our system of popular
government in order that we will not be quoted in our efforts to speak
the truth and engage in free debate?

The case for the war in Vietnam was vigorously advanced in the
competition of our free market of ideas for 5 years. It was packaged
and repackaged, hard-sold and soft-sold. It was promoted by every
dazzling technique known to Madison Avenue---with an advertising budget of Pentagon dimensions.

They even have coined such phrases as "Vietnamization," "protective reaction," "ground combat troops," which seem to have a meaning
different from that which I would understand. But Vietnam showed
itself to be an "Edsel." With everything going for it but merit the
frenetic effort to "sell" Vietnam to America has finally gone on the
rocks---a casualty of the decency, the judgment and the commonsense
of the American people.

Mr. President, for the first time since I have been a Member of
this body, my office staff is utterly swamped and unable to answer the
mail that is arriving by the hour.

The post office in the Senate Office Building, as of yesterday,
was 1 whole week behind in the delivery of mail to Senate offices
within the same building. My staff tells me mail is stacked out in
the halls as if trailer trucks had been unloaded in the hallways of
the Senate Office Building. When I left the office an hour or so ago,
before coming to the floor of the Senate, there were bundles of mail
yet untied.

The American people are aroused. They have been led to believe
that somehow, though in a drawn-out fashion, the war was being ended.
Now, in order to shorten the war, it is said, in order to save lives,
we broaden the war, widen the war, increase the casualties.

Mr. President, this invasion of a small country has taken a
tragic toll of America's moral position in the world. This country of
ours has been able to muster a majority in the United States when it
was put to the test. It has been able to do so in large part because
of its history of respect for the sovereignty of small nations. Just
as we have in our own society the principle of one man, one vote, we
have advocated in the United Nations one mission, one vote. We stood
as protector of the weak and the small.

Imagine my chagrin to sit in the White House and hear an analogy
drawn by the President of the United States between our invasion of
Cambodia and Russia's invasion of Czechoslovakia. In order that it
be not misunderstood, I wish to relate what happened. One of my colleagues inquired of the President if in his opinion the incursion,
the invasion, or the episode, whatever it is that sent thousands of
American soldiers into Cambodia, would have an adverse effect upon the
Strategic Arms Limitation Conference now underway in Geneva. The
President expressed himself negatively. I did not take down all of
his answer because I am not a stenographer, but I took down one sen-
tence verbatim because it struck me so forcefully. In the course of
his answer he said, "We expect the Soviets to protest this just as we
protested their invasion of Czechoslovakia."

Mr. President, I do not want to see my country equated with the
Russian invasion of Czechoslovakia. This has shocked our friends
around the world and the unpredictability and the instability of the
leadership which this demonstrates has shocked business leaders and
professional leaders within our own country. We do not have to go
beyond the market place to see the effect of this. I think this was
a serious mistake in judgment.

President Nixon was elected President of the United States as
the peace candidate because he said he had a plan to end the war. His
plan was kept secret, but at least he said he had a plan; he promised
to end the war and the people elected him President.

Mr. President, how do American people remain the masters of their
fate? How does their democratic system operate? Perhaps what I am
about to say may be indelicate politically, but I want to point it out
because it is the background of the frustration and bitterness that is
dividing this country.

Who was the peace candidate for President in 1964? I will not
characterize the position of my distinguished colleague, the Senator
from Arizona (Mr. GOLDWATER). History records that. I do know that
it was Lyndon Baines Johnson who promised the American people emphati-
cally that he would not send American boys into a land war in Asia
to do for Asians what Asians should do for themselves. He was elected
by the largest majority in the history of our Republic.

Who was the peace candidate in 1968? As I have said, it was
Richard Milhous Nixon.

The people elected the President on the promise to end the war.
They elected President Johnson on the promise to keep us out of war.
How does our system work?

Mr. GRIFFIN. Mr. President, will the Senator yield?

Mr. GORE. In just a moment I will. It must work, and the Senate must bear a part in making it work. I say this because a considerable number of Americans are now saying that the system has broken down, that the system is failing.

I do not share that doubt, but I ask you to share with me a determination to make it work, to implement the people's will. Every time the American people have had a chance to express themselves about the Vietnam war, it has been on the side of peace. I referred to the expression "nationwide."

I yield to the Senator from Michigan.

Mr. GRIFFIN. The distinguished senator from Tennessee was trying to make some comparison between the incumbent in the White House and his precedessor. I do not know that this serves any particular purpose, but as long as he has tried to make the comparison, I cannot very well let the occasion go by without making the statement that under the predecessor of the President who now serves, we sent more and more boys until we had over 500,000 boys in Vietnam, and I seem to be aware of the fact that under this President we now have 115,000 fewer American troops, and he has announced that another 150,000 will come home in the next 11 months, if we will give him an opportunity to do so.

I wonder if that is a very valid comparison that the Senator from Tennessee was trying to draw.

Mr. GORE. I was not attempting to draw a comparison between the Presidents or with respect to their administrations. The point I was seeking to make was that the people elected President Lyndon Baines Johnson on a promise to keep us out of war, and it was President Johnson who sent combat forces into the war soon after that election; and it was [Page S7463.] the American people who elected President Richard M. Nixon on a promise to end the war, and yet in May 1970 the war has widened, the casualties increase, and even if by next summer there are 150,000 fewer troops than there are now in Vietnam, it will still leave on the order of 250,000 Americans there, with no promise that the war will end then.

This war has been going on a long, long time; and if it continues until the summer of 1971, it means that an estimated 300,000 American boys, who have not as yet been sent to Vietnam, will be sent to Vietnam by that time. Why, mothers of 10-year-old boys are now nervous that their sons will have to go to Vietnam.

This is the longest war in our history, and our national security is not involved, in my opinion. What have we gained and what is there to gain?

Mr. President, these are some of the reasons why the American people are so wrought up on this issue. . . .

I am not a pacifist, nor have I ever been. I have not and I do not oppose any and all wars regardless of their character and causes.

Given Pearl Harbor and all the mad machinations of Hitler, I had no doubt of the justice of American involvement in World War II. But this war in Vietnam is neither just nor necessary nor in our national interest.

Despite his professed intention of ending the war, President Nixon, like former President Johnson, has now escalated and widened the war. He has offered three basic arguments---the same as President Lyndon Johnson---for continuing American involvement in Vietnam. All three, in my view, are defective.

The supposition that the war in Vietnam is part of an overall Communist plan for world conquest is without basis in fact, a scare fantasy of the radical right repudiated by every serious observer of Asian and Communist affairs---at least by most observers. It survives, nonetheless, because people in high office, who should know better, still invoke it when they are casting about for justifications for American military involvement in Vietnam. . . .

The second major argument used to justify American military interest in Vietnam is that it inspires confidence throughout the world in America's determination to honor her commitments. I wonder what commitment he has honored in invading Cambodia. In his speech of last November 3, President Nixon said that putting an end to our interest in Vietnam "would result in a collapse of confidence in American leadership not only in Asia but throughout the world."

Confidence in American leadership has now suffered a heavy blow both at home and in many parts of the world, not because we are thought to have held back in Vietnam but because we have plunged deeper into an Asian land war, plunged recklessly and on so vast a scale, because once again a U.S. President has become mesmerized with the mirage of Vietnam.

[Page S7464.] The third and most patently specious of the arguments for our interest in Vietnam is that it has something to do with the defense of freedom and self-determination. Even our policymakers are beginning to seem embarrassed when they talk about freedom and democracy in South Vietnam, because most Americans by now know something about the Saigon regime. They know that it is a corrupt military dicatorship which jails its political opponents, censors its press, and rules with no reliable popular support except that the South Vietnamese generals, big businessmen and top bureaucrats backed by the U.S. military. . . .

Wars have a momentum of their own. Once begun, their original causes are soon forgotten, and the very fact of war, the fact that the country is fighting, becomes the real reason it continues fighting. No one seems to know how to stop short of victory, yet victory has been officially ruled out by President Nixon. No one much cared about Serbia and Sarajavo once the First World War had been going for a few months, although the assassination of the Austrian archduke was supposed to have started it. And who now seriously cares about that half-imaginary skirmish in the Gulf of Tonkin 5-1/2 years ago---except for the fact that it was used to hoodwink Congress into writing the President a blank check? . . . .

Mr. MURPHY. Why do we not say, loudly and continuously, and with one voice, that the day that Moscow, and the puppets of Moscow, decide that this war should end, it will end? There is no mystery to it. I do not think one of my colleagues doubts that statement. Never in history has a nation or a people who were the leaders of a nation done as much as we over as long a period of time continuously to try to find a way and a means to end this terrible struggle.

Yet this is the longest war in history. Why? Because, once again, our military experts were not permitted to conduct the war as they wished. They were stopped and impeded by civilians, some of whom, I submit, have no expertise in these matters, and some of whom, on their record, I would submit, would be the last that I would go to for advice in this sort of problem. . . .

[Page S7470.] I can assure my colleague that there was no intent on the part of President Nixon to expand the war; that the action which he has taken was taken after careful consideration, long talks with his advisers, consideration of all the intelligence. After all, he is the only one who gets it all, as far as I can find out. It was not with the intent to expand. It was taken, on the contrary, in the hope that it would bring about a quicker end and make it possible to bring home the American troops over there not only as fast as he has promised, but faster.

Hopefully, this may be achieved, but we must remember that he does not control all the conditions. The enemy, unfortunately, has to be considered in these matters, and the enemy will certainly do everything that they can conceive of and everything they can physically do to make certain that there is a failure in our efforts to reduce our American forces and bring about peace, as President Nixon has been trying to do. There is no question about that.

One of the ways they will go about it is through the means of international propaganda. They are not youngsters at this; they are experts. We must remember that they took the process of the "Big Lie" which worked so effectively in Germany for the Nazis, adopted it, and improved it. They have been busily at work on it. I have been engaged in a study of this subject, have gained knowledge of it, have talked about it, and have planned in relation to it for 20 years. I have watched it in all sorts of areas---cultural exchange areas, motion picture festivals, music festivals, all sorts of areas [Page S7471.] where, quietly, slowly, but consistently, there is always the attempt to create the impression that anything America does is bad, and everything a Communist nation does is good.

That is not the case. The facts belie it. . . .

We must, Mr. President, therefore attempt to read the enemy's mind, to know his design and his plan, to know what he is thinking of, and hopefully be able to anticipate his strategy.

To do so, we must work from the same facts he has---all the facts, not just the few that suit our purpose, but all the conditions as they exist.

Like all of us here in this Chamber, the enemy has read the headlines about the recent protests against the President's action in Cambodia, and I am sure that he has equated the enormous volume of news coverage given to our dissenters with what he thinks is the percentage of our people who are in opposition to the President's program.

Well, as it turns out, the poll which was taken by Dr. Gallup
and lately released does not bear out that conclusion.

The enemy has also followed the resolutions and amendments which
have been offered, and others which may be introduced, in this Chamber.
Once again, I know that he must feel that our United States are becoming hopelessly and perhaps fatally disunited. That would please
him. He would have accomplished his purpose.

It was known as long ago as three years that the enemy understood
he could not win militarily in Vietnam and that his whole plan was to
do what is apparently now being done---to try to divide opinion at
home by any means, fair, foul, honest or dishonest, but somehow to
divide American opinion, destroy America's will, and destroy the determination to carry out the promises that we have made through Presidents
Eisenhower, Kennedy, Johnson, and now Nixon.

Frankly, if I were guiding the destinies of the North Vietnamese,
all I would do would be sit back and wait, under the present conditions.

There will be no need, if we continue down this path of divi-
siveness, for them to bury us. We will bury ourselves. And first we
will tear ourselves apart, piece by piece. . . .

EROSION OF CONGRESSIONAL RESPONSIBILITY*

(May 20, 1970)

Mr. MANSFIELD. [Page S7492.] Mr. President, President Nixon has
stated that all American troops will be removed from Cambodian territory by July 1, 1970, and that Americans will not reenter Cambodia in
the future. The Cooper-Church amendment is consistent with the President's pledge on Cambodia. By adopting the Cooper-Church amendment,
the Senate will be acting in concert---and let me emphasize those
words "in concert"---with his intent, even as it exercises its separate constitutional responsibility in matters of war and peace. The
Cooper-Church amendment will reinforce President Nixon's announced
expectation that the troops will be removed from Cambodia and that
they will not be ordered---without congressional sanction---back into
that nation.

It has been urged on the floor of the Senate that this action is
an attempt for the first time in history to define the limits of a
battlefield in a war. I think it is more appropriate to describe the
amendment as an effort to limit U.S. involvement, U.S. casualties,
and U.S. costs in a tragic war. It is an effort to confine the war
to a country before it spreads over a continent.

To speak of the Cooper-Church amendment as an affront to the
President as Commander in Chief is to affront the Senate. Each branch
has its own constitutional functions. The President has his duties.
We have ours. The Senate---the Congress---have fundamental constitutional responsibilities with respect to the Nation's foreign relations and warmaking. How can the assertion of this constitutional
obligation by the Senate be an affront to the President?

It seems to me that the constitutional distortion which treats
this amendment as an affront to the President is the consequence of
years of erosion, decades of erosion, of congressional responsibility
in these matters. For too long, the Senate has been all too ready to
accept this situation. It is time, now, for the Senate to stop going
along for the ride. We have reached the end of the line in Cambodia.
It is time to confront our own constitutional responsibilities in
matters of war and peace, to accept them and to act on them.

It is absurd to assert that the passage of the amendment will
cut off funds from Americans who are fighting in Cambodia and, thus,
put them in jeopardy. Not a single life will be lost because of this
amendment, but many will have been lost because it was not on the
statute books before the offensives were launched inside Cambodia.
If anything, this amendment will curb the accumulation of new casualties in Cambodia by assuring the return of American forces from the
jeopardy in which they have been placed in Cambodia without the advice
or the consent of the Senate.

The amendment is not a rash and reckless step. It is the surest
way of protecting the safety of the U.S. forces in Cambodia because it
will require their withdrawal in accordance with the President's own
timetable. Yet, to take the President at his word is now called a repudiation of the President. That is the same kind of reverse logic
which sees expanding the violence throughout Indochina and, hence,
rising American casualties and costs, as the safest and shortest path
out of Vietnam.

. . . I do know that foreign relations and warmaking are among
the most serious problems of Government which come within the purview
of the Constitution. I do know that both branches of the Government
are involved in them---expressly and implicitly---by the Constitution.
That the Congress neglected to assert a sufficient responsibility at
the outset of Vietnam---as we did neglect to do under the previous
administration---is no excuse for not facing up to it now.

If a reassertion of a constitutional obligation by the Senate
prevents expedient decisions by the executive branch in the future
that is precisely its intent. Expediency is not the highest virtue
in a constitutional democracy. Indeed, I am not sure it is a durable
virtue in any society. In any event, I believe that the cross-checks
and safeguards of the constitutional processes in matters of war and
peace must be accepted by the Senate if we are to retain free constitutional government in this Nation.

The Cooper-Church amendment, Mr. President, is a valid step in
this process. It can act in concert and again I emphasize the words
"in concert"---with the President's intent, to close out this venture
into Cambodia and to shrink our involvement in Indochina where no
vital interests of this Nation are at stake, where our casualties now
number over 325,000, including almost 50,000 dead, and are still rising, where our costs are well in excess of $100 billion and where we
have immersed ourselves in a bottomless well of war---in a tragic
conflict without a visible end.

Mr. SCOTT. Mr. President, would the distinguished majority

leader yield, with the understanding that the distinguished Senator from Ohio (Mr. YOUNG) does not have this time taken from his time?

Mr. MANSFIELD. Mr. President, I yield with that understanding.

Mr. SCOTT. Mr. President, I have listened with interest and deep and genuine understanding to what the distinguished majority leader has said. I was reading a novel this week by Charles Collingwood, the correspondent, in which he has his principal character speaking with a distinguished activist for peace.

He says to him:

> We are both for peace. The difference is that you are obsessed with the principles involved and I am obsessed with the techniques.

To a great degree that is the dilemma facing the Senate, in trying to find and bring together the essential principles of ending the war in Cambodia and ending our involvement in Vietnam, accelerating at the greatest practical rate the withdrawal of our forces from Vienam consistent with their security and consistent with the obligations we have as well, and at the same time developing the techniques whereby these things are to be accomplished.

I am delighted that the distinguished majority leader has referred to the fact that the Cooper-Church amendment is designed to operate in concert with the declared intent or declared objectives of the President. I assume there would be no objection to our continuing to make that clear as we debate the Cooper-Church amendment.

Mr. MANSFIELD. Mr. President, quite the contrary, I would hope that we would emphasize it at every available opportunity. I understand the distinguished minority leader's thoughts and thinking on these problems. And I know that he and the others on the other side of the matter are just as much concerned as those who are in favor of the proposal.

Mr. SCOTT. Mr. President, as the distinguished majority leader knows, I have never at any time taken a position that I personally am automatically against any amendments to the military sales bill. Indeed, there will be several of them that I will support.

I am most hopeful that we can work out a consensus rather than a confrontation as we proceed with these amendments.

Therefore, I am also very grateful that the distinguished majority leader has referred to the date here of the 1st of July.

I said a few moments ago to the press that I have made a completely unauthorized statement. I have discussed this with no one with regard to this statement. But it is my personal opinion that we will be out of Cambodia before the 1st of July---I did not know how long before, whether it is an hour, a day, a week, 2 weeks, or 3 weeks. But I believe that we will be out of Cambodia before that date.

I believe the operation is a tactical success. However, it has become a matter of political concern to Americans of all opinions. . . .

[Page S7493.] I myself look not so much at the map as I look at the calendar because what we are concerned with is the operation of the calendar, the passage of time, and the shortening of time, which means the less time we are in Vietnam the less casualties we incur. . . .

Mr. GRIFFIN. Mr. President, I certainly do not take issue with anything that the distinguished minority leader has said; I am in full accord with his remarks. Yet, I cannot let some of the statements made by the distinguished majority leader---and we know he speaks with deep sincerity and great conviction---stand completely unchallenged.

This is an historic debate going on in the Senate. Among Senators there are some basic and fundamental differences in points of view which cannot be clouded over and should not be dismissed. As I said on the floor the other day, if any Senator wants to offer a resolution to declare war against the Government of North Vietnam, he would certainly be within his constitutional right to do so. The Constitution makes it very clear that Congress has that responsibility. Perhaps at some earlier date, Congress should have debated such a resolution and should have taken action, one way or the other.

The fact is that when this President assumed office, we were already in a war against North Vietnam.

I feel very strongly that the Church-Cooper resolution as now worded---I do not know what changes may develop, but as it is now worded---cuts off options and ties the hands of the Commander in Chief, in areas where he has the responsibility to make what are essentially battlefield decisions.

In World War II, we did not confine ourselves to fighting the enemy in Germany. We fought the enemy where we found him.

Mr. MANSFIELD. Based on a declaration of war.

Mr. GRIFFIN. That goes back to the point I have already made in this colloquy with the distinguished majority leader. It is within the power of Congress to declare war. But that is a very broad policy decision. The Church-Cooper proposal goes far beyond such a broad policy declaration. It seeks to make what, in effect, are battlefield decisions; it would tie the hands of the President as Commander in Chief in his ability to protect the lives of American forces.

I know it is not the intention of the sponsors to aid the enemy; of course, it is not. But the amendment, if it were adopted in its present form, would have the effect of aiding the enemy by tying the hands of the Commander in Chief in a way that would prevent him from making decisions that need to be made.

I know the distinguished majority leader makes his argument with deep sincerity and he is entitled to his convictions. I hope whatever compromise can be reached here will not tie the hands of the Commander in Chief in this very, very important hour in our history. At a time when he is not sending more and more troops to Southeast Asia but he is bringing more and more troops home, the President is entitled to good-faith support and confidence in Congress.

Mr. MANSFIELD. Mr. President, allow me to reply to the extent
that I saw on the ticker yesterday where the number of troops in
Southeast Asia has been increased by 1,200. It is only momentary.

The President himself tied his own hands because he is the one
who said U.S. forces would not go beyond 21 miles; and he is the one
who said we would be out not later than July 1, 1970.

What we are trying to do, in concert, is to add strength to the
President's sinews to give him support he is entitled to and deserves
in withdrawing from Cambodia, and to make certain what he has said
will be upheld by law throughout the Government.

Mr. GRIFFIN. Will the Senator agree that there are other substantive limitations in the Church-Cooper resolution which go beyond
what the President said?

Mr. MANSFIELD. No; only to the extent that there will not be a
reentry in Cambodia after July 1, 1970. And I am sure in my mind that
the President does not contemplate that. I think the Senate should
exercise some of its advice-and-consent functions with respect to the
President, rather than to leave them to those who are around the President all the time and are not aware of what the people whom we represent in the Nation are thinking.

Mr. CHURCH. Mr. President, I wish to say, first of all, that I
heard the President himself say he had no plan to return to Cambodia
after the present operation; that if any necessity were to arise in
the future for again reaching into Cambodia to strike at those sanctuaries, he said that would be undertaken by the South Vietnamese.
So I think there is nothing in the present amendment that contradicts
the policy as delineated by the President.

[Page S7494.] However, I hope the talk of compromise would stop.
What we are trying to reach, really, is an accommodation; not a compromise. The purpose of the amendment is neither to undercut the
President, nor to question his powers under the Constitution to dis-
charge his responsibilities as Commander in Chief. Indeed, even if
we wanted to do it, we could not reduce or diminish his constitutional
power anyway.

Rather, this amendment seeks to assert a congressional responsibility to share with the President the burden of defining the outer
limits of this operation in Cambodia.

We have drawn those limits exactly where the President fixed them.
If some change in language seems to be desirable in order to make the
intention perfectly clear, without in any way affecting the substantive
thrust of the amendment, then certainly as one sponsor, I would be most
amenable. Remember, this is a bipartisan effort. Some of the most
distinguished Republican Members of this body have joined in it, and
no aisle severs this debate as between Democrats and Republicans.

Mr. SCOTT. Mr. President, if the Senator will permit, I would
be very anxious to see made clear in the debate---perhaps the language
makes clear---that in the process of withdrawal from Cambodia, the
President does have the presidential power to protect those troops as
they are going out. We all want that. That is one of the other things
that I see is perfectly feasible. I am sure we can work it out.

Mr. MANSFIELD. There is no argument about that.

Mr. SCOTT. I do not see why.

Mr. CHURCH. The President is Commander in Chief. We do not question it. But Congress has powers, too, and it is time for Congress to exercise them. If we are going to come out of this war, there is only one way to do it, and that is for Congress and the President, standing together, to assume a joint responsibility for a plan which will bring us out. This amendment is drawn in that spirit and with that intention. However it may be construed in the course of the debate, that is the spirit and intention of the amendment. . . .

Mr. YOUNG of Ohio. Mr. President. . . .

For more than 10 years we in the United States have been paying, in blood and in billions of dollars, for Vietnamization of Vietnam; and the United States has no mandate from Almighty God to police the entire world.

Mr. President, within the next few days we shall have an opportunity to take the first step toward restoring the constitutional authority of Congress in foreign policy and waging war.

At the same time the Senate can move to introduce an element of sanity to U.S. policy in Indochina. This dual opportunity is presented to us in the pending amendment sponsored by the distinguished senior Senator from Kentucky (Mr. COOPER) and the distinguished senior Senator from Idaho (Mr. CHURCH) who spoke just this morning in this Chamber and who has all along been taking a solid, sound position in support of sanity in our policy in Southeast Asia. . . .

The Cooper-Church amendment is the first of several which will at long last give Senators and Congressmen, as representatives of the American people, the chance to declare whether they favor continuation, extension, and expansion of the Indochina war, or whether they wish to bring an end to our involvement in an immoral, undeclared war in Southeast Asia within the next 13 months. Because I favor the latter course, I shall vote for the Cooper-Church amendment.

This is not only an immoral and undeclared war, but it is the most unpopular war and longest war the United States has ever fought. It has cost a tremendous toll of killed in action and wounded. . . .

Mr. President, it has been stated that President Nixon rejected the advice of his Secretary of Defense and Secretary of State in ordering the invasion into Cambodia by men of our Armed Forces. I do not know about that. I am not privy to what goes on in the White House. But I do know that the President yielded to the CIA, the leaders of the military-industrial complex and the generals---including the Attorney General from Wall Street. The result is that thousands of American ground combat troops have been sent into battle in another distant Southeast Asian land. That decision was a tragic mistake involving grave risks.

The folly and failure of this latest adventure into Indochina are becoming increasingly evident. I note in an article before me that when President Nixon ordered American forces into Cambodia on May 1, he told the American people the mission was to destroy the central office for South Vietnam---COSVN, that is the Communist's jungle pentagon. President Nixon, in his demagogic television address to the American people announcing that the invasion of Cambodia had taken place, said U.S. troops were wiping out the Cambodian sanctuaries and that the main objective was to destroy the "headquarters for the entire Communist military operation in South Vietnam located in Cambodia" and that our troops would penetrate not to exceed 21 miles into Cambodia and that this entry into Cambodia and the operation would be completed by July 1.

That headquarters, known as COSVN, has not, in fact, been attacked by American or South Vietnamese forces, though that was the purpose, it was said, of this adventure across the border of a nation, Cambodia, whose neutrality we had guaranteed.

But it appears now, that this headquarters has not been found and destroyed, and that American military intelligence and the CIA are guilty of the most serious blunder since the time they assured General MacArthur that if he invaded North Korea the Chinese would not cross the Yalu and enter the Korean conflict. General MacArthur disregarded his instructions from President Truman, advanced into North Korea close to its northerly border and the Chinese Army crossed the Yalu and hurled our forces back into South Korea with great slaughter. This was an equally horrendous blunder. Our CIA and military intelligence were again proven wrong. Now the public relations men at the Pentagon ---and they have 300 or more personnel doing nothing but that---and Defense Secretary Laird glibly say that COSVN or the military headquarters directing the Vietcong and North Vietnamese forces is mobile and has been moved somewhere in Cambodia.

[Page S7495.] We did not hear about this mobile headquarters until we suddenly invaded, and then it eluded our forces.

As a result of our invasion of Cambodia there has been a strengthened resolve on the part of North Vietnam and an increased willingness to help on the part of China and the Soviet Union. Now they are finally getting together; and no doubt these great superpowers will be more than happy to replace every weapon and every round of ammunition captured by the United States in the Cambodian sanctuaries. If we force the North Vietnamese to seek closer alliance with the Chinese and to become dependent upon the Chinese, we will have created a situation which could doom all of Southeast Asia to another 20 years of war.

The most serious consequence of the decision to invade Cambodia has been the terrible division within our own country. Students on our college campuses and thoughtful citizens of all ages felt that they had been betrayed by their leaders. They feel that way now. . . .

Mr. President, on this floor we frequently hear from Senators who are regarded as war hawks, who favor all-out invasion, even to the extent, perhaps, of involving some of our allies, and sinking the British freighters which come from Hong Kong into Haiphong Harber. We have heard them speak out, time and again, saying that while we should never have been in Vietnam in the first place, now that we are there, we must see it through.

Mr. President, 2,500 years ago Confucius said that a man who

makes a mistake and does not correct it makes another mistake. Mr.
President, that goes for the U.S. Government also. Now we have compounded our mistake by extending combat in Cambodia and in Laos.

In 1965 and 1966, Pentagon officials released optimistic reports
on an early end to the Vietnam war. They persuaded President Johnson
to begin the escalation which has led to the death of more than 50,000
young Americans and maiming and wounding more than 281,000 other Americans, and the waste of hundreds of billions of dollars. In addition,
many of our soldiers and military advisers overseas from 1961 to the
present have been afflicted with malaria fever, bubonic plague, and
other tropical and jungle diseases. Some of them have died from those
diseases, and thousands and thousands of others will suffer malaria
fever and other diseases as long as they live. The generals of our
Armed Forces win wholesale promotions, so we have a flock of major
generals, lieutenant generals, and brigadier generals. They attain
wholesale promotions, but the bombing of North Vietnam and other military escalation and expansion of our involvement in a civil war in
Vietnam proved it is impossible to bomb a determined people into sub-
mission.

That is a civil war in Vietnam. I was in Vietnam in 1965 and
again in 1968. On my visit in 1968, General Westmoreland told me that
the bulk of the Vietcong fighting us in the Mekong Delta were born and
reared in the Mekong Delta. General Stilwell, then the deputy commander, told me that it was 80 percent. I mentioned that, therefore,
it was a civil war. He did not like that. He said it might be considered an insurrection. . . .

The Cooper-Church amendment before us should be sustained. It is
a declaration of the Senate that this unwinable war must be ended.
Adoption of the Cooper-Church amendment is our declaration of the will
and determination that civilian authority in the United States is supreme, just as the Founding Fathers proclaimed when they wrote our
Constitution. Let us try to return to that. . . .

The CIA and the generals of the Joint Chiefs of Staff have been
unable to understand that political considerations and human values
must often override military strategy. The tragedy of our intrusion
into Cambodia is the revelation that President Nixon has accepted the
simplistic rhetoric of the same generals and admirals who have led us
into the Southeast Asian abyss under the guise of victory. . . .

PRINCIPLES OF FOREIGN POLICY*

Mr. YOUNG of Ohio. [Page S7542.] Mr. President (Mr. GRAVEL). . . .

The war's most significant feature is the enemy's use of the pattern of guerrilla combat. That this has been the basic pattern for
what the Communists call "wars of national liberation" had already
been demonstrated earlier in other countries. Looking back, we see
that this was the pattern used by Tito's Partisans in Yugoslavia.
It was used again in the attempt to take over in Greece. It has been

tried and has failed in Malaya and the Philippines, it was tried in the Dominican Republic, and is still continuing in Thailand, and now in Cambodia. Of course, for us the most vivid and embarrassing example was Castro's takeover of Cuba with a handful of men.

By now, it is obvious that we have made steady progress against the guerrilla warfare in Vietnam.

Not only have we reduced its intensity in Vietnam, but we have also pushed the guerrillas back into their illegal Cambodian sanctuaries. This having happened, the logical next step was to destroy, or at least weaken, those sanctuaries. I believe that President Nixon was farsighted in seeing this necessity, and in moving to take advantage of it. He possessed the courage to move, in order to take advantage of it. . . .

It is clear to me that in all these little wars, the United States has been reacting in accordance with its traditional policies. Contrary to belief of some, we have not been improvising our foreign policy in Vietnam. We have been pursuing there the same objectives that we held in Europe when we opposed the Kaiser, Hitler, and Stalin, and in Asia when we opposed Japan. It has been our policy not to allow one nation, either directly or through proxies like North Vietnam, to dominate whole regions of the globe.

Today, the task is harder because the current threat used the cutting edge of communism, and for a while at least that has an appeal to people who have been impoverished and held down previously under a colonialist's thumb. But the principles for which we stand and our objectives are the same. Any changes we detect in our attitude then and now are simply those made necessary by differences in time, circumstances, and tactics.

At least four American principles stand out, and in every war of this century we have sacrificed much blood and treasure rather than give them up. Let me list them:

First. Devotion to the principle of personal freedom as a fundamental concept of government.

Second. Our belief that all other peoples who desire to live with these same freedoms should have the right to do so, and that when we protect their freedom, we are also protecting our own.

Third. A willingness to help other peoples improve their economic conditions, even to the extent of opening our own markets and sharing our own wealth with them if necessary.

Fourth. A determination never to be an aggressor or to embark on a policy of colonialism.

In listing these, it should go without saying that we believe such a policy will always be in our own national self-interest, and result in long term benefits to ourselves as well as to our friends. I am sure that in this present contest with communism in South Vietnam, there is no essential conflict between our own goals and the hopes of those we seek to help.

Of course, the application of these four principles has varied with the changing circumstances of our expanding history. Its first major expression was for the protection of the infant Latin American Republics when early in the 19th century they began to try to throw off the yoke of European colonialism. Because this principle was laid down during the Presidency of James Monroe, the principle has been known since as the Monroe Doctrine. Our commitment to this principle led us into our war with Spain in the Philippines at the end of the 19th century, and this in turn brought us for the first time into Southeast Asia more than 70 years ago. That experience, now two-thirds of a century behind us, set the precedent for our more recent intervention in Japan, Korea, Taiwan, the South Seas, and now South Vietnam.

Since this has been the latest of many confrontations between our foreign policy and that of the Communists, perhaps we should pause to look at Vietnam in terms of these principles. When we do, it is obvious: First, that there has been a challenge to a people seeking to establish freedom as the basis for their own self-government; second, that we have come to the aid of a nation so challenged, and, third, that we have been generous with our economic aid.

I want to dwell a little longer on my analysis of the fourth aspect of our foreign policy, that we have never been the aggressor nor succumbed to the temptation of neocolonialism.

[Page S7543.] If there is one case in which this might not have been true, it is the Philippines. But over the years, certainly we have made up for any partial failure of our devotion to that principle in the service we have given to those people.

If ever a nation was in a perfect position to take advantage of a world situation, that nation was the United States after World War II. During the troubled years since, we could easily have become the world's greatest neocolonial power, a label which now very obviously fits the great Communist nations. We could easily have turned our economic aid programs into international mortgages and foreclosed them to gain territorial control in many parts of the world.

When World War II ended, all of Europe was broken and prostrate and Japan was helpless. If the Communists had been in our place, all these countries would have been dragged behind the Iron Curtain. But our devotion to the moral values in self-government has been stronger among us than the urge to dominate other people.

We could have conquered and held Japan; instead we chose to rebuild it as an independent democracy. And so well did we succeed that today it challenges us for our place in the world economy. Our success in Japan holds promise for what we can do for the people in Vietnam. The successful growth of free government in Japan is proof that Buddhism is not incompatible with the essential concepts from which democracy must grow.

The same spirit shines through our record in Taiwan. By supplying military protection and foreign aid, we have helped make that once-backward nation economically independent, and its example stands as a beacon of hope to the other nations of Southeast Asia. We have provided them with foreign aid so effectively that they have reached a point that we have determined that they no longer need it.

As I have tried to demonstrate, our presence in Vietnam is in keeping with our long time foreign policies. We are there to protect ourselves and our own interests by protecting the existence and interest of still another small nation. We are doing this: First, because our own security requires that Red China or Russia not be allowed to become the dominant nation in Asia; second, because we cherish freedom, and third, because we believe such help rather than territorial acquisition or colonial control is better for us and the whole world.

Having indicated my belief that we are in this war as a logical expression of our long-established foreign policy based essentially on self-interest, I am led naturally to reask my third question: Has our intervention already created benefits for Vietnam and for those other countries in Southeast Asia who love freedom? I think the answer is a resounding "Yes."

Had we not been there, Vietnam at least would have been behind the Iron Curtain, with a real chance that her neighbors would have long since joined her.

I think there is great value in the fact that South Vietnam is still a free country, free enough at least to adopt a new constitution and elect the new officers it provided for, both by popular vote. But of greater worldwide significance is the indirect effect of our intervention in preserving the freedom of other countries in Southeast Asia. Before we put our military power in South Vietnam, several had already been set up for Communist takeover, and all would probably have been lost by now. . . .

ENEMY SANCTUARIES AND PROTECTION OF AMERICAN TROOPS*

Mr. BENNETT. . . .

Most experts recognize the Vietnam confrontation as crucial. It has been building up for nearly 15 years now, and if we should allow the Communists to prevail, storm warnings would immediately rise around the world. Our premature withdrawal would demonstrate that Communists have at last found the key to victory in a war. If we allow this to happen, all free nations, particularly the small ones, would be justified in believing that we are unworthy to be trusted as the leader of the free world. Those other countries to which we have given promises of support would properly doubt whether our help would be forthcoming when they needed it, especially when the going got tough. In other words, our friends would lose faith in us, and we would deserve it.

If we ever lost the right to lead the free world, Communist power would be unchallenged, and communism could eventually become the wave of the future. One by one, the smaller free countries would have to bow under its yoke, and the day conceivably could come when we stood isolated and alone. Obviously, we must not risk that great tragedy by trying to isolate ourselves from freedom's problems now.

Our capitulation would put all the free nations now along the Pacific coast of Asia into great and immediate jeopardy, including the giant Japan---which under the terms of peace we dictated has no military establishment except an internal defense force---the now stable Formosa, the still struggling Korea, Thailand and the remarkable Indonesia.

Because we know that communism hates Christianity, we might soon
expect religion to disappear in Asia as the Philippines, then Austra-
lia and New Zealand were outflanked and overrun.

Am I seeing nightmares? The Japanese almost did all this less
than 30 years ago from a much weaker power base. . . .

[Page S7545.] I am sure it is obvious that it is for the same
reasons that I am opposed to the various amendments now pending before
the Senate designed to limit the President's authority in Vietnam and
Cambodia. This does not mean that I believe the President should have
unlimited authority to expand the war. It means that I think such
amendments as those before us are unnecessary and illtimed particularly
under the circumstances. It is interesting to note that the sponsors
of the pending amendments have fastened upon the power of the Congress
to appropriate money as a means of stopping the President. It is my
feeling that this attempt to use the power of the purse usurps the
responsibility clearly vested in the President to issue orders for the
protection of our Armed Forces. The President has determined that the
limited actions he has ordered within Cambodia are necessary for the
protection of our forces in South Vietnam. The proposed amendments
would try to substitute the judgment of the Congress on that question
for the judgment of the President. Knowing a little about both the
Congress and the President, having been a Member of Congress for 18
years, and knowing my own weakness in this respect, I am choosing the
Commander in Chief in this instance. . . .

The Senate now finds itself participating in a debate over Presidential powers and their relationship to the powers of Congress. In
a sense, this shows that the American Government---in spite of some
weaknesses---has a great deal of vitality. This ongoing debate goes
back to the beginning of our history. It began in earnest in the Constitutional Convention. Even then among the great men who forged the
Constitution, it was not resolved; for Madison and Hamilton and the
other men present in Philadelphia either could not or did not see fit
to specify in great detail the powers of the President and the powers
of the Congress in the field of foreign policy, with its underlying
issue of war powers. I suppose this debate has been one of the longest
in American political history and, as we are obviously learning again
this week, the issue has not been resolved.

While fascinating to political scientists and legal scholars, it
has been frustrating to the Congress and perhaps confusing to the American public. . . .

Under the Constitution, the President's powers for the direction
of our Armed Forces abroad are derived from those parts of article II
which make him the Commander in Chief of the Army and the Navy of the
United States and which give him a special responsibility in the field
of foreign affairs. Congress, for its part, is given the power to declare war, to raise and support armies, to make rules for the Government, and regulation of land and naval forces, and other powers important to the conduct of foreign affairs and to the national defense.
However, it is clear to me that these powers of Congress may not lawfully be used so as to undermine or replace the powers of the President
as Commander in Chief.

Mr. President, until the fall of Prince Sihanouk, Cambodia had retained a facade of neutrality, but everyone knew it was only a facade because North Vietnamese Communist and Vietcong troops have been using Cambodian and Laotian sanctuaries and supply routes for many years. Prince Sihanouk could not enforce that neutrality; and when he was deposed, the facade was stripped away. In the past month, the sanctuaries have become a much greater threat to South Vietnam and allied forces.

Unfortunately, the entire role of the sanctuaries in this war has been generally ignored by virtually everyone but the fighting man in the field. I am certain that the fighting man, who knows the situation best, does not have any qualms in striking back at the enemy where it hurts.

I have felt for a long time that the American public has found it difficult to understand how guerrilla warfare is conducted. An absolute necessity in this type of warfare is a safe area to which the guerrilla fighters can return to rest, resupply, refill their ranks, and treat their wounded. In the Vietnam war we have allowed him unmolested use of "over the border sanctuaries" for 6 long years. It has never made sense to me [Page S7546.] to chase a Communist across the border into a very unneutral part of a supposedly neutral country only to have him come back a week later, well rested, with a stomach full of "neutral" Cambodian rice, to shoot at Americans again with his new Russian-made machinegun just shipped down the Ho Chi Minh Trail through neutral Laos.

The contest would have been much different had the Cambodian Government had both the willpower and the means to deny these sanctuaries to the enemy. The truth, of course, is that the Cambodian Government did not. To me it is an incontestable fact that Communist violation of Cambodia and Laotian neutrality has been a key factor in keeping Hanoi and its Communist forces in the war. The supply lines down the Ho Chi Minh Trail and the sanctuaries which have been the terminal points of those lines have been absolutely vital to the Communist war effort south of the 17th parallel.

Now, for the first time in several years, we have a President who decided to quit watching helplessly while the enemy crossed the border, and America has had the courage to deny to the enemy this major military advantage. . . .

Mr. President, in summary, I again restate my support of President Nixon's action. I am pleased that there is growing support for his foreign policy decisions of the past 3 or 4 weeks and I, for one, think that in the end his action will be well justified and hailed as a success. I think that the present attempts by Congress to tie the President's hands are grossly unfair not only to him but also to our fighting men overseas. I, for one, do not want to go down in history as having voted to cut off arms and ammunition, supplies and materiel, funds, wages, and support for our fighting men in the rice paddies of Indochina.

If the Cooper-Church amendment comes before us without acceptable modification I shall vote against it. I hope it will be possible for those with both points of view who are sincerely concerned about this problem to develop an adjustment of these two points of view in the American tradition so that every Member of the Senate can vote for it. . . .

Mr. FONG. [Page S7550.] Mr. President, I am opposed to the third committee amendment, which includes the so-called Cooper-Church amendment, primarily because if enacted the Cooper-Church language would endanger the more than 400,000 American troops ordered to duty and now serving our country in South Vietnam.

I am as concerned as any other Member of this body about the risk involved in the President's decision to clear out the enemy sanctuaries in Cambodia.

I am as concerned as any Member of this body about the constitutional prerogatives of the Congress and the constitutional prerogatives of the President.

But, today, we are not debating whether Congress should authorize our troops to be ordered into Cambodia. We are [Page S7551.] faced with the fact that they have been ordered there and that thousands of Americans are presently in Cambodia as well as Vietnam.

At such a time and in such circumstances where the lives of more than 400,000 Americans as well as millions of South Vietnamese people are at stake, the Senate of the United States should take no action that would jeopardize our forces under fire.

It is my firm belief that the Cooper-Church amendment would indeed jeopardize American men now in Southeast Asia. . . .

[Page S7552.] The Senate of the United States is in no position to anticipate every situation, every contingency, every confrontation in a war.

We do not know what the enemy will try to do. But we do know he has been very resourceful, very flexible, and very clever so far.

When he cannot win big battles, he reverts to guerrilla war, harassment, terrorism, and small engagements.

When he finds out he cannot protect his forces inside South Vietnam, he takes refuge in sanctuaries in Cambodia and Laos.

To tie the hands of our Commander in Chief and our troops in the field under his command by legislative enactment, which could be changed only by another legislative enactment, could leave our troops at the mercy of a clever and resourceful enemy who is backed by one of the world's super powers and also by one of the world's most belligerent regimes. . . .

[Page S7553.] Whatever else other Senators may decide to do, and I respect their right to their views, the Senator from Hawaii does not intend to jeopardize the lives of 400,000 American men by voting for the Cooper-Church amendment. . . .

Mr. CHURCH. Mr. President. . . .

[Page S7556.] I have listened to the inflated, exaggerated, and distorted charges made by the Senator from Hawaii (Mr. FONG). He has charged that this amendment will somehow endanger our troops in the field. He has charged that it will jeopardize their lives; that it will constitute an abandonment of the men we have sent to Vietnam to fight. How can that be? How can that possibly be, when all we have done is to fix the line where the President himself has set it? There is not a word in the amendment that undercuts the President, let alone puts our troops in jeopardy.

The President has limited his objectives in Cambodia. We accept his limits. We say we will share with the President the responsibility for fixing those limits. Yet the Senator from Hawaii protests that we seek to tie the President's hands; that we would place obstacles in his way; that we would pull the rug out from under him; that we would bind and straitjacket the President. So amazed was I to hear such charges that I carefully reread the amendment. Again, I am at a loss to find where any limitation at any place conflicts with the stated purposes of the President, as they have been explained to Congress and the American people, concerning the current operation in Cambodia.

. . . We had better know now if there is some other policy that has not yet been revealed which involves assuming a whole new set of obligations to defend the Cambodian regime. We had better know now, because there is nothing on the public record to suggest that any one of these provisions conflicts in any way with the stated policy of the administration. . . .

Mr. GOLDWATER. . . . [Page S7559.]

What is there in the air around Washington, D.C., that makes Senators and Representatives feel that they were formed after the pattern of von Clausewitz and are automatically military tacticians superior to any that might exist in the Joint Chiefs of Staff, in the National Security Council, or in the Office of the Commander in Chief? . . .

Mr. President, again, not exactly in a political way but to keep the record straight, only one President has done anything about deescalating the fighting, and about withdrawing American fighting men.

That President is the one we have today, Richard M. Nixon. He is the only President in the last three who has come up with a viable and workable plan for the replacement of American fighting men with forces of the South Vietnamese. . . .

The fact of the matter is, every move the President has taken in Southeast Asia has been designed to bring about a safe and intelligent withdrawal of American forces. It is, of course, very easy to charge the President with all kinds of evil designs and attach them to one word---Cambodia. . . .

[Page S7561.] I, for one, do not want to be a party to any of this high-sounding but ill-conceived nonsense that is being pushed in this Chamber under the guise of peace or a design carrying the false label of a device to "end the war."

What we are talking about here---though I hate to say this---is a measure to force an American surrender. To some Senators it would seem like the manly thing to do to stand up and announce that we were wrong and that we are withdrawing from Vietnam. And I might say, Mr. President, that that could be done. It is not that simple, however. How would we describe in later weeks and months the bloodbath that would ensue in Southeast Asia if we were to withdraw either precipitately or in accordance with a legislatively fixed deadline? Would we not then shoulder a different kind of responsibility? Would we not then look to all the world as a Nation which went to war for the cause of freedom, grew tired of the effort, and found an excuse to turn tail and run while leaving millions of defenseless Asians at the mercy of Communist aggressors?

Mr. CRANSTON. [Page S7564.] Mr. President. . . .

The Cooper-Church amendment is essentially a conservative document based on a strict constructionist view of the Constitution of the United States.

I view the amendment as a second step in an effort to restore Congress to its proper role in controlling the funding of military operations and giving the people a greater voice in the issues of war and peace through their elected representatives. . . .

I want to make it clear that the Cooper-Church amendment is a document of restraint---not isolation.

In no way are its supporters advocating a return to "fortress America."

Action taken by the Senate in no way impairs American commitments to Israel or other allies throughout the world.

The war has gone on despite the wishes of a majority of the people that it be halted.

Our involvement in Southeast Asia endangers peace in the world.

The issue of the war in Vietnam has become so vital and significant to America in the last 10 days that references to the intent of the Founding Fathers in granting Congress the power to fund and declare war have become more than patriotic sloganeering.

At stake is the separation of powers upon which our experiment in democratic government is based. . . .

Mr. TOWER. . . . [Page S7646.]

If we are going to assert the constitutional authority of the U.S. Senate in the conduct of foreign policy, why can we not do it in a dispassionate climate, one in which we are not faced with a particular kind of crisis? Why can we not, when the dust settles, sit down and consider the whole business of the tripartite separation of powers of the Government of the United States? This is a unique form of government. Very few nations in the world have it. No other major nation in the world has it. There are three separate, relatively independent branches of Government, each with its common source of authority, the Constitution of the United States. Why can we not---in a dispassionate climate, not at a time when the President has to deal with a crisis with speed and dispatch---sit down and talk about the constitutional prerogatives of the President, of Congress and, indeed, of the Supreme Court?

How many times has the legislative power of Congress been usurped by this agency, that agency, this department, that department, or the courts of the United States, and yet we have done nothing?

The fact of the matter is that our power over the conduct of foreign policy is essentially a negative power. We have the right to ratify treaties. We have the right to confirm appointments. We have the right to raise the stop sign. But seldom in our history have we gone over to the positive business of saying, "You may not do something in the future that we think you might do."

The supporters of this amendment have contended that this is in pursuance to what the President has said he will do: this is pursuant to presidential policy. Why not nail it down to this specific respect? If it is pursuant to presidential policy, then I submit that it is redundant for us to seal it into law here, in a really unprecedented action, at a time when we run the risk of convincing the world that we all disagree with our President, that we are not going to allow him to implement his policy and, from this point forward, "Ye shall know, be ye friend or foe, what the United States of America is going to do. We tie our hands."

In the Soviet Union, does the Presidium of the Supreme Soviet tell us what its limitations are? Does Hanoi tell us what its limitations are? Does Peking tell us what its limitations are? No. What we are doing is ourselves creating a strategic or tactical disadvantage for the United States in the face of aggressor powers in this world that are not concerned with all the niceties of being responsive to popular will, without concern for world opinion, without concern for Judeo-Christian concepts of law and right. We are putting ourselves at a grave disadvantage with a cynical, disciplined, dedicated force in this world that seeks to control; and I think it is a foolish thing for us to do. . . .

NATIONAL SECURITY AND CONGRESSIONAL FUNDS*

(May 25, 1970)

Mr. SYMINGTON. [Page S7740.] Mr. President. . . .

The Constitution tells us that the power to declare war and to appropriate funds for the waging of war is reserved to Congress. The Constitution also provides that the President, under his powers as Chief Executive and Commander in Chief, has the power to respond quickly to an immediate threat to national safety or the safety of our troops.

These two principles are not inconsistent; the Constitution dictates that they be balanced. But a proper balance will result only if both Congress and the President are aware of their separate responsibilities and are prepared to act to fulfill them.

The principle which emerges from the debates over the formulation and adoption of the Constitution, and its application in the early years of our history, is that Congress should have the power and responsibility to decide when American forces will be used to achieve national security objectives, with the single limited exception that the President should have discretion to commit troops to battle when the threat to the safety and survival of the Nation itself is immediate.

The most obvious example of this limited exception is nuclear war. If we should be attacked with nuclear weapons, only the President can respond in the few minutes time that action is possible and meaningful. Thankfully, this remains only a future possibility.

On the other hand, the Constitution does not give the President discretion to act alone if a possible threat to our national security is not so immediate as to preclude a few days of congressional consideration.

In the middle of the last century an attempt was made in the House of Representatives to censure the President for "unnecessary and unconstitutional" action in committing American troops to a war with Mexico without providing Congress with all of the information needed to make a sound judgment on whether such intervention was justified. That attempt at censure was supported by perhaps our greatest President, when he was still a Member of the House---Abraham Lincoln---as well as by another Member who had formerly been a President---John Quincy Adams.

The history of the constitutional balance in the intervening century has proven that congressional inaction can be disastrous. The President's inherent powers to respond to immediate emergencies has been expanded far beyond the original intent to justify his unilateral assumption of the power to decide between war and peace.

Commitments of large numbers of troops for an indeterminate length of time to a war in a far-off land is not the sort of decision which the Constitution delivers to the sole discretionary power of the President. It is certainly not a decision to respond immediately to a threat to the safety of our troops.

[Page S7741.] Such commitments may be a decision as to what is essential to our national security, but not one which need be---or should be---made precipitously.

I find the distinction between an immediate threat to national safety and a general threat to national security a nice one---and I conclude that Congress should participate in decision as to the proper response to the latter.

President after President in this century, however, has made this sort of decision privately, without any deference to congressional authority; and often without even consulting the legislative branch. We have seen how the traditional power of Congress has atrophied, as time after time the Executive has committed and dispatched American forces to foreign conflict; occasionally, as I have emphasized previously, under cover of secrecy.

Part of the blame, of course, belongs to Congress. We have for too long passively accepted the President's ability to commit our troops to battle, to use the awesome military establishment with which we have provided him as the equivalent of a Constitutional power to do so, and so as to preclude Congressional attention to the issue.

Time after time we have justified these involvements by invocation of the magic words of "national security" as a means of foreclos-
ing either congressional scrutiny or public examination.

To invoke the words "national security" or even "safety of our
troops," with nothing more, is merely to beg the question of what our
national security really requires in troop commitments, and of what the
safety of our troops really means. . . .

The result of the repeated and specious invocation of the concept
of "national security," which has been used to justify giving unbridled war power to the President, has been a series of private executive
decisions in which Congress has played no meaningful role; and the
most striking example of the executive's arrogation of the power to
make such private decisions about what constitutes our national security, is the whole conduct of the war in Indochina, by administrations
of both parties.

First, we had the Tonkin Gulf joint resolution. Certainly, none
of us foresaw that the measures required then to protect our ships---
whether or not they had provoked attack by the North Vietnamese---would
require the eventual commitment of hundreds of thousands of our
troops---Army, Navy, and Air Force---to a protracted war on the Asian
mainland.

The decision that our security required such a commitment, with
the ensuing heavy cost in lives, treasure, and domestic distress, was
made exclusively in the secret counsels of the executive branch of
the Government.

A second example of a private executive decision as to what the
national security required was the decision that led to our deep involvement in the conflict in northern Laos. Not only was the decision not made by Congress, but the truth about the situation was not
made available to Congress.

Time after time I have pointed out the grave danger incident to
the veil of secrecy which the administration drew over our role in
that area.

If the President's power to respond to immediate threats justified
those combat actions in an area far removed from any American combat
forces, his discretionary powers would allow him to commit our forces
to battle just about anywhere in the world. But the President did engage our forces, and in such a manner as to exclude congressional
participation in the decision.

A third, and the most recent and dramatic example of a private
Executive determination of what national security required was the
decision to send troops into Cambodia. The situation posed there was
certainly not an immediate threat to our security as a Nation, by any
standard.

It was a situation which could have been dealt with in consultation with the Congress. Instead, the executive branch has been quite
proud of its ability to keep the plans for this venture a secret for
a considerable period. Their pride in preserving this secrecy illus-
trates precisely how much the original allocation of the war power has
been twisted and distorted.

Today I am sorry to state that the balance has tipped heavily to one side. This tipping is not solely the fault of the present President. It is a process that has been going on for years under several Presidents. And Congress must carry its share of the blame for failure to meet its constitutional responsibilities.

Passing the Cooper-Church amendment will not by itself redress the balance and undo the current misallocation of decisionmaking power. It will be only one step, the first step, in what I hope will be a growing list of instances where Congress exercises its share of this power. The weight of precedent and the powers of the Presidency are so strong that only continued awareness and sensitivity by Congress can guard the congressional prerogatives which remain, and recoup those which have been defaulted in recent years.

Furthermore, it is fitting that we begin the process of reasserting our responsibilities by addressing the most recent example of executive arrogation of the power to make decisions about the national security; namely, the venture in Cambodia, a nation hitherto not included in even the most diffuse and distorted conceptions of national security.

The President's unilateral decision must be balanced, and balanced immediately, by a firm and clear expression of the will of Congress. The amendment proposed by Senators COOPER and CHURCH is an example of the kind of action that is necessary, and it addresses itself to that Presidential action which stands out most prominently at the moment as an arrogation of the power which rightfully belongs to Congress. . . .

Mr. TYDINGS. [Page S7765.] Mr. President. . . .

The significance of each Senator's vote on this matter must be measured not only in terms of its affect on hastening the conclusion of this disastrous war, important as this may be. The votes will also test whether the Senate shall continue to be nothing more than a mute sister unwilling to make the hard decisions when it comes to guiding the Nation into or out of war, or whether the Senate shall at long last reclaim and exercise its rightful authority to help make these important decisions. The vote shall test whether the checks and balances of our governmental system are to remain asleep or whether they shall be revived to doublecheck and oversee and, if necessary, refrain the President from committing our Nation to a war of any scope, against any adversary and for any duration. The vote shall test whether one man or one Government is to have control over the contraction or expansion of a war which has already cost our country so dearly in blood and treasure. The Church-Cooper vote shall test whether the people of this Nation, through their chosen representatives, shall regain control over their own destinies with regard to the most important issue facing them---that of sacrificing their lives and their treasure in battle. . . .

. . . the facts are that the plain meaning of our Constitution, the recorded intentions of our Founding Fathers who framed this great document, the opinions of the Justices of the Supreme Court, and the statements and actions of the leaders of our country throughout its history squarely support the authority of Congress to enact the Church-Cooper amendment.

Congress' fundamental authority to keep Federal funds from being used for military matters in Cambodia after July 1, 1970, is founded in two important clauses in the Constitution. First, in clause 1 of article 1, section 8 of the Constitution it is provided that Congress shall have the power "to lay and collect taxes, duties, in posts and excises, to . . . provide for the common defense." Second, in clause 11 it is provided that Congress shall have the power "to declare war, grant letters of marque and reprisal, and make rules concerning captures on land and water."

Our forefathers were indeed wise in giving to Congress both the power to initiate and generally control war and the power of the purse to ensure that its wishes with regard to war were not abused. They remembered the long history of kings and rulers who plunged their countries into disastrous wars without the approval of their parliaments and people. They sought to insure that no U.S. President would ever involve this country in a war without the stated consent of the peoples' elected representatives in the Congress.

Thus, at the Constitutional Convention in 1787, the framers sought to employ language that would clearly show that the power to embark on war rested solely in Congress. To this end, the words "to make war" were used in the first draft of the Constitution to describe Congress' complete control over this area.

It is significant to note that during the debate over this provision, it was suggested that the warmaking powers be given to the President instead. Voicing opposition to this suggestion, George Mason, the great Virginian, said the President could not safely be trusted with it. Others also voiced their objection, and the suggestion was forever put aside.

However, James Madison moved to substitute the phrase "declare war" for "make war." In suggesting this change, his recorded intention was to keep the warmaking authority in Congress but to leave to the President the "power to repel sudden attacks." Roger Sherman agreed, stating that the Executive "should be able to repel and not commence war." With this understanding, Madison's change of language was adopted.

Thus, as the debate reflects, the framers of our Constitution intended Congress to retain control over the power to make war, with the exception that the President was empowered to repel unilaterally sudden attacks upon our shores.

In contrast to the broad warmaking powers entrusted to Congress, the founders of our country envisioned the Commander in Chief powers to be similar to the power possessed by any high military or naval commander. This was the view of Hamilton as expressed in "Federalist Paper No. 69." Hamilton wrote:

The President is to be Commander in Chief of the Army and Navy of the United States. In this respect his authority would be nominally the same with that of the King of Great Britain, but in substance much inferior to it. It would amount to nothing more than the supreme command and direction of the military and naval forces as first General and admiral of the Confederacy; while that of the

British King extends to the declaring of war and to the
raising and regulating of fleets and armies, all which, by
the Constitution under consideration, would appertain to
the legislature.

There is no question what Alexamder Hamilton had in mind. There
is no question what James Madison had in mind. There is no question
what any of the drafters of our Constitution had in mind. It is
rather amazing to me that my distinguished colleague from North Carolina (Mr. ERVIN), a man who prides himself on his strict construc-
tionism approach to the Constitution, would advocate such a loose and
liberal interpretation of the Constitution, which could hardly ever
be justified in the light of the language of the document itself, or
the recorded words and intentions of our Founding Fathers who framed
the Constitution.

Mr. President, the framers of our Constitution could hardly have
imagined that when they vested in Congress the power to commit our
Nation to war and made the President the Commander in Chief of our
Nation's troops, they were creating in one man, the President, the un-
fettered power to make for all the Nation a decision to send our
troops across recognized boundaries into foreign nations for any time
and at any expense.

Likewise, our forefathers could hardly have imagined that in
giving Congress the power to initiate war it failed to also give Congress the power to limit a war or, indeed, to end it.

The leaders of our young Nation demonstrated an awareness of Congress' broad constitutional power with regard to engaging in war outside our shores. They recognized that congressional authorization was
a constitutional prerequisite to committing American troops to battle
outside of our country. And they understood that in limited wars,
Congress was intended to retain control over the scope and boundaries
of American military involvement.

Our first war, which lasted from 1789 to 1801, was a limited
naval war with France. Although American shipping was endangered,
Alexander Hamilton cautioned President Adams not to take action against
the French fleet without congressional authority. Hamilton wrote:

In so delicate a case, in one which involves so important a consequence as war, my opinion is that no doubtful authority ought to be exercised by the President.

President Adams listened to the advice of Hamilton and elected to
follow the lead of Congress.

The supremacy of Congress with regard [Page S7766.] to the making
of war was likewise voiced by President Jefferson, President James
Monroe, Secretary of State John Quincy Adams, and Secretary of State

Daniel Webster.   For example, during a dispute with Spain in 1805
over the boundary between Louisiana and Florida, Jefferson told
Congress:

>   Considering that Congress alone is constitutionally
> invested with the power of changing our position from peace
> to war, I have thought it my duty to await their authority
> before using force in any degree which could be avoided. . . .
> The spirit and honor of our country require that force
> should be interposed to a certain degree. It will probably
> contribute to advance the object of peace.
>
>   But the course to be pursued will require the com-
> mand of means which it belongs to Congress exclusively to
> yield or deny. To them I communicate every fact material
> for their information and the documents necessary to enable
> them to judge for themselves. To their wisdom, then, I look
> for the course I am to pursue, and will pursue with sincere
> zeal that which they shall approve.

The words of Monroe and Adams are equally enlightening. In 1824,
President Monroe addressed himself to the activities of Cuban-based
pirates who plundered American shipping and fled again to the safety
of Spanish territory. In his annual message to Congress, Monroe said:

>   Whether those robbers should be pursued on the land, the
> local authorities be made responsible for these atrocities,
> or any other measure be resorted to to suppress them, is sub-
> mitted to the consideration of Congress.

In 1824, Colombia, then an infant nation, informed the United
States that it was threatened by France and needed protection. Even
though the Monroe Doctrine had been announced the preceding year, the
President would not commit the Nation to defend Colombia. In a letter
to former President Madison, Monroe wrote that "the Executive has no
right to commit the Nation in any question of war." Three days later,
Secretary of State Adams formally wrote to the Minister of Colombia
that "by the Constitution of the United States, the ultimate decision
of this question belongs to the legislative department of the Government."

Over the history of our Nation, the Supreme Court has also addressed itself to the relative roles of the President and Congress in
the warmaking process. Three very illuminating decisions of the Supreme Court involve cases which grew out of the French-American naval
war. The first case, Bas against Tingey, decided in 1800, involved
a claim by the owner of a French vessel that his vessel could not be
seized and salvaged by an American naval commander because the United
States was not offically at war with France. This case raised the
question whether Congress had the power to initiate a limited or
"imperfect" war and whether the Congress was empowered to so determine
the scope of this war. The Supreme Court stated that Congress may
both establish and set the boundaries of limited war. Justice Chase
said:

Congress is empowered to declare a general war, or
Congress may wage a limited war; limited in place, in
object, in time . . . if a partial war is waged, its extent and operation depend on our municipal laws.

Justice Patterson agreed. He said:

As far as Congress tolerated and authorized the war
on our part, so far may we proceed in hostile operations.

Chief Justice John Marshall was not on the Supreme Court when Bas
against Tingey was decided, but he had an opportunity to discuss the
war in Talbot against Seeman. Upholding the right of a U.S. ship of
war to take a prize, he said:

The whole power of war being, by the Constitution of
the United States, vested in Congress, the action of that
body can alone be resorted to as guides in this inquiry.

The third case is Little against Barreme, decided in 1804. This
case involved a law of Congress which authorized the President to instruct the Navy to seize any American ship "sailing to" any French
port. In contrast, President Adams instructed naval commanders to
seize American vessels "bound to or from French ports." A Danish
vessel bound from a French port was mistaken for an American vessel
and seized. In affirming a lower court decision awarding damage against
the American captain, Chief Justice Marshall, writing for the Supreme
Court, held that the naval commander was not authorized to follow the
instructions of the President and seize an outward bound ship because
Congress, pursuant to its warmaking power, had already legislated
otherwise.

Thus, Chief Justice Marshall, the man whose court laid down so
many of the fundamental constitutional law decisions of our Nation's
jurisprudence, opined that the acts of Congress enacted pursuant to
its war-declaring power are superior to the actions of the President
undertaken pursuant to his commander in chief power, and that the
President must comply with the boundaries established by Congress for
fighting a limited war.

Moreover, in 1850, the Supreme Court in Flemming against Page
stated that as Commander in Chief the President's "duty and power are
purely military" and the Court held that this power cannot be expanded to include certain powers conferred on Congress by the Constitution.

In 1863 in the prize cases the Court again turned its attention
to the power of the legislative and executive branches over war. The
Court said:

By the Constitution, Congress alone has the power to
declare a national or foreign war . . . [the President] has
no power to initiate or declare a war against a foreign
nation.

Aside from these Supreme Court decisions, aside from the plain meaning of the Constitution, aside from the "Federalist Papers," and aside from the words and explanations of Madison, Mason, Hamilton, and Sherman, and their deeds and actions and those of the rest of the delegates of the Philadelphia Convention, more recent events serve as ample precedent for congressional action designed to keep our troops out of Cambodia. I am referring to the Selective Service and Training Act of 1940 which set clear geographical limits on the use of our troops abroad. This act provided that:

> Persons inducted into the land forces of the United States under this act shall not be employed beyond the limits of the Western Hemisphere except in the territories and possessions of the United States, including the Philippine Islands.

In brief, it is clear that the war-declaring clause of the Constitution independently empowers Congress to specify the outer boundaries of our Nation's involvement in the war in Southeast Asia.

Some might conclude that the President's decision to send American troops into Cambodia without congressional authorization represents an infringement of Congress' warmaking authority and an abuse of his own authority as Commander in Chief. I am somewhat puzzled by the way this matter has been answered. For while it has been argued on the Senate floor that the Gulf of Tonkin resolution, supplies adequate authority for the President's action in Cambodia, the administration has told us that it is not relying on the Tonkin Gulf resolution as support for its Vietnam policy.

However, it is not my purpose to question the President's Commander in Chief authority. Rather, the point I wish to make is that the argument of the distinguished Senator from North Carolina (Mr. ERVIN), that Congress does not have the constitutional right to limit the perimeters of U.S. military activity is completely without support in the constitutional history of the Nation; indeed, it is contrary not only to the language of the Constitution but also to the words of the Founding Fathers and the great opinions of the Supreme Court that were addressed to this vital matter.

It is clear that Congress has been granted by the Constitution, at the very least, an equally important role to play with regard to the issue of war and peace. We must no longer ignore that responsibility. . . .

Mr. ALLEN. [Page S7774.] The Senator from Idaho has emphasized the fact that the amendment does not question the warmaking power of the President as Commander in Chief. I should like to ask the Senator from Idaho if it is not a fact that the amendment applies not only to the present Cambodian conflict but also it applies ad infinitum, that it does restrict the President in taking emergency action to protect the interests of this country if at some future time he deems that to be necessary; and, is it not a fact, that while no question is raised as to his power to have started the present military action in Cambodia, the effect of the amendment is to say to the President, "In the future, we will not support with our resources or with appropriations any future action on your part in Cambodia as

Commander in Chief"; and, does it not, thereby, restrict the powers of
the President of the United States as Commander in Chief of the Armed
Forces to take emergency action in the best interests of the country
in the future?

Mr. CHURCH. Mr. President, that question can be answered, I think,
the way many questions in the law must be answered; namely, by applying
the standard of the reasonable man.

It is next to impossible to draw a precise line between the powers
of the President under the Constitution and the powers of Congress in
the matter of war. A gray area exists between the two. So, the amendment was drafted in such form as to avoid that gray area as much as
possible.

It is one thing to conjure up a situation in which the President
might act reasonably, owing to the immediate needs of our troops in the
field. Even if his action were not in strict accordance with the letter of the amendment, I am sure that if the circumstances showed the
action was necessary for the protection of our troops, no one in Congress would raise a question---

Mr. ALLEN. Yes, but may I say---

Mr. CHURCH. Let me finish my thought---but if, on the other hand,
the President were to say that the protection of the American troops
we have sent to South Vietnam required us to invade North Vietnam---a
far more important sanctuary of the enemy---or, to think of a more extreme case, if the President were to say, as Commander in Chief, "I
have decided that the adequate protection of our troops in South Vietnam necessitates the bombing of China or an all out attack on the
Soviet Union," well then, I doubt anyone in the Senate would argue that
the President has inherent power, in order to protect our troops in
South Vietnam, to start a third world war or initiate a nuclear exchange that could bring an end to civilization.

No, it is a question of reasonable interpretation of power.

As matters now stand, the President does have broad discretion in
determining the extent we will involve ourselves in Cambodia, which
adjoins the present theater of operations. But, if the amendment is
enacted, and the President signs it into law, then we have exercised
congressional power to establish the outer limits in Cambodia. We
establish those limits where the President himself has fixed them. As
law, the matter would then take a different shape. If the President
later decided we should go in and occupy Cambodia, or assume the
obligations of defending the Lon Nol government, then he would have to
come back and present his case to Congress and ask Congress to lift
the limitations.

So I say to the Senator, as best I can, that although it is not
possible to define the precise line between the power of the President
and the power of Congress in a case of this kind, it is possible to
proceed to assert the authority of Congress under this amendment. And
the consequences that would flow from that are those I have attempted
to describe.

Mr. ALLEN. Mr. President, to take any further action with respect to Cambodia after all troops have been withdrawn by July 1, it would be necessary for the President to do, not what he did on this occasion, but to come back to Congress and, in effect, ask for permission to take this action. Is that not correct?

Mr. CHURCH. Mr. President, if this becomes a part of the Military Sales Act which is signed by the President into law, the Senator is correct. That would be the requirement insofar as a future action in Cambodia is concerned. . . .

Mr. ALLEN. [Page S7775.] Mr. President, the Senator from Idaho has pointed out on several occasions on the floor that the effect of the amendment is merely to take the President at his word and work in concert with him with respect to the withdrawal of our troops from Cambodia. But the junior Senator from Alabama seems to recall that the President in his address to the Nation mentioned the fact that it might be necessary in the future to go again, after the withdrawal from the sanctuaries, into Cambodia and recapture them.

Yet the amendment offered by the distinguished Senator from Idaho would require that before doing that, he must come back to Congress and get permission by way of an appropriation or some expression of congressional approval.

Mr. CHURCH. Mr. President, I do not know to what the distinguished Senator from Alabama alludes when he says that the President has indicated that it may be necessary to go back into Cambodia again after the sanctuaries.

That precise question was asked the President in his last press conference.

He said in answer to the question: "And what we have also accomplished is that by buying time, it means that if the enemy does come back to these sanctuaries, the next time the South Vietnamese will be strong enough and well enough trained to handle it alone."

So the President has not indicated any intention of going back. And he has based the justification for his present action on buying time to proceed with his withdrawal from South Vietnam.

I say to the Senator that the line we draw in this amendment conforms in every particular to the best evidence we can get as to the limits the President himself has set.

I think that if, at some later date, he decides the United States should expand the war and go back into Cambodia, or that we should go to the defense of the new Cambodian regime, or to the rescue of the South Vietnamese, who have now apparently decided to stay in Cambodia, he should come to Congress.

Mr. ALLEN. Mr. President, insofar as Cambodia is concerned, it would be necessary for the President to come back to Congress and, in effect, get permission to take any action in Cambodia, even though he thought it was necessary to protect the lives of American soldiers in South Vietnam.

Mr. CHURCH. Mr. President, I say to the Senator what I have said before, because I know he does not want to place words in my mouth.

I have said, and I restate it once again, that the precise limits of the President's authority under the Constitution to protect American troops in the field defies exact definition. The very nature of that authority is such that one cannot enclose it within a certain verbal framework.

This amendment does not challenge the President's right as Commander in Chief to take any action reasonably required to protect our troops in the field; he takes such action under authority that he derives from the Constitution.

We could not, even if we wanted to do it---and we do not. The last thing we want to do---as I am sure the Senator from Alabama will concede, is to place American troops in jeopardy in the field.

Mr. President, what we are trying to do in this amendment is not to define the President's authority, which we can neither diminish nor enlarge. Rather, we seek to assert the authority that Congress possesses over the expenditure of public money in such a way that if the President should later want to exceed limits he himself has defined, he would be required to come back to Congress and get approval.

Mr. ALLEN. Mr. President, it would be possible for him to send troops in. But, without the approval of Congress, those troops could not be supported.

Mr. CHURCH. No. That is not correct. It may be that I am failing to express myself clearly.

Mr. President, I can only restate once more what I have said before, and that is that whatever power the President has under the Constitution to protect American troops in the field, we do not attempt to reach, and we could not reach, even if that were intended. But Congress is the keeper of the public purse strings. And there is a reasonable line of demarcation between action that can be justified as necessary for the protection of American troops and action that involves a new national commitment to go to the defense of a foreign government.

Mr. ALLEN. Mr. President, the Senator says that he is not going to interfere with the President's action as Commander in Chief. Yet, at the same time, he says that he is not going to support that action by appropriations unless the President comes back to Congress and asks for it.

Mr. CHURCH. Mr. President, it is not properly within the President's power as Commander in Chief to commit the United States to the defense of the new regime in Cambodia.

If Congress has any power at all under the Constitution of the United States, it has the right to determine the necessity of such an action, and the Senate itself has the power to ratify or to reject treaties that go to this very question. And we have no treaty with Cambodia.

Mr. ALLEN. Mr. President, I am not talking about protecting the

government of Cambodia. I am talking about protecting the lives of
American servicemen.

Mr. CHURCH. But this amendment relates to support for Cambodian
forces and support for the Cambodian Government.

Mr. ALLEN. That is not what it says. It says retaining American
forces in Cambodia. It does not say for what purpose.

Mr. CHURCH. As I stated to the Senator, the retention of American forces in Cambodia is based on a date which the President himself
declared to be the date by which he intends to withdraw them. We have
merely set the time for their withdrawal on the very date the President
himself set. . . .

Mr. WILLIAMS of Delaware. . . . [Page S7778.]

Much is said about the President's usurping the powers of Congress.
As one who has served here for 23-1/2 years I am just as jealous as any
Member of Congress of the powers of the Senate. But let us face it:
The criticism of the President's usurping the powers of Congress is
not the President's fault. It is because we in Congress have delegated to the President many of these powers which we should have kept
right here in the Congress and discharged ourselves. This matter of
easy delegation of powers I shall discuss further in a moment. Congress has delegated these powers, oftentimes, and then acted as a Monday morning quarterback after the decision was made. If the President's decision through these powers works out well we take the credit.
If it is bad we can then say it is all his fault.

I think Congress should stop this delegation of these broad powers
to the President and then trying to second guess him after it is over
with as to whether he should or should not have acted.

Mr. MANSFIELD. Mr. President, will the Senator yield?

Mr. WILLIAMS of Delaware. I yield.

Mr. MANSFIELD. Let me say that I am in accord with what the distinguished Senator has said. It is not the fault of the President that
the executive branch has been able to retain these powers over the past
4 decades; it is because we gave those powers. We did not try to pull
them back. If there is any blame, I would attach it to no President,
but I would attach it to Congress as a whole, because we have been
derelict in our duty and derelict in facing up to our responsibilities
in that regard.

Mr. WILLIAMS of Delaware. The Senator from Montana has said it
better than I could.

I mentioned particularly that the Secretary was primarily before
the committee on that Monday, before the President made the decision
regarding Cambodia, to discuss with us and to get our opinion on the
question of large-scale shipment of arms for the Cambodian Government
which had been requested. There is no secret about this. It was in
the press, so we can mention it. Yet under the powers which Congress
in earlier years delegated to the President he did not have to come to
Congress. He did not have to come to the Committee on Foreign Relations

and get our opinion on this question of arms for Cambodia because in
the passage of these bills in past months and years we delegated to
the President the power to grant these arms to any nation in the world
if he thought it was in the best interests of the U.S. Government.

Mr. MANSFIELD. That is inherent in the bill under discussion.
I do not think that the Foreign Relations Committee was aware of just
how all embracing, how far embracing the authority in this bill is
until the bill was before us a week or two ago.

As the Senator has said, the President, on his own initiative,
can empty the arsenal of the United States and give it to any country
or any set of countries he wants to. Is that correct?

Mr. WILLIAMS of Delaware. That is correct both under prior laws
and so far as this bill is concerned. The bill before the Senate
carries appropriations of $250 million in cash sales of military equip-
ment and $350 million in credit sales, which is approximately $600 million. Under this pending bill the President will have the authority
to use that $600 million to furnish military equipment, either sales
or guarantee credits, to any nation in the world where he thinks it
is in the best interests of the United States Government. The only
requirement in the existing law or the bill before the Senate is that
the President reports to Congress at the end of the fiscal year and
tells us what he has done with it. This pending bill is only one of
three such laws.

There is also the military sales under the Foreign Aid Act, where
we sell surplus military equipment. All told, the figures given to
our committee indicate that there is about $600 million in this bill.
But there is approximately $2-1/2 billion a year in authority for
military sales that is permitted under three acts. Under all those
acts as well as under the pending bill we delegate to the President
the authority to make these weapons of war available to any nation in
the world, except those nations that we spell out such as under the
Cooper-Church amendment, which says "except Cambodia." But Congress
has delegated him this authority.

That is the reason I am discussing it here today, to point out
that the criticism should be directed to us right here in Congress.

I made the point in the Foreign Relations Committee hearings---the
chairman is in the Chamber, and he will recall---when a witness from
the Defense Department testified. I said that I did not think we
would ever regain control of [Page S7779.] the sale of these military
supplies until such time as we stopped delegating this authority to
the President. This is no reflection on President Nixon. I trust him
just as much as any other President. But I think this is our responsibility in Congress, and we should assume it. And if Congress
dodges its responsibility and insists upon delegating these powers to
the President then let us stop criticizing him for using it. This
broad delegation of powers has been done during the administrations
of the past several Presidents. We should stop it. We should let
the President of the United States---whoever he may be and whatever
his political affiliation---if he wants arms for X country, come before Congress and ask us to approve the appropriations for so many
planes for this country, so many tanks for that country. It should
be done as a line item, country by country just as would be done with

the construction of a public building in my State, or a dam in Colorado or Idaho, or the dredging of a river in Ohio. We specifically approve each as a special project; we appropriate the money, and the Executive cannot transfer it to other areas.

I do not think Congress will get control of this until we stop this delegation of authority. The irony of the present situation right here is that Congress under the Cooper-Church amendment would be questioning the word of the President. I cannot get away from the fact that approval of the amendment as proposed to be modified would write into law that the troops must be out by July 1, which is an indication that we are accepting the President at his word but are not quite sure he means it and that therefore Congress is going to write into law a penalty if he does not keep his word. Immediately thereafter, the next vote would be to delegate to the President broad powers to sell $600 million in military equipment anywhere in the world---Thailand, Taiwan, Israel, or even Red China if he desired. Yes, any nation in the world? Does this make sense?

We have had the situation, as Senators know, in Pakistan and India where we were furnishing arms to both sides. When one got ahead of the other we would give arms to the other country. The result is that in any border dispute whoever got killed on either side had the satisfaction of being killed with an American bullet.

I think we must stop this practice. That is how we have been getting involved in all areas of the world. We as a nation just cannot afford to act as policeman for the world. This is not the way to make friends, nor is it a path to peace.

Mr. CHURCH. Mr. President, will the Senator yield?

Mr. WILLIAMS of Delaware. I yield.

Mr. CHURCH. I concur in much of what the Senator has said. I wanted to make the point that when this bill was up for hearing before the committee, we discovered, in the course of the questioning of witnesses, that the President had unlimited authority to distribute excess or surplus weapons. He would declare them surplus, and if he did declare them surplus, he had unlimited power to transfer as many as he cared to any country that was otherwise eligible for military assistance. In the committee, we undertook to impose a ceiling on that authority which had not existed prior to the action of the committee in bringing the bill in its amended form to the floor.

Mr. WILLIAMS of Delaware. That is correct.

Mr. CHURCH. So this bill would, for the first time, impose a ceiling on the amount of equipment the President can simply declare as surplus and transfer at pleasure to foreign governments. I think this bill represents a stride in the right direction, one that we probably should have taken a long time ago, and that we are now getting around to taking in the light of recent developments.

Mr. WILLIAMS of Delaware. But even after that modification, which I supported, it still leaves over $2 billion worth of equipment. This bill is for another $600 million, again with complete delegation of all congressional powers to the President.

The point I am making is this: If we want to regain the power
of Congress why do we not just say we are going to stop delegating
this authority to the President? In the future let there be line
items in the appropriation bills for each country by name. Then Congress can accept or reject the request.

The question is raised as to the disadvantage of Congress assuming its own responsibility. The disadvantage of it from the standpoint of various Members of the Senate is that we would have to stand
up and be counted when country A wanted arms or country B wanted
planes. Our constituents would know how each Senator had voted in
approving or disapproving arms or weapons requested for X country,
whereas under the delegation of powers we can go into those areas of
the state where it is popular and say, "Yes, we gave authority to the
President, and we are glad he approved country B's request for planes."

In an area where his decision was unpopular we can say, "The
President is a so and so for having made that decision."

I do not think Congress can retain the opportunity to second-
guess the President and ride both sides of the question. I think the
Senate ought to be on record as to the weapons we are going to give
or sell to the respective countries, wherever in the world it may be.

Should Congress reject this approach and insist upon a continued
delegation of our powers and authority to the President then it should
stop criticizing or second-guessing his decisions.

I cannot understand the reasoning or the logic behind an argument
that we need to adopt an amendment to make sure that the President
backs up the word he has given to Congress when he said he would get
our troops out of Cambodia by July 1. How can we say: "We don't
quite trust you, so we're going to write something in the law to make
sure you do it. But we do trust you with the sale at your sole discretion of $2 billion of equipment that you can send to any nation in
the world except Cambodia." This delegation of powers would not even
bar sales to Red China. Surely this is no way to run a government.

It was agreed in the committee that, assuming that this Cooper-
Church amendment is written into the bill in its tightest form it
would still not achieve its objective if a President wished to circum-
vent its intent. For example: We will take country Y. Suppose we
are furnishing 80 percent of the military equipment for that country,
and they are paying 20 percent. They cannot transfer any of that 80
percent to Cambodia or to any other country because they are prohibited by this act, but they can transfer any part of the 20 percent
which they themselves are paying for to Cambodia or to any other
country that they wish. All the President would have to do to circum-
vent the intent of the Cooper-Church amendment would be to raise the
amount we pay from 80 percent to 90 percent. They could then give
half of the equipment they had been paying for to the country barred
by this amendment. There is only one way to proceed, and that is to
stop the delegation of power---period. Congress should say that in
disposing of military weapons, either by sale or gifts, anywhere in
the world, no matter what the nation is, the administration should
come down to Congress and justify it as a special line item in an
appropriation bill for that particular country.

In the bill before us Congress would delegate to the President authority to sell or guarantee payment of $600 million in military equipment to any country anywhere in the world---to Red China if he wants---there is no prohibition except that the President cannot make the equipment available to Cambodia.

Mr. GRIFFIN. Mr. President, will the Senator from Delaware yield?

Mr. WILLIAMS of Delaware. I yield.

Mr. GRIFFIN. I think the Senator has made his point very well, namely, that it would not be unfair, as a result of the explanation of the Senator from Delaware, to say that Congress, in this legislation, delegates to the President and trusts the President with respect to any country in the world except Cambodia, if the Church-Cooper amendment is adopted. Is that correct?

Mr. WILLIAMS of Delaware. That is correct. There is no question that it does not bar sales to Thailand, or to Red China, or even to Russia, if that is desired. Under the bill even with the Cooper-Church amendment $600 million can be disposed of completely at the President's discretion if he certifies that it is in the best interests of the country. The time has come for Congress, especially the Senate, to stop criticizing the President for usurping the powers of Congress or else to stop delegating those powers. Let us assert our own responsibility by acting on these amounts as line items, as we would for any other project.

The administration could justify those items if it wanted to, whether they be for countries in South America, the Mid East, or in Southeast Asia.

Mr. FULBRIGHT. Will the Senator from Delaware yield?

Mr. WILLIAMS of Delaware. I yield.

Mr. FULBRIGHT. First, I would certainly [Page S7780.] join the Senator in support of limiting the arms aid and sales program further. But I thought that we obtained about as many improvements as was feasible during the committee's work on the bill. I supported those changes and I believe the Senator did also. I would be perfectly willing to go further in limiting giveaway of excess arms, for example. There was a good deal of discussion in the committee on that problem. I thoroughly agree with the Senator that Congress has been improvident in giving extraordinary discretion to Presidents past as well as present. This practice of giving them vast authority did not start with President Nixon. . . .

The only reason we did not go further than we did is that we did not think we had the votes to support more drastic changes.

I agree with much that the Senator has said. About 3 years ago the Senate put in strict controls on the number of countries that could receive aid without further congressional approval. But we could not hold that provision in conference.

Whenever we have made efforts to restrict military aid and sales activities, we have often found that we did not have the votes either here or in the House.

I do not think the Senator can deny that the Military Establishment, through its powerful and distinguished leaders in both Houses of Congress, have for all practical purposes dominated Congress on these matters. Whenever efforts have been made to do some of the things the Senator has suggested, we have failed for lack of votes.

Congress is certainly much at fault in not having imposed restrictions as the Senator has suggested. . . .

[Page S7781.] The efforts of the Foreign Relations Committee have been in this direction over the last several years. But last year, for example, the Foreign Relations Committee, of which the Senator is a distinguished member, tried to cut off aid to Greece. That was, in effect, a line-item approach. The committee approved an amendment to cut off aid and on the floor, the prohibition was stricken by a fairly close margin.

On most efforts that have been made---and there have been a number of them---the Military Establishment has won practically every time in either the Senate or the House.

We are trying to impose additional restrictions through this bill. There were some substantial changes added in the committee. But they have nothing to do with the Cooper-Church amendment. Whether the Senate will agree to these new restrictions, I do not know. And an even greater question is whether the House of Representatives will agree to them.

The Senator is well aware of the extent of the influence of the Military Establishment on the other body. It is very powerful.

Mr. WILLIAMS of Delaware. Mr. President, I point out that the Military Establishment is not responsible for my vote in the Senate. The Senator is correct that Congress has tried on occasion to limit sales with respect to certain countries. Greece was one country, and we have tried to limit sales to other countries.

The point I make is, why approve a bill which provides $600 million and delegates the President this broad authority only by negative action then to say that the authority is good anywhere in the world, "except in Cambodia and maybe Greece"?

Why single out two or three countries? That is always embarrassing for diplomatic reasons. Why not take our action affirmatively? Why delegate this $2 billion and this $600 million of authority and then start limiting this authority by two or three countries? Why not act affirmatively? Let the administration come down and ask for the authority, mentioning each country by name and amounts, and then let congress vote on the specific request.

Mr. FULBRIGHT. Mr. President, I agree with the Senator.

Mr. WILLIAMS of Delaware. If the Senator will join with me we will defeat the bill where it is and at least stop the delegation of the power to use this $600 million.

Mr. FULBRIGHT. Mr. President, I would like to stop it. But the

Senator is confusing two very different things. One is the sale of military weapons. The second is the question of this President's right to go into Cambodia without coming to Congress.

We have not delegated, and the Congress would not allow us to delegate, wide open authority for the President to go to war with any country in the world. Going to war is supposed to be done only in accordance with constitutional procedures.

We have never been faced with a situation quite like the present one.

It is not the arms sales program in which we are particularly interested. The Cooper-Church amendment does not involve the arms sale program. We are concerned in this amendment with the Congress' powers in the field of foreign affairs. I do not think it contributes to public understanding to confuse those two issues.

I say again that I agree with the Senator on the matter of arms sales. I think that it has been a bad program and is not in the national interest.

Mr. WILLIAMS of Delaware. Mr. President, unfortunately the Senator came in when I was half or two-thirds through with my remarks. I discussed that earlier. I was not trying to say these two points were exactly related, but they are part of the same bill. And the Senator from Idaho and the Senator from Florida discussed the constitutionality of the action.

I am speaking of the long-range viewpoint. My own position is that if one has two neighbors and they are having difficulties, and if one of the neighbors is my friend and I give him a gun with which to shoot the other fellow, that man is just as apt to shoot me for furnishing the gun as the other neighbor. That is how our country got involved in the Vietnam war. We first sent them weapons and then we sent them advisers to tell them how to use them. Then we sent soldiers to protect the advisers.

We cannot separate the two points during a discussion of the pending bill because there is $600 million in new authority provided in the pending bill.

If Congress gives this broad authority to the President we have no way to control it.

Congress has lost its authority in the past because we have been negligent in assuming our responsibilities.

Even here today there is a tendency to criticize the President for his alleged resumption of congressional powers and then to turn right around and vote him more extended broad powers. Such hypocrisy. . . .

Mr. HOLLAND. Mr. President, I certainly enjoyed this exchange between two very able Senators whom I respect very much. I do not think I ever heard so much wisdom coupled with so much unrealistic idealism in my life, and that goes back a number of years.

The fact is that everyone in the Senate knows the President has to have consent with reference to furnishing arms where they are badly needed. There is not a citizen in the United States who does not know how he has been pressed to furnish very much needed planes to Israel. Most of the people in the United States feel the President is using proper restraint. I do not suppose you will find one person in ten who does not admit that there has to be somebody in power to act and act when the facts require it.

The same thing is true with reference to this whole question of supplying arms. We live in a world that moves fast.

A while ago I reported to the Senate that the ticker tape indicated that within an hour four different things had happened at an airport in Phonm Phen, halfway around the world. They were very interesting things, too, because they differed so greatly in importance. We live in a fast world, and somebody has to be empowered to act. We love the republican form of government and we like to live under what we call a democracy. But we know its greatest weakness is the inability to act fast unless we delegate some power for fast action in those areas that require it.

With all due respect to my distinguished friend from Delaware and my distinguished friend from Arkansas, I know that they know that Congress does not act fast. They know the Senate frequently exercises its prerogatives for long hearings, for exhaustive reports, and then long debates before it ever acts. At the other end of the Capitol, something of the same situation exists when one considers the long time taken by the Rules Committee to act. So we have to delegate authority.

In this important question of trying to supply arms where they are needed to keep weakness from being overthrown by force and innocence to be overthrown by violence, we have to give the power to somebody, and the President, chosen by all the people in the Nation, is the one who should receive such power. It is utter idealism to suggest he should not have that power. . . .

U.S. PRESTIGE

(May 28, 1970)

Mr. STEVENS. [Page S7981.] Mr. President. . . .

There is one aspect of our policy in Southeast Asia which I have not yet discussed. The United States has been effective in maintaining peace in this area and in the rest of the world because of two factors: prestige and credibility. China backed down from its planned invasion of Quemoy and Matsu because they knew the 7th Fleet was ready to repel their efforts. They respected both our position as a world power and our determination to use that power in the defense of those islands. Prestige and credibility---these two factors make the United States a world power.
In the Cuban missile crisis, the Soviet Union also decided that discretion was the better part of valor and withdrew their missiles from that island. Again, prestige and credibility prevented World War III.

When the Chinese invaded India in 1962, we indicated our intention to help India repel this attack and the Chinese withdrew. Again prestige and credibility were our key to success.

The conflict in Indochina has done, I believe, some damage to our credibility. We have not achieved a military victory, because we have not sought one. But in the eyes of those who think we were trying for such a victory, it appears that we were incapable of achieving it. This has resulted, I believe, in the feeling among some revolutionary elements in the world that the United States cannot be effective in [Page S7982.] aiding a government beset by guerrilla warfare.

It is therefore important that our policy toward Vietnam also consider the credibility of the United States as a power that can effect its will once it has decided that such action is in its national interest.

"Precipitous withdrawal"---that is, the immediate and pellmell retreat with enemy soldiers chasing our last troops out---is unacceptable. It would, indeed, be a humiliating defeat that would severely cripple our credibility as a world power. For this reason President Nixon has rejected "precipitous withdrawal."

But "precipitous withdrawal" is a far cry from the orderly withdrawal that President Nixon has announced. By replacing our combat units with newly trained and equipped South Vietnamese combat units, we can withdraw without military defeat, leaving the South Vietnamese to defend their nation after we have gone. This policy will permit us to end our direct military involvement in this area while retaining our credibility and simultaneously accomplishing our other goals.

The second factor in our ability to keep world peace---prestige--- has, contrary to much that has been said by critics of this war, not seriously been injured. No one doubts our sincerity or purpose at this point. But our prestige could suffer serious damage if we "precipitously withdrew." Even a country with credible power is not to be believed if it does not have will to carry out its announced intentions in international affairs. All four of our most recent Presidents have commented on the importance of our prestige to keeping world peace.

President Eisenhower wrote in his memoirs:

> One possibility was to support the French with air strikes, possibly from carriers, on Communist installations around Dien Bien Phu. There were grave doubts in my mind about the effectiveness of such air strikes on deployed troops where good cover was plentiful. Employment of air strikes alone to support French forces in the jungle would create a double jeopardy; it would comprise an act of war and would also entail the risk of having intervened and lost. Air power might be temporarily beneficial to French morale, but I had no intention of using United States forces in any limited action when the force employed would probably not be decisively effective.

And President Kennedy, in an interview with NBC newsmen Chet Huntley and David Brinkley, said:

The fact of the matter is that with the assistance
of the United States and SEATO, Southeast Asia and indeed all of Asia has been maintained independent against
a powerful force, the Chinese Communists. What I am
concerned about is that Americans will get impatient and
say, because they don't like events in Southeast Asia or
they don't like the Government in Saigon, that we should
withdraw. That only makes it easy for the Communists.
I think we should stay. We should use our influence in
as effective a way as we can, but we should not withdraw.

President Johnson, in a message to Congress, stated:

There are those who ask why this responsibility
should be ours. The answer is simple. There is no one else
who can do the job. Our power is essential, in the final
test, if the nations of Asia are to be secure from expanding communism. Thus, when India was attacked it
looked to us for help, and we gave it gladly.

We believe that Asia should be directed by Asians.
But that means each Asian people must have the right to
find its own way, not that one group or nation should
overrun all the others.

Make no mistake about it. The aim in Vietnam is not
simply the conquest of the South, tragic as that would be.
It is to show that American commitment is worthless. Once
that is done, the gates are down and the road is open to
expansion and endless conquest. That is why Communist China
opposes discussions, even though such discussions are clearly
in the interest of North Vietnam.

President Nixon addressed himself to the importance of our prestige in his November 3 address to the Nation:

A Nation cannot remain great if it betrays its allies and
lets down its friends. Our defeat and humiliation in South
Vietnam would without question promote recklessness in the
councils of those great powers who have not yet abandoned
their goals of world conquest.

This would spark violence wherever our commitments help
maintain peace---in the Middle East, in Berlin, eventually
even in the Western Hemisphere.

Ultimately, this would cost more lives. It would not
bring peace but more war.

We must, therefore, accomplish our announced goal of withdrawing
all combat troops from Vietnam in a manner which will preserve both
our prestige and credibility. . . .

[Page S7984.] Mr. President, I have asked the Department of Defense to provide me with a list of the countries to which we provide military aid or training under the Foreign Assistance Act of 1961. This is dated May 28, 1970. This information shows that we provide assistance to the following countries:

Afghanistan	Greece	Nicaragua
Australia	Guatemala	Pakistan
Argentina	Honduras	Panama
Bolivia	India	Paraguay
Brazil	Indonesia	Peru
Ceylon	Iran	Philippines
Chile	Jordan	Portugal
Nationalist China	Lebanon	Saudi Arabia
Colombia	Korea	Senegal
Congo	Liberia	Spain
Dominican Republic	Libya	Tunisia
Ecuador	Malaysia	Turkey
El Salvador	Mexico	Uruguay
Ethiopia	Morocco	Venezuela
Ghana	Nepal	

Three countries are receiving assistance under the defense appropriations bill---namely, Laos, Thailand, and Vietnam.

I note that the pending amendment would prevent the executive branch from furnishing military instruction to Cambodian forces or providing military instruction in Cambodia. . . .

I cannot see why we should cut off from Cambodia the training we are giving to so many other nations to increase their own ability to defend themselves. I can understand full well why some of the other provisions of the Cooper-Church amendment were offered, but I do not understand the prohibition against military instruction to Cambodian forces or military instruction in Cambodia. It would prevent us, for example, from training their pilots. It would prevent us from training any of their people in Vietnam or in Cambodia itself. This is a provision of the Cooper-Church amendment which I just do not understand, and I would be very willing to listen to anyone who wants to explain it.

I am informed that every time we either give or sell military equipment to a foreign nation, we provide advisers who instruct them in the use of that equipment. Why is it that Laos, Thailand, and Vietnam should receive this advice and this service in providing for their own defense, while we simultaneously prevent the President from giving similar instruction---or ordering the military to give similar instruction---in Cambodia or to Cambodians? I think this is one of the serious defects of the Cooper-Church amendment. . . .

THE WAR: A DOMESTIC DISASTER*

Mr. FULBRIGHT. [Page S7988.] Mr. President, having participated in a filibuster or so myself in the past on issues that were, I thought, quite legitimate, I am sympathetic to those now conducting a

filibuster. Thus, I thought it would not be inappropriate for them
to give me some time today so that I could make a few remarks and
relieve them of some of the onerous duties of holding the floor until
some time next week. I hope that they will appreciate that properly,
because my remarks are germane to the matter of the Church-Cooper
amendment.

Mr. President, President Nixon keeps assuring us that he wants
peace, as if his decision for peace were a matter in doubt. In fact,
I know of no one in the Senate who questions the President's desire
for an end to the war, but many of us are very doubtful, indeed, that
his present course can lead to peace, or to anything but endless,
spreading war in the jungles of Indochina.

When we come right down to it, the enemy almost certainly wants
peace too but, like the President, they want peace on their own terms.
Neither side can be said to have shown a fondness for fighting for its
own sake, but neither side has shown any willingness to make significant concessions for peace. Both are bent on a victory as they conceive
that term, and until one side or the other achieves it, the fighting
will go on.

That is the heart of the matter, and it benefits us not at all to
use the enemy's stubbornness as an excuse for our own. If we want
peace, someone must take the first step, and while many of us would
welcome such an initiative on the part of the Vietnamese, we also
should recognize that as the smaller, weaker party to the war, fighting
as they are on their own part of the world where they belong, they must
find it far more difficult than should we, to break the impasse. Even
if it were clear on the merits that they ought to take the first step,
that judgment should not serve as a policy for us. The fact is they
have shown that they are settling in for the long haul of indefinite
guerrilla warfare, and we are not able to control the decisions that
are made in Hanoi. We can only control the decisions that are made
in Washington, and that, basically is why it is up to us to take an
effective step toward peace.

It is indeed incumbent upon us, and [Page S7989.] urgently so,
because this war has become a domestic disaster for the American people.
Our economy is racked by unchecked inflation and, perhaps even worse,
by signs of collapsing confidence in the economy on the part of the
financial community. Morally and socially, we are in a condition beyond mere division among ourselves. We are in a condition indicative
of social disintegration. The students are not the only people who
have become alienated from the Government and its policies; as the
stock market shows, the bankers and businessmen are losing confidence
in the Government's policies, if not indeed in our national leadership
altogether. If it was not clear before, it is crystal clear now that
this war has become a moral and economic disaster for America. That
is why we cannot wait the enemy out. That is why we must take the
first step.

Step by step the administration has hedged, backed off, and now
all but repudiated the President's confident prediction of South Vietnamese withdrawal. . . .

From the narrow viewpoint of the Saigon dictators, getting in
over their heads in Cambodia is by no means a "silly argument of silly

people." It serves the double purpose of advancing traditional Vietnamese designs on Cambodia and of drawing the United States further
into the swamp.

Besides Thieu and Ky, the only people who appear to be delighted
by the American invasion of Cambodia are the Chinese. Assuming that
the Chinese wish to expel American military power from Asia, to curb
Soviet influence and expand their own, they cannot fail to take pleasure in seeing the Americans blunder into a new hopeless military adventure. From the Chinese point of view, the extension of the war
into Cambodia serves to drain American resources and isolate the
United States internationally, while giving the Chinese an opportunity
to displace Soviet influence with the Indochinese Communists by dem-
onstrating their own more militant support. In addition, the "protracted war" to which the Vietnamese Communists are now settling down
can only serve, from China's standpoint, to bring a dependent and ex-
hausted North Vietnam even further under Chinese influence. . . .

[Page S7990.] Anticipating protracted warfare, China appears to
have pledged full backing to the Communist forces in all three Indochinese countries. The Chinese indicated long ago that they welcome
American involvement in Asian wars of attrition. It is worth recall-
ing a significant editorial which appeared in the People Daily of
Peking on August 30, 1966: "To be quite frank," the editorial stated,

> if United States imperialism kept its forces in Europe and
> America, the Asian people would have no way of wiping them
> out. Now, as it is so obliging as to deliver its goods to
> the customer's door, the Asian people cannot but express
> welcome. The more forces United States imperialism throws
> into Asia, the more will it be bogged down there and the
> deeper will be the grave it digs for itself. . . .
>
> The tying down of large numbers of United States troops
> by the Asian people creates a favorable condition for the
> further growth of the anti-United States struggle of the
> people in other parts of the world. With all the people
> rising to attack it, one hitting at its head and the other
> at its feet, United States imperialism can be nibbled up bit
> by bit.

We are being "nibbled up bit by bit," not only in Indochina but,
far more seriously, by the repercussions of the Indochina war within
our own country. It is most urgent, therefore, that we change our
course and seek a political settlement based on the two general principles which the North Vietnamese have repeatedly indicated will
motivate them to engage in serious bargaining. These two principles
are, first, the establishment of a transitional coalition government
for what would become an independent, neutralist South Vietnam; and
second, a commitment to a definite schedule for the ultimate total
withdrawal of American forces.

The major single obstacle to serious negotiations on these
bases is the disastrous notion that there is a connection between our
own national interests and the survival and power of the Saigon military dictatorship. We do not have to impose anything on Mr. Thieu
and Mr. Ky or on anybody else in order to open the way to negotiations.

We have only to put them on notice that they are at liberty either to join us in negotiating a compromise peace or to make some arrangement of their own. Should they prefer to continue the war, that would be their privilege, and they have an army of over a million men of which to do it. All that I would take away from the Thieu-Ky regime is their veto on American policy.

Perhaps the really difficult thing for Americans is not in recognizing what needs to be done but in recognizing the disastrous consequences of what has already been done. The nature of this dilemma was summed up eloquently by Rabbi Irving Greenberg in a statement before the Committee on Foreign Relations on the moral impact of the war:

> Shall we now go to the parents of the 40,000 (American dead) and say; we have erred and your children have died in vain? Shall all this patriotism and sacrifice mean nothing? I realize the full force of this dilemma. But the only corresponding answer must be: Shall we condemn another 10,000 Americans and another 50,000 Vietnamese to death rather than not admit?

> But inability to accept the tragic, the ironic, the possibility of mistake and failure is to be less than fully human. Perhaps this is our national problem.

Looking beyond this war which has so drained our substance and spirit, things need not look so bleak for America after all. Drawing a parallel between American feelings about Vietnam and British anxieties over the revolt of the American colonies two centuries ago, an English military analyst, Correlli Barnett, points out that the British leaders of that day suffered feelings of failure and frustration no less acute than those of our own leaders today. But, Mr. Barnett writes:

> Once the American war was liquidated, Britain's mood changed with astonishing speed. National hope and self-confidence were reborn. Instead of the decay and disintegration to which men had looked forward, Britain's greatest wealth, greatest power and greatest influence in the world were yet to come.

With some commonsense and moral courage, the same might be arranged for America. . . .

PRESIDENT NIXON'S STATEMENT ON CAMBODIA

(June 4, 1970)

Mr. GRIFFIN. [Page S8346.] Mr. President. . . . concerning President Noxon's address to the Nation last evening.

The President's address was a convincing statement of the wisdom and the success of the sanctuary operation.

I believe he made it abundantly clear again that all American troops will be out of Cambodia before the end of June and that 150,000 troops will be coming home on schedule.

In my view, his forthright statement demonstrated that there is no need for the pending Church-Cooper amendment, and I believe that a majority of the Senate will come to that conclusion.

As he has done before, President Nixon reaffirmed his confidence in the American people---and I am hopeful that confidence will be reciprocated.

I ask unanimous consent that the text of the President's address be printed in the Record.

There being no objection, the text of the President's address was ordered to be printed in the Record, as follows:

Radio and Television Address by the President on the Cambodian Sanctuary Operation

Good evening, my fellow Americans.

One month ago, I announced a decision ordering American participation with South Vietnamese forces in a series of operations against Communist-occupied areas in Cambodia which have been used for five years as bases for attacks on our forces in South Vietnam.

This past weekend, in the Western White House in California, I met with Secretary Laird, General Abrams and other senior advisors to receive a firsthand report on the progress of this operation.

Based on General Abrams' report, I can now state that this has been the most successful operation of this long and very difficult war.

Before going into the details which form the basis for this conclusion, I believe it would be helpful to review briefly why I considered it necessary to make this decision; what our objectives were; and the prospects for achieving those objectives.

You will recall that on April 20, I announced the withdrawal of an additional 150,000 American troops from Vietnam within a year---which will bring the total number withdrawn, since I have taken office, to 260,000. I also reaffirmed on that occasion our proposals for a negotiated peace.

At the time of this announcement I warned that if the enemy tried to take advantage of our withdrawal program by increased attacks in Cambodia, Laos, or South Vietnam in a way that endangered the lives of our men remaining in South

Vietnam, that I would, in my capacity as Commander-in-Chief of our Armed Forces, take strong action to deal with that threat.

Between April 20 and April 30, Communist forces launched a series of attacks against a number of key cities in neutral Cambodia. Their objective was unmistakable---to link together bases they had maintained in Cambodia for five years in violation of Cambodian neutrality. The entire six-hundred-mile Cambodian-South Vietnam border would then have become one continuous hostile territory from which to launch assaults upon American and allied forces.

This posed an unacceptable threat to our remaining forces in South Vietnam. It would have meant higher casualties. It would have jeopardized our program for troop withdrawals. It would have meant a longer war. And---carried out in the face of an explicit warning from this Government---failure to deal with the enemy action would have eroded the credibility of the United States before the entire world.

After very intensive consultations with my top advisors, I directed that American troops join the South Vietnamese in destroying these major enemy bases along the Cambodian frontier. I said when I made this announcement: "Our purpose is not to occupy these areas. Once the enemy forces are driven out of the sanctuaries and once their supplies are destroyed, we will withdraw."

That pledge is being kept. I said further on that occasion, "We take this action not for the purpose of expanding the war in Cambodia, but for the purpose of ending the war in Vietnam." That purpose is being advanced.

As of today I can report that all of our major military objectives have been achieved. 43,000 South Vietnamese took part in these operations, along with 31,000 Americans. Our combined forces have moved with greater speed and success than we had planned; we have captured and destroyed far more in war material than we anticipated; and American and allied casualties have been far lower than we expected.

In the month of May, in Cambodia alone, we captured a total amount of enemy arms, equipment, ammunition and food nearly equal to what we captured in all of Vietnam in all of last year.

Here is some film of the war material that has been captured.

This is some ammunition you see. We have captured more than 10 million rounds of ammunition. That is equal to the enemy's expenditures for nine months.

Here you also see a few of the over 15,000 rifles
and machine guns and other weapons we have captured.
They will never be used against American boys in Vietnam.

This reality was brought home directly to me a few
days ago. I was talking with a union leader from New
York. His son died in Vietnam this past February. He
told me that---had we moved earlier in Cambodia---we
might have captured the enemy weapon that killed his son.

Now you are looking at some of the heavy mortars,
rocket launchers and recoilless rifles that have shelled
U.S. base camps and Vietnamese towns. We have seized over
2,000 of these along with 90,000 rounds of ammunition.
That is as much as the enemy fires in a whole year. Had
this war material made its way into South Vietnam and had
it been used against American troops, U.S. casualties would
have been vastly increased.

Here you see rice, more than 11 million pounds of rice.
This is more than enough rice to feed all the enemy's combat
battalions in Vietnam for over three months. This rice will
not be feeding enemy troops now, but rather war refugees.

Now with the rainy season now beginning, it will take
the enemy months to rebuild its shattered installations and
to replace the equipment we have captured or destroyed.

The success of these operations to date has guaranteed
that the June 30 deadline I set for withdrawal of all American forces from Cambodia will be met. General Abrams advises me that 17,000 of the 31,000 Americans who entered
Cambodia have already returned to Vietnam. The remainder
will return by the end of this month. This includes all
American air support, logistics and military advisory personnel.

The only remaining American activity in Cambodia after
July 1 will be air missions to interdict the movement of enemy troops and material where I find that is necessary to
protect the lives and security of our men in South Vietnam.

Our discussions with the South Vietnamese government
indicate that their primary objective remains the security
of South Vietnam, and that their activity in Cambodia in the
future---after their withdrawal from the sanctuaries---will
be determined by the actions of the enemy in Cambodia.

When this operation was announced, the critics charged
that it would increase American casualties, that it would
widen the war, that it would lengthen our involvement, that
it might postpone troop withdrawals. But the operation was
undertaken for precisely the opposite reasons---and it has
had precisely the opposite effect.

Let us examine the long-range impact of this operation.

First, we have eliminated an immediate danger to the
security of the remaining Americans in Vietnam, and thereby

reduced our future casualties. Seizing these weapons and
ammunition will save American lives. Because of this operation, American soldiers who might not otherwise be ever
coming home, will now be coming home.

Second, we have won precious time for the South Vietnamese to train and prepare themselves to carry the burden
of their national defense, so that our American forces can
be withdrawn.

From General Abrams' reports and from our advisors in
the field, one of the most dramatic and heartening developments of the operation has been the splendid performance of
the South Vietnamese army. Sixty percent of all the troops
involved in the Cambodian operations were South Vietnamese.
The effectiveness, the skill, the valor with which they
fought far exceeded our expectations. Confidence and morale
in the South Vietnamese army has been greatly bolstered.
This operation has clearly demonstrated that our Vietnamization program is succeeding.

Third, we have insured the continuance and success of
our troop withdrawal program. On April 20, I announced an
additional 150,000 Americans would be home within a year.
As a result of the success of the Cambodian operations, Secretary Laird has resumed the withdrawal of American forces
from Vietnam. Fifty thousand of the 150,000 I announced on
April 20 will now be out by October 15.

As long as the war goes on, we can expect setbacks and
some reversals. But, following the success of this effort,
we can say now with confidence that we will keep our timetable for troop withdrawals.

Secretary Rogers and I have been particularly encour-
aged by the resolve of 11 Asian countries at the Djkarta
Conference to seek a solution to the problem of Cambodia.
Cambodia [Page S8347.] offers an opportunity for these 11
nations, as well as other countries of the area, to cooperate in supporting the Cambodian government's efforts to
maintain Cambodian neutrality, independence and territorial
integrity. We shall do what we can to make it possible for
these Asian initiatives to succeed.

To the North Vietnamese tonight I say again---the door
to a negotiated peace remains wide open. Every offer we
have made at the conference table, publicly or privately, I
herewith reaffirm. We are ready to negotiate, whenever they
are ready to negotiate.

However, if their answer to our troop withdrawal program, and to our offer to negotiate, is to increase their
attacks in a way that jeopardizes the safety of our remaining forces in Vietnam, I shall, as my action five weeks ago
clearly demonstrated, take strong and effective measures to
deal with that situation.

As all of you know, when I first announced the decision
on Cambodia, it was subjected to an unprecedented barrage of

criticism in this country. I want to express tonight my
deep appreciation to the millions of Americans who supported me then and who have supported me since in our efforts to win a just peace.

But I also understand the deep divisions in this
country over the war. I realize that many Americans are
deeply troubled. They want peace. They want to bring the
boys home. Let us understand once and for all that no
group has a monopoly on those concerns. Every American
shares those desires; I share them very deeply.

Our differences are over the best means to achieve
a just peace.

As President I have a responsibility to listen to
those in this country who disagree with my policies. But
I also have a solemn obligation to make the hard decisions
which I find are necessary to protect the lives of 400,000
American men remaining in Vietnam.

When I spoke to you a month ago, a clear threat was
emerging in Cambodia to the security of our men in Vietnam.

Ask yourselves this question: If an American President
had failed to meet this threat to 400,000 American men in
Vietnam, would those nations and peoples who rely on America's
power and treaty commitments for their security---in Latin
America, Europe, the Middle East or other parts of Asia---re-
tain any confidence in the United States? That is why I
deeply believe that a just peace in Vietnam is essential, if
there is to be a lasting peace in other parts of the world.

With this ammouncement tonight, we have kept the pledge
I made when I ordered this operation, that we would withdraw
from Cambodia on a scheduled timetable---just as this Administration has kept every pledge it has made to the American
people regarding the war in Vietnam and the return of American troops.

Let us look at the record.

In June of 1969 I pledged a withdrawal of 25,000 troops.
They came home. In September of the same year I said I would
bring home an additional 35,000. They came home. In December
I said an additional 50,000 Americans were coming out of Vietnam. They, too, have come home.

There is one commitment yet to be fulfilled. I have
pledged to end this war. I shall keep that promise. But I
am determined to end the war in a way that will promote peace
rather than conflict throughout the world. I am determined
to end it in a way that will bring an era of reconciliation
to our people---and not an era of furious recrimination.

In seeking peace, let us remember that at this time
only this Administration can end this war and bring peace.

We have a program for peace---and the greater the support
the Administration receives in its efforts, the greater
the opportunity to win that just peace we all desire.

Peace is the goal that unites us. Peace is the goal
toward which we are working. Peace is the goal this
government will pursue until the day that we reach it.

Thank you, and good night.

SENATORIAL REACTION TO PRESIDENTIAL STATEMENT*

Mr. MUSKIE. [Page S8357.] Mr. President, in his television address to the Nation last evening, President Nixon made far-reaching
claims as to the military success of the Cambodian invasion. I
question those claims and their relevance to our long-term interests
and objectives in Southeast Asia.

As I said in my reaction to the President's speech, last night,
captured weapons and supplies may give the appearance of military
victory, but that cannot obscure the fact that we have widened the
war and added to the uncertainty as to our prospects in Southeast
Asia. The President's action has, in addition, made a negotiated
settlement much more difficult.

By supporting expanded South Vietnamese military action in Cambodia, we have helped to spread their forces thinner. By increasing
military pressure on the Vietcong and the North Vietnamese in Cambodia, we have driven them farther into the arms of the Communist
Chinese. Most important, we have complicated our political problems
in Southeast Asia and in Europe by raising new obstacles to a political settlement in Indochina. In South Vietnam we have tied ourselves
more closely to the fortunes of the Saigon regime. In Cambodia we
have injected ourselves into a more complex political situation, where
we do not even have a bargaining partner. . . .

Mr. GRIFFIN. [Page S8365.] Mr. President, in his television address to the Nation last night, President Nixon briefly outlined the
accomplishments in the Cambodian sanctuary operations and reported that
"all of our military objectives have been achieved."

As the President indicated, allied sweeps in the Cambodia/Vietnam
border area have located a number of major base complexes used by
North Vietnamese and Vietcong troops. One of the largest of these
bases taken by allied forces was discovered by elements of the U.S.
1st Air Cavalry Division on May 5, 1970, in Cambodia's Fishhook area.
It is an immense complex some 3 square kilometers in an area dubbed
"The City" by the U.S. cavalrymen.

The logistical part of "The City" was located in three separate
areas and included approximately 182 storage bunkers. [Page S8366.]
About 80 percent of these bunkers, each measuring 16 by 10 by 8 feet,
were being utilized and contained enemy war supplies. Sixty percent
or 87 of these 145 bunkers were filled to capacity. The bunkers
contained munitions, weapons, food stocks, medical supplies, and quar-
termaster clothing and equipment. The largest quantity of a single

type was ammunition including AK-47 and 57 mm. recoilless rifle rounds. Generally, all types of equipment and supplies were in an excellent state of preservation and in good operating condition when captured. All bunkers were serviced by bamboo-matted trails from 3 to 8 ft. in width.

After a thorough investigation of the area, its contents and documents captured in the area, it is apparent that "The City" was well organized and was capable of rapid receipt and issue of large quantities of supplies. Judging from the general condition of the oldest bunkers, and from captured supply documents found in the area, it appears that the storage depot had been in operation for some 2-1/2 years. The bunkers in the northern part of the complex appeared to have been constructed within the last 6 months.

An analysis of the documents and earlier reports indicate that this complex was a supply depot with the primary mission of obtaining supplies and equipment within Cambodia and then delivering these supplies to Communist forces in South Vietnam. In addition, this depot provided supplies to a number of training and headquarters elements. When considering the type and amount of supplies captured, the loss of this depot will certainly reduce the enemy's offensive capabilities in the III Corps area of South Vietnam. . . .

In addition to the logistical storage facilities, the complex contained a training area consisting of a large classroom, small-arms firing range, and mess facilities to support the training area. Also located in the southeastern part of the complex was a small animal farm. These facilities and training aids, including silhouette targets and dummy grenades as well as a large stock of items of personal clothing and equipment, indicate that a portion of this base area was used to provide refresher military and political training to recent replacements from North Vietnam. Colocated with the supply depot, the training center could also readily outfit the replacements while providing the refresher training.

Materiel captured in "The City" base complex includes the following:

Individual weapons: 50 AK-50 rifles, 922 SKS rifles, 36 MAS rifles, 48 Thompson submachine guns, 42 Chinese Communist grease guns and 13 AK-47 rifles.

Crew-served weapons: Three 14.5 twin barrel AA guns (complete with sights), 1 20-mm. machine gun, 15 7.62-mm. machine guns, 60 .30-cal. AA machine guns, 6 .51-cal. AA machine guns (with 80 extra barrels), 40 60-mm. mortars, 6 82-mm. mortars, 3 4.2-in. mortars, 5 120-mm. mortars, 22 RPG rocket launchers, 8 75-mm. recoilless rifles, and 33 Chinese Communist light machine guns.

Ammunition: 319,000 .51-cal./12.7-mm. ammo, 152 anti-tank mines, 710 Chinese Communist grenades, 25,200 14.5-mm. AA machine gun rounds, 411 82-mm. mortar rounds, 84 4.2-in. ammo, 303 57-mm. recoilless rifle rounds, 127 75-mm. recoilless rifle rounds, 142 B-50 rocket rounds, 1,559,000 AK-47 rounds, 1,400 rifle grenades, 17 122-mm. rockets, 58,000 lbs. plastic explosives, 250 cases detonating cord, 144,000 non-electric blasting caps, 270,000 ft. time fuse, 2,700 fuze lighters, 42,670 7.5-mm. machine gun rounds, 22 cases anti-personnel mines,

400,000 .30-cal. rounds, 13 107-mm. rockets, 10 85-mm. field gun
rounds, 780 60-mm. mortar rounds, 168 120-mm. mortar rounds, 200
electrical blasting caps, and 16,920 propelling charges for 120 mm.
rounds.

Miscellaneous: 2,800 rucksacks, 607 shovels, 470 picks, 120
entrenching tools, 45 AK-47 magazines, 4 cases AK-47 repair parts,
1 blow torch, 18 cases 106 mm. repair kits, 500 bicycles, 2,750
bicycle tires, 100 pair shoes, 75 pair socks, 320 mess kits, 15 cases
122 mm. repair parts, 8 two-wheeled carts, 37 gunners quadrants, 118
.51-cal. ammo cans, 40 aiming stakes, 20 60-mm. mortar sights, 14
82-mm. mortar service kits, 20 60-mm. mortar service kits, 4 82-mm.
mortar base plates, 2 panoramic mortar sights, 3 cases B-40 components,
25 plastic sheets, 3 hydraulic test kits, 80 batteries, 8 field tele-
phones, 9 PRC-6 radios, 27 cases RPG-7 repair parts, 200 lbs. medicine,
86 cases coagulent medicines, and 550,000 ampules.

Food: 30 tons rice, 8 tons corn, 1,100 lbs. salt, 10 pigs, 25
chickens, and 50 baby chicks. . . .

Mr. DOLE. [Page S8401.] Mr. President. . . .

I detected in the statement by President Nixon perhaps an effort
by the President to extend at least the tip of the olive branch to Congress. It was a very conciliatory message. The President made clear
that after July 1 we would carry on very limited operations in Cambodia, not with ground troops, but only through air interdiction to
protect American forces.

I share the view of the Senator from Oklahoma the amendment of
the Senator from West Virginia (Mr. BYRD) is an improvement. If the
Byrd amendment could be agreed to, while the President might not en-
dorse the Cooper-Church amendment, he might not oppose it. The Byrd
amendment makes it very clear that the President would have the
right---as he should have, and as he does have under the Constitution---
to protect American forces.

I would reiterate, as the Senator from Oklahoma has pointed out,
it is difficult to understand how we can question the credibility or
the actions of President Nixon, when he is the first President to deescalate the war in Southeast Asia. He announced again last night
that another 50,000 troops would be withdrawn by October 15 of this
year, which indicates to me, as it does to the Senator from Oklahoma
that President Nixon is on a path for peace, that he has a plan for
peace, and that it is working notwithstanding enemy efforts to disrupt
those plans.

. . . what we need now is, unity in America. What we need now is
probably unity in this body. I do not believe the timing of the so-
called Church-Cooper amendment is particularly appropriate, again because President Nixon has kept his faith with the American people,
again because President Nixon is deescalating the conflict in Southeast Asia, and again because he is Commander in Chief and has the inherent right under the Constitution to protect American forces. To
me, that is the crux of the entire debate today, and has been for the
past couple of weeks, and may be for some time in the future. Does
the President, as Commander in Chief, have the right to protect American forces? Does the President, as Commander in Chief and Chief

Executive Officer, have the right to make peace? Or should those functions be left to Congress---the Senate and the House? I do not believe they can be or should be. . . .

[Page S8402.] We have every right to support our President. If President Nixon had escalated the war, if President Nixon had invaded another country to make war against that country, whatever the country, then we could question his credibility, we could question his powers; but it is clear that he has charted a course for peace, as are those who support him. . . .

Mr. HANSEN. . . .

Mr. President, with a great many other Americans, I had the privilege last night of hearing the President make a progress report on the situation in Southeast Asia. I noted that President Nixon reaffirmed that the timetable to withdraw 150,000 additional American troops from Vietnam will go according to schedule, as will the plan to withdraw all American troops from Cambodia by June 30. The President advised that already 17,000 of the 31,000 Americans who entered Cambodia to seize the arms, ammunition, food, and the munitions and to clean out the enemy sanctuaries, have returned to Vietnam. The President further advised that the military objectives of the Cambodian action have been achieved.

Mr. President, this is further evidence of President Nixon's ability to establish attainable goals, to report to the Nation what the goals are, and to see that those goals are accomplished within the period of time promised.

Because the President does keep his word, there is no credibility gap in the Nixon administration. The President has the confidence of a majority of the American people. This is evidenced in the nation-wide polls which indicate strong approval of the wisdom in the President's decisions. . . .

The President has the confidence of the majority of the American people, and he has their support. In my opinion, it will be most appropriate for Congress likewise to express its confidence in the President---the confidence of the people's elected representatives.

For Congress to do otherwise is to give the world a misleading picture of the courage, the patriotism and the fortitude of the great majority of the American people. In my view, the passage by either the House or the Senate of any legislative proposal designed to discredit, in an unusual manner, the foreign policy decisions of our President, decisions that have proved successful, will confuse foreign nations.

Such an act would at best astound our allies, and we know from experience that any such move will be twisted by the enemy to feed their propaganda mill and encourage the will of their people to prolong the war, in the hope that the spirit of America will be not long in breaking. . . .

Mr. BAKER. [Page S8406.] Mr. President. . . .

One of the most extraordinary things about the national reaction

to the President's speech on April 30, and to his press conference
on May 8, was the emotional criticism of his stated intentions. Many
people, especially in the academic community, in the national news
media, and in the Congress, apparently, simply refused to believe what
the President had said.

Time and time again I have asked students and faculty members who
came to my office to discuss these issues and these developments,
whether they believed that American troops would be withdrawn from
Cambodia by July 1.

To my astonishment, almost invariably, they replied that they did
not. Almost invariably, they replied that they did not believe the
representations made by the President of the United States.

On some occasions, I have asked on what basis they asserted this
disbelief that the previous representations which had been made by the
President of the United States had not been kept, or kept only partially, which gave them enough of an intellectual basis for thinking that
this representation was untrue or would not be kept.

I asked why they did not believe the explicit statements of fact
or intention that were made by the President of the United States.

I found, on almost all occasions, that their skepticism about the
accuracy of the representations of the President was far more emotional
than it was rational.

They answered that the Government has been less than candid in
the past, and, more often than not, they referred to the past as extending beyond January 1, 1969.

Therefore, it follows necessarily that the new President taking
office at that time and the administration over which he presided cannot be believed, either.

It seems to me, Mr. President, that this situation which I found,
not once, but on a number of occasions, and with different groups who
visited my office expressing concern over the American involvement in
Southeast Asia, and Cambodia in particular, is strictly illogical.

While I do not question the depth of feeling that the critics of
the President exhibit about him personally, and about his policies in
Indochina, I do question the objectivity and the fairness with which
they approach these complex and difficult public issues.

Mr. President, I have, on occasion, put this question to more
than one group:

Assume for the moment that July 1, 1970, has come and gone and
that American involvement in Cambodia has ended; assume, for the moment, that in the fall of 1970, further, that additional troop withdrawals from Southeast Asia are accomplished, and that by the spring
of 1971 an additional 150,000 have been withdrawn from Southeast
Asia, as the President has promised to do; assume, for the moment,
that, as time goes by, say in the fall of 1971, substantially greater
numbers of troops are withdrawn from Southeast Asia to the point that
there are virtually no American combat troops remaining in Southeast

Asia, and that there is only a residual core of support troops; and assume, further, that the President has indicated previously, as long ago as 1970, that he intended regularly and methodically to reduce those numbers; but assume most of all that, during his campaign in 1968, the President of the United States assured and then reiterated that he intended to end the war in Southeast Asia, and that he is . going to do so---as you assume all those things, for the sake of argument, and assuming them to be true, would you still protest this action, and would you feel the disenchantment that you apparently do with the judgment and the policies of the President and his adminis- tration?

Mr. President, many of my colleagues in this body are lawyers. They recognize that this question which I put has more than rhetorical but rather a valid and historical basis for placing a hypothetical proposition.

Assuming certain hypothesis as being true, then what would your answer be?

I think that most Senators would recognize the form of the ques- tion I have just outlined as being a valid basis for judging an ulti- mate conclusion that is based on an intellectual as distinguished from an emotional basis as one examines a given issue.

[Page S8407.] It is interesting to me, then, that most of the groups to whom I put this hypothetical question refused to answer.

Sometimes, on occasion, some of them would answer that, of course, if that were the case, they would not be exercised about the situation and that, of course, not only would they not question the validity of the judgment made by the President and his administration, but they would commend him for having done what should have been done a long time ago; namely, to disengage American combat troops from war in Indochina, but that, after all, was more often than not the case. "We do not believe that" or, "We refuse to assume that" or, "We think it is extremely unlikely that it would occur," they reply to these assumptions that I have asked them to make.

To those who listened to the assumption I have just outlined, it will be recognized that many of them have not only transpired but have been fulfilled.

They will also recognize, I believe, that none has been trans- gressed, that none of the hypotheses I asked them to accept in this situation, in this hypothetical question, has been unfulfilled.

We recognize further that some of them are yet to be fulfilled. And it is the purest speculation on my part, but of the specific recom- mendations of the President, the most general and the broadest and meaningful one was, "I shall end the war," a representation and a com- mitment made by the President during his campaign for the Presidency in 1968 and reiterated as late as last night in his very splendid, frank, and candid address to the Nation by the President of the United States.

The point of the matter is that I am stunned that people will not accept these hypotheses, at least to the extent that they have already

been fulfilled. And I am shocked that they will not believe the representations made by the President as to his future intentions and
commitments.

I think the President of the United States has, the majority of
the time, a track record for candor and honesty in his representations
with respect to Southeast Asia that is so good that he richly unde-
serves to be disbelieved in these representations.

I believe then that there is ample and abundant reason to think
that the shrill criticisms of the President's policy in Southeast Asia
and his determination to deprive, not Cambodians, but North Vietnamese
invaders, of their privileged sanctuary in Cambodia and of their right
to strike with impunity the American forces, I believe that the criticism of these policies would be less shrill if it were not for some
other factors that the critics have not yet examined.

I wonder, then, in the interest of pure, sweet reason and impar-
tial judgment if it must not be concluded that many students, acade-
micians, and others whose motives I do not doubt, have succumbed to
the unscholarly and unintellectual devices of basing their response
and evaluation on the basis of prejudice and emotion outside of the
range of the facts and circumstances supplied by the hypotheses themselves.

If that is the case, then the reaction to Cambodia by so many,
especially in the academic community, is a remarkable situation, indeed, because not only must the academic community be free of turmoil
in terms of partisan conflict, if it is to act in the university
tradition, but it must also be the bastion of intelligence and civilization that requires people to move for the good of the country,
and not to react---as one person suggested that many do---to the
President as if he were running against Helen Gahagan Douglas for the
U.S. Senate.

Some have said, and I am not sure that it is wrong, that there
is a core or group of people in the United States that simply do not
like the President and have not since he defeated Helen Gahagan
Douglas. And nothing will change their minds.

That may be true. If it is, it is unfortunate. But it is understandable.

His decisions have to do entirely with deciding the best course
for the United States in terms of terminating hostilities in Southeast
Asia and providing for the common defense of the United States. That
is the universal belief of most Congressmen and of most people in the
United States. . . .

                         THE FIRST BYRD AMENDMENT*

    Mr. LONG. . . . [Page S8414.]

I think that the pending amendment by the distinguished Senator
from West Virginia (Mr. BYRD) has a great deal merit, and I think it

should be carefully and fully considered. I know that it will be, and
I would not be surprised if the vote on his amendment proved to be the
decisive vote on this whole matter.

In summing up, I believe that the President of the United States
has performed with the most unusual personal and professional skill
and courage throughout this entire episode. I think that, when all
the smoke has cleared, he will have earned and will be given the grati-
tude and admiration of the American people. I think that his speech
last night was one of the best of his career, and I think that it should
demonstrate to his persistent critics that the man should be trusted.
I do not believe that the President has usurped any power from the Congress or anyone else during the course of the past few weeks, and I am
confident that the Congress will not repudiate him.

Mr. BYRD of West Virginia. Mr. President, will the Senator yield?

Mr. BAKER. I am happy to yield.

Mr. BYRD of West Virginia. I thank the Senator for his very inci-
sive statement. I am glad to know he feels that the vote on the amendment which I have offered, and which is cosponsored by several Senators,
will be the decisive vote. I share that feeling. I feel that this is
the key amendment. I believe that, if this amendment is adopted, it
will then allow some of us who are presently opposed to the Cooper-
Church language as presently written to vote for the Cooper-Church
amendment as amended by my amendment.

I personally would like to vote for the Cooper-Church language in
large part, but unless this amendment which I have offered is adopted,
I would find it impossible to vote for the Cooper-Church amendment. I
think that the amendment which I have offered has great merit.

I believe that the great majority of the American people, if they
understand the full intent of my amendment clearly, will support it.

Our U.S. Government has sent American servicemen to Vietnam. We
have 428,000 American servicemen there now. They were sent there by
the U.S. Government. Some of them---most of them, I would say---went
through no choice of their own. I think it is the responsibility of
the U.S. Government to protect their lives while they are there, and
to do everything possible to see that they return home safely. This
is all that I and other Senators who are supporting my amendment are
trying to accomplish. We just want to make sure that the President
has flexibility, and that he has authority and power---which we think
he has in any event, but we want to make it doubly clear to the enemy
and to everyone concerned that the President has this power, this
authority, and this flexibility---to take whatever action is necessary
to protect the lives of the American servicemen who have been sent by
the U.S. Government to South Vietnam and to do everything possible
to bring them back home safely.

I think the parents, the grandparents, the other relatives and
the friends of servicemen throughout this country would say "Amen"
to my amendment, if we can just get the message out to the people of
the country as to exactly what the amendment would do.

I thank the Senator for his contribution. I agree with him in his evaluation that this will be a decisive vote, and once it is taken, if the amendment is adopted, I feel that all ranks can close here, and that most of us---or certainly many of us who cannot now do so---can then vote for the Cooper-Church language, and that it will be an improved amendment by virtue of the adoption of my perfecting language. . . .

[Page S8415.] If my amendment is agreed to, as far as I am concerned, I shall be ready to vote on the Cooper-Church amendment. However, I am only 1 of 100 Senators. . . .

Mr. HANSEN. Mr. President. . . it could very well be that the vote on the Byrd amendment will be the decisive vote on the whole proposition that has been before this body for some days. I say that, first of all, because it is my conviction that the language itself cuts right down to the basic issue that must be faced by the people of America. I read from the amendment:

> Except that the foregoing provisions of this clause shall not preclude the President from taking such action as may be necessary to protect the lives of United States forces in South Vietnam or to facilitate the withdrawal of United States forces from South Vietnam.

The reason why I commend the Senator from West Virginia for having presented this body with an opportunity to face up to this issue is that he has focused attention upon the very purposes that prompted the President to move American forces into Cambodia in the first place. This is true despite the cries of anguish and dismay by many who said that this holds broad import for all Americans because it constitutes an invasion of yet another country and those who say that it reflects an expansion and an escalation of the war.

I think, by contrast, the amendment focuses attention upon the precise thought that the President of the United States had when he entered Cambodia. These two objectives, to protect the lives of United States forces in South Vietnam and to facilitate the withdrawal of forces from South Vietnam, are exactly what he had in mind, and it is well that we face up to that issue. . . the Byrd amendment is the key amendment. So far as I know, it really brings the issue into sharp focus and calls upon each Member of this body, as well as every other American, to examine his own conscience; to see if we want to take steps now that might bind the President's hand and deny him the opportunity to accomplish the goals which constitute an important part of the prayers of every American.

I hope that we will understand, as I believe some do---as I hope many will---that what the President has done directs itself to the attainment of ending the war and bringing peace. It is a matter that will require some understanding and some explaining; because the very fact that we have had so many people coming into this city in the last several weeks and so many writing to us, saying, "Support the peace amendment; support the end of the war amendment," indicates to me that not everyone does understand. Only by understanding what the issues are can we hope to clarify the issues, increase the determination of this country and add strength to the present ability of this country to achieve these goals. They are commendable goals. . . .

PRESIDENT NIXON SUPPORTS THE BYRD AMENDMENT

(June 5, 1970)

Mr. GRIFFIN.   [Page S8420.] Mr. President. . . .

Last night, the Senator from Pennsylvania (Mr. SCOTT) received a letter from the President regarding the pending Byrd amendment to the Cooper-Church amendment.

I ask unanimous consent that the letter from the President to the Republican leader be printed at this point in the Record.

There being no objection, the letter was ordered to be printed in the Record, as follows:

The White House,
Washington, June 4, 1970.

Hon. Hugh Scott,
U. S. Senate,
Washington, D.C.

Dear Hugh: You have requested my views on an amendment offered by Senator Robert Byrd of West Virginia to the Cooper-Church amendment to the Foreign Military Sales bill now being considered by the Senate.

As you know, I am opposed to the language of the Cooper-Church provision in its present form. Nevertheless, I fully appreciate the concerns of many Senators anxious that the Cambodian expedition not involve our nation in another Vietnam-type conflict. As I reported to the American people last night, this has been the most successful operation of this long and difficult war and will be completed by June 30. The results will be fewer casualties and continued withdrawals from Vietnam---objectives that Senators share with me.

The Byrd amendment reaffirms the Constitutional duty of the Commander in Chief to take actions necessary to protect the lives of United States forces and is consistent with the responsibilities of my office. Therefore, it goes a long way toward eliminating my more serious objections to the Cooper-Church amendment.

You will recall that last year in Guam I outlined the Nixon doctrine establishing a policy for Asian nations to de-fend themselves, with American material assistance and tech-nical help. If a stable lasting peace is to [Page S8426.] emerge in that beleaguered region, it is important that we promote regional cooperation. Therefore, I should hope that the Senate would also adopt an amendment supporting the Nixon doctrine of American material and technical assistance toward self-help.

I appreciate your continued deep interest in this subject

and the untiring effort you and your colleagues have made
in an effort to achieve meaningful legislation in the best
interest of the American people.

Sincerely,

Richard Nixon.

DEBATE ON THE FIRST BYRD AMENDMENT*

Mr. DOLE. [Page S8455.] Mr. President, I wish to commend the
President of the United States on the letter forwarded to our distinguished minority leader, the senior Senator from Pennsylvania (Mr.
SCOTT), in which the President indicates his willingness to compromise
and to work out some accommodation with the Senate with reference to
the pending business, the so-called Cooper-Church amendment.

The President indicates in clear and concise terms his support
for the Byrd amendment. He states that the Byrd amendment does reaffirm his constitutional power and the constitutional power of any
Commander in Chief to take necessary action to protect the lives of
American forces consistent with his responsibilities and obligations.

I believe that the President by indicating his intentions is saying to the Senate that now is the time for compromise, not the time for
confrontation.

I believe that the President has clearly indicated his sincere
desire to work out this accommodation. He has indicated his clear
concern and clear recognition that we do have certain powers and responsibilities in the Senate when it comes to declaring war and ap-
propriating money for any engagement.

At the same time, the President recognizes, as any Commander in
Chief would, his responsibility and his overriding responsibility to
protect American forces.

He also suggests in the letter that there be some minor amendment to section 3 of the Cooper-Church amendment so that it does not
in any way negate and conflict with the so-called Nixon Asian doctrine
announced in Guam last year.

I again must emphasize that President Nixon is the power to peace
in Vietnam. He wants to cooperate with the Senate and with the House
of Representatives. And he has so demonstrated in his letter to the
minority leader under date of June 4, 1970.

Mr. HANSEN. [Page S8470.] Mr. President, it has become the
fashion today for the vocal minority to undertake a game of second
guessing the President of the United States. It is increasingly apparent to all of us that this minority, which takes pride in using
clear hindsight, will question the President on every move he makes. . . .

[Page S8472.] It is evident that the President's plan of Vietnamization is working. There has been progress toward the Vietnamese

takeover in the war in Vietnam. Nevertheless the President's critics
have been so enamored with their own movement that they refuse to see
the progress. Their rhetoric is consistent. Translated it says "we
have lost the war so we must get out now---regardless of the consequences."

This is easy for the demonstrator to say. He can clothe himself
in the raiments of self-righteousness declaring that love, peace, and
individual liberties are his goals and that anything that conflicts
with his view is immoral, brutal, and dehumanizing. Some go so far
as to resort to the practice of reading the names of the Vietnam war
dead claiming they speak for those who have died as heroes for their
nation. How insulting it would be if these young men could hear their
names being used by those opposing that for which they died. They died
proving their allegiance to each of us and the Nation. They deserve
better treatment for their sacrifice.

During the last weeks, there have been many who have decried the
invasion of Cambodia. Unfortunately, they have falsely accused the
President. Our action in Cambodia does not even resemble an invasion.
As President Nixon has stated, the areas in which these attacks were
launched are completely occupied and controlled by the North Vietnamese forces. Our purpose is not to occupy these areas. Once enemy
forces are driven out and their sanctuaries and military supplies destroyed, we will withdraw.

I believe the President when he said it was not necessary to the
Vietnamization program to knock out these North Vietnamese strongholds
and I believe him when he says he does not intend to remain in Cambodia. Nevertheless, let me say that if events develop which would
force the President to stay in Cambodia past June 30 or would force the
return of American troops into that area, the President must have the
power to make these decisions.

There are those who say the President should not have gone into
Cambodia without first consulting with Congress. That he must not be
empowered to make necessary decisions. . . .

[Page S8473.] Mr. President, the old phrase "When the going gets
tough, the tough get going" was never more applicable or relevant
than today. It is easy to sit in our overstuffed chairs and question
the President. It would be even easier to just say "I quit." Indeed,
that seems to be the general idea behind some of the statements I
have heard on the floor recently.

I do not subscribe to that philosophy. I applaud and compliment
the President for taking measures, as unpopular as they might be with
some, which he feels he must in order to protect lives in Vietnam.

The present assault by Congress on the powers of the President
is viewed in different light by different dissenters.

For some, it is simply a matter of being against the war in Vietnam. For others, the problem becomes a complex constitutional argument over the prerogatives of the Congress as opposed to the Executive.
For still others, this is a matter of returning to the principles
and the intentions of the Founding Fathers. For a few, I suspect
their stand is based on political prejudice and bias.

But it is really far more than any of these things. What the argument is all about is, in fact, the role that the United States should play in the world today. What we are witnessing could turn out to be the greatest resurgence of classic isolationism that has been seen in this country for nearly half a century.

The matter we are debating today goes far beyond the borders of Vietnam, Cambodia, Laos, or Thailand. When we cast our vote on the Cooper-Church amendment we will be making policy which is going to have a direct effect on our position in Latin America, and most certainly Israel.

Looming in the backdrop of this amendment is the question of how far the Congress will go in restricting the President in the next international clash. For instance, are we going to allow the Arab nations to run over Israel? Given the mood of some Americans, they would be willing to accept an Israel defeat. That course might, for the time being, avoid war. Undoubtedly, that is what dissidents want---to avoid war.

In this regard, let me say that I was one of the Senators who signed the letter which was sent to the White House urging the President to sell needed jets to Israel. Although I was in Wyoming when the letter was circulated and was somewhat tardy in having my name added to the letter, I felt that it was most important that the President take this action in order to maintain a balance of arms between the Arab countries and Israel. Based on my knowledge of the situation. I believe that these jets are necessary and the President should proceed with this sale.

Nevertheless, I must admit that I am somewhat puzzled by the overwhelming support of some of the Senators who saw fit to sign this letter to the President on the one hand and who persist in their contentions that we must bind the President's hands in Cambodia on the other. In fact, for the most part, those who propose that we should limit the President's authority to make necessary military decisions concerning Cambodia and Southeast Asia are also the same ones that have urged the President to sell jets to Israel. . . .

To sign a letter urging that jets be sold to Israel while at the same time urging withdrawal and limitation of the President's authority in Southeast Asia seems to me to be a completely inconsistent position. I realize that there are those who try to reconcile their inconsistency by pointing out that the Middle East is much more strategically important to the United States than Vietnam. I take issue with those who assert this position. The Russian-built aircraft which apparently justify our selling jets to Israel is not any different from the Russian-built rockets, mortars, rifles, and machineguns that have made it necessary for us to go into Cambodia. I believe it is an extremely difficult position to say that we must sell jets to Israel so as to protect against Russian-supplied aggressors in the Middle East and then to turn around and advocate a policy whereby the President is without the power to make decisions which he feels are necessary to protect against Russian and Communist supplied aggressors in Cambodia.

Let me say again, I certainly concur with all the Senators who signed the letter urging the President to sell jets to Israel. My only contention is that there is a blatant inconsistency in urging the President to get out of Cambodia and Vietnam and then turning around and urging the sale of these jets. . . . (June 9, 1970)

Mr. DOLE. [Page S8620.] Mr. President, today a debate rages over President Nixon's decision to send American troops into Cambodia. Arguments are being made by sincere men for new initiatives by the Congress to curb the President's power. . . .

[Page S8621.] The limits of the President's power as Commander in Chief are nowhere defined in the Constitution, except by way of negative implication from the fact that the power to declare war is committed to Congress. However, as a result of numerous occurrences in the history of the Republic, more light has been thrown on the scope of this power. . . .

The questions of how far the Chief Executive may go without congressional authorization in committing American military forces to armed conflict, or in deploying them outside of the United States and in conducting armed conflict already authorized by Congress, have arisen repeatedly through the Nation's history. The President has asserted and exercised at least three different varieties of authority under the power as Commander in Chief;

First. Authority to commit military forces of the United States to armed conflict, at least in response to enemy attack or to protect the lives of American troops in the field.

I might add that this is precisely the type of authority we are talking about today, with reference to the Church-Cooper resolution.

Second. Authority to deploy U.S. troops throughout the world, both to fulfill U.S. treaty obligations and to protect American interests; and

Third. Authority to conduct or carry on armed conflict once it is instituted, by making and carrying out the necessary strategic and tactical decisions in connection with such conflict. . . .

It is clear that the President, under his power as Commander in Chief, is authorized to commit American forces in such a way as to seriously risk hostilities, and also to actually commit them to such hostilities, without prior congressional approval. However, if the contours of the divided war power contemplated by the framers of the Constitution are to remain, constitutional practice must include Presidential resort to Congress in order to obtain its sanction for the conduct of hostilities which reach a certain scale. Constitutional practice also indicates, however, that congressional sanction need not be in the form of a declaration of war. . . .

The notion that such advance authorization by Congress for military operations constitutes some sort of an invalid delegation of congressional war power simply will not stand analysis. A declaration of war by Congress is, in effect, a blank check to the Executive to conduct military operations to bring about subjugation of the nation against whom war has been declared. The idea that while Congress may do this, it may not delegate a lesser amount of authority to conduct military operations . . . is utterly illogical and unsupported by precedent.

[Page S8623.] What must be regarded as the high-water mark of Executive action without express congressional approval is, of course, the Korean war. Although Congress never expressly sanctioned the President's action in committing U.S. forces by the hundreds of thousands to the Korean conflict, it repeatedly voted authorizations and appropriations to arm and equip the American troops. This is not to say that such appropriations are invariably the equivalent of express congressional approval; the decision as to whether limited hostilities, commenced by the Executive, should be sanctioned by Congress may be one quite different from the decision as to whether American troops already committed and engaged in such hostilities shall be equipped and supplied. . . .

This is not to say however that every conceivable condition or restriction which Congress may by legislation seek to impose on the use of American Military Forces would be free of Constitutional doubt. Even in the area of domestic affairs where the relationship [Page S8624.] between Congress and the President is balanced differently than it is in the field of external affairs, virtually every president since Woodrow Wilson has had occasion to object to certain conditions in authorization legislation as being violative of the separation of powers between the executive and the legislative branch. The problem would be compounded should Congress attempt by detailed instructions as to the use of American Forces already in the field to supersede the President as Commander in Chief of the Armed Forces. . . .

The duration of the Vietnam conflict and its requirements in terms of both men and materiel have long since become sufficiently large to raise the most serious sort of constitutional question, had there been no congressional sanction of that conflict. However, as is well known, the conflict in its present form began following an attack on U.S. Naval Forces in the Gulf of Tonkin in August, 1964. At that time, President Johnson took direct air action against the North Vietnamese, and he also requested Congress "to join in affirming the national determination that all such attacks will be met" and asked for "a resolution expressing the support of the Congress for all necessary action to protect our Armed Forces and to assist nations covered by the SEATO treaty."

On August 10, 1964, Congress passed the so-called Gulf of Tonkin resolution. I ask unanimous consent that the text of the resolution, 78 Stat. 384 (1964), be printed at this point in the Record.

There being no objection, the resolution was ordered to be printed in the Record, as follows:

SOUTHEAST ASIA RESOLUTION[1]

Whereas naval units of the Communist regime in Vietnam, in violation of principles of the Charter of the United Nations and of international law, have deliberately and repeatedly attacked United States naval vessels lawfully present in international waters, and have thereby created a serious threat to international peace; and

[1]Text of Public Law 88-408 [H.J. Res. 1145], 78 Stat. 384, approved Aug. 10, 1964.
Department of State Bulletin, Aug. 24, 1964, pp. 272-274

Whereas these attacks are part of a deliberate and systematic campaign of aggression that the Communist regime in
North Vietnam has been waging against its neighbors and the
nations joined with them in the collective defense of their
freedom; and the President, as Commander in Chief, to take
all necessary measures to repel any armed attack against
the forces of the United States and to prevent further
aggression.

Sec. 2. The United States regards as vital to its national interest and to world peace the maintenance of international peace and security in southeast Asia. Consonant
with the Constitution of the United States and the Charter
of the United Nations and in accordance with its obligations
under the Southeast Asia Collective Defense Treaty, the
United States is, therefore, prepared, as the President
determines, to take all necessary steps, including the use
of armed force, to assist any member or protocol state of
the Southeast Asia Collective Defense Treaty requesting
assistance in defense of its freedom.

Sec. 3. This resolution shall expire when the President
shall determine that the peace and security of the area is
reasonably assured by international conditions created by
action of the United Nations or otherwise, except that it may
be terminated earlier by concurrent resolutions of the Congress.

Mr. DOLE. Mr. President, in connection with this resolution,
Congress noted that whatever the limits of the President's authority
acting alone might be, whenever Congress and the President act together, "there can be no doubt" of the constitutional authority.

Since that time, Congress has repeatedly adopted legislation recognizing the situation in Southeast Asia, providing the funds to
carry out U.S. commitments there, and providing special benefits for
troops stationed there. By virtue of these acts, and the provision
in the Gulf of Tonkin resolution as to the manner in which it may be
terminated, there is long-standing congressional recognition of a
continuing U.S. commitment in Southeast Asia.

While seeking a negotiated peace and furthering "Vietnamization,"
President Nixon has continued to maintain U.S. troops in the field in
South Vietnam. The legality of the maintenance of these troops in
South Vietnam, and their use to render assistance to the South Vietnamese troops in repelling aggression from the Vietcong and the North
Vietnamese, would be subject to doubt only if Congressional sanction
of hostilities commenced on the initiative of the President could be
manifested solely by a formal declaration of war. But the numerous
historical precedents previously cited militate against such reasoning.

A requirement that congressional approval of Presidential action
in this field can come only through a declaration of war is not only
contrary to historic constitutional usage, but as a practical matter
would curtail effective congressional participation in the exercise
of the shared war power. If Congress may sanction armed engagement
of U.S. forces only by declaring war, the possibility of its retaining

a larger degree of control through a more limited approval is foreclosed. While in terms of men and materiel the Vietnam conflict is
one of large scale, the objectives for which the conflict is carried
on are by no means as extensive or all-inclusive as would have resulted from a declaration of war by Congress. Conversely, however,
there cannot be the slightest doubt from an examination of the language of the Gulf of Tonkin resolution that Congress expressly authorized extensive military involvement by the United States. To
reason that if the caption "Declaration of War" had appeared at the
top of the resolution, this involvement would be permissible, but
that the identical language without such a caption does not give effective congressional sanction, would be to treat this most nebulous
and ill-defined of all areas of the law as if it were a problem in
common law pleading. Mr. Justice Grier, more than a century ago, in
the Prize cases said:

      This greatest of civil wars was not gradually developed
   by popular commotion, tumultuous assemblies, or local un-
   organized insurrections. However long may have been its previous conception, it nevertheless sprung forth suddenly from
   the parent brain, a minerva in the full panoply of war. The
   President was bound to meet it in the shape it presented
   itself, without waiting for Congress to baptise it with a
   name; and no name given to it by him or them could change the
   fact.

      If substance prevailed over form in establishing the right of
the Federal Government to fight the Civil War in 1861, substance
should equally prevail over form in recognizing congressional sanction
for the Vietnam conflict by the Gulf of Tonkin resolution, even though
it was not in name or by its terms a formal declaration of war.

      Viewed in this context, the President's determination to authorize
incursion into Cambodian border area by U.S. forces to destroy sanctuaries utilized by the enemy is a tactical decision traditionally con-
fided to the Commander in Chief. From the time of the drafting of the
Constitution, it has been clear that the Commander in Chief has authority to take prompt action to protect American lives in situations
involving hostilities. Faced with a substantial troop commitment to
such hostilities made by the previous Chief Executive, and approved by
successive Congresses, President Nixon has an obligation as Commander
in Chief of the country's armed forces to take steps he deems necessary to assure their safety in the field. A decision to cross the Cambodian border to destroy sanctuaries being utilized by North Vietnamese
in violation of Cambodia's neutrality, is wholly consistent with that
obligation. It is a decision made during the course of an armed conflict as to how that conflict shall be conducted, rather than a determination that some new and previously unauthorized military venture
shall be undertaken.

      By crossing the Cambodian border to attack sanctuaries used by the
enemy, the United States has in no sense gone to "war" with Cambodia.
United States forces are fighting with or in support of Cambodian
troops, and not against them. The Cambodian incursion has not resulted in a previously uncommitted nation joining the ranks of our en-
emies, but instead has enabled us to more effectively deter enemy aggression heretofore conducted from the Cambodian sanctuaries.

Only if the constitutional designation of the President as commander in chief conferred no substantive authority whatever could it be said that prior congressional authorization for such a tactical decision was required. Since [Page S8625.] even those authorities least inclined to a broad construction of presidential power concede that the commander in chief provision does confer substantive authority over the manner in which hostilities are conducted, the President's decision to invade and destroy the border sanctuaries in Cambodia was authorized under even a narrow reading of his power as commander in chief. . . .

So I say again today, as I have said time after time after time concerning the constitutional right and the constitutional power and constitutional obligation a President has, as, what harm can it do to adopt the language of the Byrd amendment and make it part of the Cooper-Church amendment.

Mr. President, I am one of those who believe that Congress has grave responsibilities. Those responsibilities are clearly defined in the Constitution---the power to appropriate money for the Armed Forces, the power to declare war. I believe that we should accept the responsibilities. I believe we should now compromise any differences that exist with reference to the Church-Cooper amendment in the same spirit the President has offered to compromise those differences.

But in the process I would say to my friends and the sponsors of the Cooper-Church amendment that if they sincerely believe that nothing in that amendment ties the hands of the President and that there is nothing in the amendment to prevent the President from protecting American forces, then agreeing to the amendment of the Senator from West Virginia (Mr. BYRD) would strengthen the Cooper-Church amendment; it would be a recognition of the President's right, power, and obligation to protect American forces and a recognition by this body that the President has that right, and that we expect him to use that power and to carry out his obligation. . . .

Mr. SCOTT. [Page S8626.] Mr. President, we have been engaged in debate now for several weeks on issues which are most fundamental to our Government. We have been discussing, both from a policy and constitutional point of view, questions concerning the allocation of warmaking authority between the President and the Congress. We have addressed ourselves to the question whether the President's action in ordering incursions into Cambodia was consistent with the Constitution, and at the same time we have discussed the power of Congress to limit or terminate a war presently being fought.

I believe this debate has been a useful one, and I hope that we shall continue to air our views on these most vital questions regarding the commitment of American forces to combat abroad. Specifically, I shall address myself to the Cooper-Church amendment and to the perfecting amendment which has recently been proposed by the distinguished Senator from West Virginia.

The Cooper-Church amendment contains four sections. The first would prohibit the use of appropriated funds for the purpose of retaining U.S. forces in Cambodia after July 1, 1970, unless Congress should specifically so authorize in the future. At present, subsection (1) contains no qualifications and it would purport to place a limit

on the President's actions even where he believes it is necessary to
station American troops in Cambodia in order to protect our men in
South Vietnam.

I may add, parenthetically, it is my personal conviction he has
no intention whatsoever of doing so.

Subsections (2), (3), and (4) contain broad prohibitions against
the use of either U.S. personel or hired volunteers either to provide military instruction in Cambodia or to engage in combat activities
in support of Cambodian forces. Air combat activity in support of Cambodian forces is specifically prohibited. While I generally agree that
Congress should have a say as to whether we commit American soldiers
in support of the Cambodians, I would note that the prohibitions in
subsections (2) and (3) are so broad as to prohibit even the furnishing
of military instruction to the Cambodian forces.

This I believe to be inconsistent with the President's doctrine
announced at Guam last year, when he stated that while America would
no longer be willing to carry the burden of war for nations in Southeast Asia, it would attempt to cooperate and assist those nations in
helping themselves.

The main thrust of my remarks, however, is not addressed to the
breadth of subsections (2) through (4). I shall address myself instead to subsection (1) and to Senator Byrd's perfecting amendment
which would make it clear that the President is not precluded from
taking such action as he deems necessary to either protect the lives
of our forces or to facilitate their withdrawal. I support this perfecting language. Indeed, it is difficult for me to understand the
reason for opposing it.

Those opposing the perfecting amendment apparently do so on the
theory that the United States should not become embroiled in a new
war, unless Congress has so authorized. I would agree that we should
not become involved in a new war which would sap our human, financial,
and moral resources, unless Congress determines that such a commitment is in the national interest. Congress does have a constitutional
role to play in the decision as to whether combat should be initiated
with foreign nations. That, however, is not the issue here.

Cambodia does not raise the question of initiating a new war
with a new enemy. This is vitally important to recognize, and I believe that it is this point which is at the very heart of the dispute
between those who support the Cooper-Church amendment as now con-
stituted and those who, like myself, believe that Senator Byrd's
perfecting amendment is absolutely necessary. The fighting in Cambodia is not a new war. Cambodia is but an extension of the South
Vietnamese battlefield. I believe that the President, as Commander
in Chief of the Armed Forces, has the sole authority to direct military
operations on the field of battle. If the Constitution's designation
of the President as Commander in Chief means anything, it must mean
that he, and he alone, is responsible for the strategic and tactical
decisions in the field.

Both judicial and historical precedents recognize the President's
exclusive authority to conduct military campaigns. . . .

[Page S8627.] Senator Byrd's amendment would eliminate the unconstitutional feature of the Church-Cooper proposal. It would expressly
provide that the President would not be precluded from taking the action he deems necessary to protect the lives of our forces in the
field or to facilitate their withdrawal.

If the Senate defeats the proposal of the Senator from West
Virginia (Mr. BYRD), it will be the first time that either House of
Congress has attempted to interfere with the prosecution of an existing military operation. One of the leading students of Presidential
power, E. S. Corwin, in his work "The President: Office and Powers,"
has observed:

> Actually Congress has never adopted any legislation
> that would seriously cramp the style of a President at-
> tempting to break the resistance of an enemy or seeking
> to assure the safety of the national forces. Corwin,
> Op. cit., 4th Rev. Ed., p. 259.

I urge my colleagues just as strongly as I can not to break with
this salutary lesson of the past. As Mr. Justice Black, dissenting
in Johnson v. Eisentrager, 339 U.S. 763, at 796 (1950), has so aptly
put it:

> It has always been recognized that actual warfare can
> be conducted successfully only if those in command are
> left the most ample independence in the theater of oper-
> ations.

Senator Byrd's perfecting amendment is consistent with this principle, and I shall vote for it. We should recognize the President's
constitutional prerogatives and responsibilities, not hamper them. . . .

Mr. CHURCH. [Page S8630.] Mr. President, it has now been revealed
that the President supports the amendment offered by the Senator from
West Virginia.

This should not come as a surprise to Senators. Of course, the
President would favor it; any President would. All Presidents like
blank checks, and that is just what this amendment is. No President
likes to deal with Congress, as the Cooper-Church amendment requires.
Unpleasant as this may be to them, however, it is an unavoidable and,
I think, important requirement under our constitutional system.

Six years ago the Congress, to its sorrow, gave President Johnson
a blank check. He was quick to whip out a copy of the Gulf of Tonkin
resolution whenever questioned about his authority to fight an undeclared war half-way around the world. Make no mistake about it---the
Byrd proposal could readily become a second Gulf of Tonkin resolution,
an open invitation to the President to do what he wills in Cambodia,
without the further approval of the Congress---as long as he does
it in the name of protecting our forces in Vietnam.

In saying this, I do not in any way question the President's intention to get our men out of Cambodia and to keep them out. But

other men, and subsequent and unforeseen events, will be constantly
working to undermine the President's determination. And, with the
existence of another blank check on the statute books, their voices
will be more persuasive than would be the case otherwise. This administration has stated that it does not depend on the Tonkin Gulf
resolution as "legal or constitutional authority for its present conduct of foreign relations, or its contingency plans." I hope that
the Senate demonstrates, in voting on this amendment, that it can
profit from experience and that it will not volunteer a replacement
for that ill-fated resolution.

The amendment of the Senator from West Virginia states, in effect,
that the President can send U.S. ground forces back into Cambodia
after July 1 anytime he considers it necessary to protect the lives
of American troops in South Vietnam. But the Cooper-Church amendment
does not deny, as has been charged so often in the course of this debate, the President's constitutional power as Commander in Chief to
protect the safety of American forces. It recognizes that the Congress cannot---by passage of a mere bill---add to or take away from
the President's powers and responsibilities as [Page S8631.] Commander
in Chief. Without question, the President has a responsibility to protect U.S. troops in Vietnam---and no doubt he will do so. He does not
need a mandate from the Congress for this purpose. Thus, the amendment of the Senator from West Virginia is both superfluous and unnecessary.

The point that Senators should bear in mind is that the Senate
has constitutional responsibilities also---both in the making of foreign policy and in deciding how public funds are to be spent. President Nixon, as a former Member of this body, knows that very well. I
remind my colleagues of what he said in this Chamber last November 13
during a short visit to the Senate:

>   I find, looking back over this period of time, that
> this administration has been subjected to some sharp criti-
> cism by some Members of this body, both from the Democratic
> side and from the Republican side. I want the Members of
> this body to know that I understand it. I recognize this
> as being one of the strengths of our system, rather than one
> of its weaknesses, and I know that, in the end, out of this
> kind of criticism and debate will come better policies and
> stronger policies than would have been the case had we simply
> had an abject Senate---or House of Representatives, for that
> matter---simply approving whatever ideas came from the exec-
> utive branch of the Government.

>   This does not mean that we do not feel very strongly
> about our proposals when we send them here. It does mean
> that I, as a former Member of this body, one who served
> in it and who presided over it for 8 years, recognize this
> great tradition of independence, and recognize it as one
> of the great strengths of our Republic.

We in the Congress have been derelict far too long in placing adequate restraints on the executive branch in the commitment of our men
and dollars abroad. As Senators we should concern ourselves primarily

with seeing that Congress carries out its responsibilities, not with
the duties of the President. We should worry, not so much about preserving the President's powers which he will faithfully uphold---let
there be no doubt about that---but preserving our own. This debate
should be focused, not on whether this proposal ties the President's
hands---it does not---but on whether it will help to untie the knots
by which Congress has shackled its own powers. The Cooper-Church
amendment is a step in righting the imbalance in our system. While
the Senator from West Virginia's amendment would not add to the President's legal or constitutional powers, it would have the practical
effect of tipping the scales of political power even further toward
executive domination.

     Passage of this amendment would also be a retreat from the prin-
ciple established by the 80 to 9 vote of the Senate last year, which
prohibited the use of American ground troops in Loas or Thailand. No
Senator raised a question during the debate on the Cooper-Church amendment last December concerning the need to spell out the President's
authority to protect our forces. I remind my colleagues on the other
side of the aisle that the language of that amendment was worked out
in consultation with, and was fully endorsed by, the White House. . . .

     On May 8, President Nixon told the American people that---

          What we've also accomplished (in Cambodia) is that by
     buying time it means that if the enemy does come back into
     those sanctuaries, the next time the South Vietnamese will
     be strong enough and well trained enough to handle it alone.

     The Senator from West Virginia's amendment would have the Senate
go beyond the President's own stated intentions, by giving him our consent in advance to going back into Cambodia after all.

     If the Senator's amendment were approved and the Cooper-Church
amendment subsequently adopted, the Senate would have said, on the one
hand that we should get out of Cambodia and stay out and, on the other
hand, that we really do not mean it---that the President can go back
in whenever he chooses.

     Instead, Mr. President, of taking a historic step in the process
of beginning to restore the Senate to the role the Constitution intended, we would have acted, not like a great forum, but like a fudge
factory and rendered the Cooper-Church amendment so largely meaningless
that it would then be questionable whether we should proceed to adopt
it, in its modified form, at all.

     I say to the Senate in all sincerity that the adoption of the
Byrd amendment would blow a hole in the Cooper-Church amendment large
enough to drive a whole new war through, without the President ever
having to return to Congress for authority or consent.

     In summary, Mr. President, the pending amendment would repeat the
errors of the past and give the President a blank check to go back into
Cambodia. It would tip the political balance of power still further
in favor of the executive branch. And it would fly in the face of the
Senate's action on Laos only 6 months ago. I hope that it will be defeated. . . .

     [Page S8634.] Whatever powers the President holds under the Con-
stitution cannot be affected by anything we pass in the Senate. My
concern is not that the adoption of the Byrd amendment would affect

any power the President may already possess under the Constitution.
My concern is that it could and in the light of past experience, might
well be interpreted by the President in the future as giving our consent in advance for a return to Cambodia on a mass scale.

That is why I think it would be a grave mistake to adopt it. . . .

Mr. MANSFIELD.   [Page S8636.] Mr. President. . . .

Six years ago the U.S. military presence was confined largely to
Saigon and a few coastal Vietnamese cities. The U.S. involvement was
still indirect and peripheral. Now 6 years after the Tonkin Gulf resolution, U.S. servicemen are scattered through Vietnam, Laos, Thailand, Cambodia. The involvement is direct and, notwithstanding the so-
called Vietnamization program, it is central to the entire structure
of the war in Indochina.

I do not recall this history without a painful awareness of the
Senate's part in its writing. Yet, it must be recalled. It must be
recalled because the Senate is, again, face to face with another
Tonkin Gulf resolution. I refer to the Byrd-Griffin modification which
is now pending to the Cooper-Church amendment.

Once again, the Senate is **asked**, in effect, to accept what the
executive branch has done, what it is doing, and what it may do with
regard to Cambodia. That is the price the Senate is quoted if we
would retain even a promise of preventing the further spread of the
war under the Cooper-Church amendment. We are asked by the Byrd-
Griffin modification to give legal endorsement to whatever course may
be set by the executive branch in Cambodia. We are asked to subscribe
not only to what is done in Cambodia in the name of the Commander in
Chief under this President but, if the war persists, under his successor, whomever he may be and, perhaps, his successor's successor.

That is the nub of the Byrd-Griffin modification. It would establish for the Cambodian policies of the executive branch the same
legal basis that the Tonkin Gulf resolution fashioned for the Vietnamese involvement 6 long years ago. The Byrd-Griffin modification
says that Cooper-Church will not apply unless the executive branch
decrees that it should apply. Under Byrd-Griffin, the statutory wall
of Cooper-Church against the spread of our involvement into Cambodia
stands or falls on a word from the White House.

Let the executive branch affirm that what it does in Cambodia is
for the purpose of protecting our forces in Vietnam. Let the executive
branch assert that what it does in Cambodia is to facilitate the withdrawal of U.S. forces from Vietnam. Let either be said by the executive branch at any time and the Cooper-Church limitations are nullified.
No matter that the Senate is not consulted. No matter that the Congress is ignored. No matter how long U.S. forces remain in Cambodia,
no matter how many Americans may die in Cambodia, no matter how many
more billions are spent in compounding the tragedy of Vietnam, it will
all be done with the legal sanction of the Senate.

I know that the authors of the Byrd-Griffin modification do not
expect the modification to work in that fashion. I know that the Senator from West Virginia and the Senator from Michigan want not to prolong but to end the involvement in Cambodia. They want to protect

American servicemen in Vietnam, not jeopardize others in Cambodia. That is what we all want.

Is it not what we wanted---all of us---when we passed the Tonkin Gulf resolution 6 years ago?

The Byrd-Griffin modification is a direct descendant of the Tonkin Gulf resolution. The clay carries the same imprint. The door to further involvement in Cambodia is not closed by Byrd-Griffin. Byrd-Griffin opens the door wider. It sanctions an in-and-out entanglement in Cambodia. It sanctions a direct or indirect entrapment in Cambodia. It sanctions an ad infinitum involvement in Cambodia even as the Tonkin Gulf resolution did the same for the open-ended involvement in Vietnam.

Byrd-Griffin lifts the Congressional counterweights which Cooper-Church seeks to place against the pressures for expanding involvement in Indochina. It shackles the Senate's responsibility to join its separate constitutional authority with that of the President in a common effort to confine the war and withdraw U.S. forces.

If Byrd-Griffin is adopted on Thursday next, let there be no Monday morning regrets. Let there be no shocked indignation later. Whatever our intent, we will have cleared the way for another Vietnam in Cambodia and, perhaps, for still others elsewhere. The time to face the implications of Byrd-Griffin is now. It is not next year or the year after. . . .

I am aware that the President has expressed some sort of unofficial endorsement of the pending modification. The White House has written a letter. That is the President's right and his comments---solicited or unsolicited---deserve the most careful consideration of the Senate. Let us be clear, however, on one point. The President's constitutional responsibility in this matter does not begin at this time. His constitutional responsibility is not activated unless and until this legislation has passed, not only the Senate but also the House. Then and only then does the measure become subject to the President's approval or rejection. Then and only then does it become the Constitutional business of the President.

Now it is the Senate's responsibility. Now, the disposition of the Byrd-Griffin modification is a matter for the Senate alone. We have had the President's letter. We have also had citizens' letters, by the hundreds of thousands. We have had lobbying and lectures. That is appropriate and proper. But the obligation now---the constitutional obligation---is for the Senate alone, for 100 Senators. . .

[Page S8637.] The hour is late, very late.

The Byrd-Griffin modification, in my judgment, is the critical vote of this issue. Reject it and the Senate will say that the way out of Vietnam is not by way of Cambodia. Adopt Byrd-Griffin to Cooper-Church and the Senate will still say that the way out of Vietnam is not by way of Cambodia, but only if the executive branch also says the same thing.

The Constitutional message of Cooper-Church without this proposed addition is clear. The Senate acts in concert with the President's expressed determination but under its own legal responsibility in an effort to curb the further expansion of the war in Indochina. The Byrd-Griffin modification clouds that message.

In my judgment, the Senate should keep the Cooper-Church amendment free of distortion. The credibility of the Senate demands it. The urgencies of the Nation require it. . . .

Mr. GRIFFIN. Mr. President, I appreciate very much the fact that the distinguished majority leader has yielded to me briefly so that I might make a brief response.

I have listened with close attention to the remarks of the majority leader. With the greatest respect for him, and he knows I have great respect for him, I must say very candidly that he has reached a long way to fashion an argument against the Byrd amendment. His characterization of the Byrd amendment is somewhat colorful but entirely inappropriate. The Byrd amendment is only a qualification or limitation of the Church-Cooper amendment. It could reach no higher in terms of authority than would be the case if there were no Church-Cooper amendment at all.

I wish to emphasize that the Byrd amendment touches only one of four subsections of the Church-Cooper amendment; so it could not be said that it goes so far as to nullify the Church-Cooper amendment. But even if one were to give the widest and most far-reaching interpretation to the Byrd modification; the most that it could possibly be said is that it would nullify the Church-Cooper amendment. Certainly to nullify the Church-Cooper amendment is not to adopt a Gulf of Tonkin resolution, which the majority leader indicated was tantamount to a declaration of war.

So I respectfully suggest that the characterization is most unfair and most unreasonable under the circumstances.

I think it is very important to look at what the Byrd amendment provides. It would add language to that one particular subsection having to do with the retention of U.S. troops in Cambodia. It states:

> Except that the foregoing provisions of this clause shall not preclude the President from taking such action as may be necessary to protect the lives of United States forces in South Vietnam or to facilitate the withdrawal of United States forces from South Vietnam.

Surely the distinguished majority leader, I know, does not object to that last clause reading "to facilitate the withdrawal of U.S. forces from South Vietnam."

It is very difficult for me, of course---and I respect our differences---to see how he could oppose recognition of the constitutional power of the Commander in Chief to protect the lives of American forces in South Vietnam.

Mr. MANSFIELD. Nobody is opposing that, may I say. That is the first time I have heard that question raised on the floor of the Senate during this debate.

Mr. GRIFFIN. I say it is very difficult for me to understand opposition to language which would recognize the authority of the Commander in Chief to protect the lives of American forces in South Vietnam. I think it is clear that is the purpose of the Byrd amendment.

Mr. MANSFIELD. Mr. President, will the Senator yield at that point?

Mr. GRIFFIN. I yield.

Mr. MANSFIELD. May I point out that this question has been raised time and time again: to safeguard American lives to further the withdrawal of U.S. troops from Vietnam. Nobody in this Chamber is against that. All 100 Members of the Senate are for it. The chief proponents of the Cooper-Church amendment have said that time and time and time again, but the question is always raised.

I am willing to take the word of a Senator---certainly the chief proponents of an amendment when asked a question and they give an answer---because who knows more about it than the proponents and who are more qualified to answer the questions?

If the Senator will yield further, I wish to point out that the President has unilateral constitutional powers as Command in Chief to take measures to protect the lives of U.S. servicemen, not only in Vietnam, but also U.S. citizens, including servicemen, anywhere in the world. He does not need congressional sanction for that purpose because he already has that power, authority, and responsibility. But the executive branch does not have the unilateral constitutional power to commit this Nation to an involvement which requires a continuing input of men and money in a country, even in the name of defending U.S. forces, or for some other objective in a second country. That interpretation is underscored by the national commitments resolution which the Senate enacted earlier in this Congress.

If the executive branch does make such a broad commitment on its own in Cambodia directly or indirectly it treads on highly questionable constitutional ground.

Furthermore, if it were to make such a commitment on its own, if and when Cooper-Church, as is, is enacted, the executive branch would break the law.

It would tread then on the most dangerous constitutional grounds. But if it wished to act unilaterally, should Byrd-Griffin be enacted, then the executive branch could do what it pleased in the way of a broad commitment in Cambodia---forces, aid, or whatever, without further reference to Congress. Indeed, the Senate would have given its approval in advance to whatever the executive branch did in Cambodia, whether it was wise or foolish, necessary or unnecessary, responsible or irresponsible, whether it led to a wider war or not, provided what was done was done in the name of withdrawing U.S. forces from Vietnam or protecting U.S. forces in Vietnam. . . .

Mr. GRIFFIN. Of course, the differences between the majority leader and the junior Senator from Michigan, go to what are the constitutional responsibilities of the President and what are the constitutional responsibilities of the Congress. I am one of those who

believe the Senate should exercise its constitutional responsibility
to the fullest. However, I am convinced that the Church-Cooper amendment goes too far, and seeks to get the Senate involved in what are
essentially battlefield decisions. The proposed amendment would tie
the hands of the Commander in Chief, and would play into the hands of
the enemy, making it more difficult for the President to carry out his
objective of getting American troops out of Vietnam and bringing them
home.

This administration is not sending more and more troops to Vietnam. This President is bringing troops home. This President needs
and deserves the good faith and support of the Congress, and I [Page
S8638.] sincerely believe he would have a much better chance of a-
chieving the objectives we all want if we would give him our support.

Mr. MANSFIELD. May I say, before I yield to the distinguished
Senator from Kentucky, that no one is tying the President's hands,
but what we would be doing, and doing very nicely, in the Byrd-
Griffin modification is tying the hands of the Senate. I think we
have a responsibility, too. We would like, not to act against a
President, but to act in concert with a President.

What we are trying to do is to strengthen the President's hand,
to give him added stamina, added muscle, to give him a place to which
he can come for recourse, a body in which he served for over 8 years,
among people whom he knows. We are trying to counterbalance the
pressures which are on him constantly, which are on any President,
to give him a chance not to act precipitately, but to think a little
while before making a move, to discuss this matter with his friends
in the Congress and to give recognition to the fact that under the
Constitution the Congress of the United States is a coequal branch in
the Government, along with the executive and the judiciary.

I think the intent of what we are trying to do is being taken in
the right spirit. Despite these differences among us---and I question
no one's position, no one's. I am sure that those who favor Byrd-
Griffin are just as concerned and just as patriotic and have just as
much integrity as those on the other side.

I would emphasize that what we are really trying to do is protect the President of the United States. For some reason or other,
it is hard to get that point across. Some people are looking for
cards under the table. They are trying to pull up the rug to see if
they can find something which does not exist. They are afraid to
take us at our word, even though we have said time and time again,
privately, publicly, and in print, and in as many ways as we know how,
that we want to work with the President because we think working with him
in concert will help the Republic, and will be to his advantage, and
not ours primarily. . . .

Mr. GRIFFIN. [Page S8369.] If I may have a moment, I would
simply like to say for the record that the Byrd amendment would not
approve in advance any action that the President might take. Adoption
of the amendment would not indicate approval of particular actions.
It would merely declare that if the President, as Commander in Chief,
does have the authority to protect the lives of our forces in South
Vietnam, the Church-Cooper amendment, as it would be amended, would
not take it away. That is the extent of the effect and the purpose
of the amendment. . . .

(June 10, 1970)

Mr. CHURCH. [Page S8765.] Mr. President. . . .

The key word in the Cooper-Church amendment is "retaining." Subsection 1 of the amendment prohibits the retention of American forces in Cambodia after June 30. I agree with the Senator from Kentucky that our amendment is intended to prohibit a permanent or quasi-permanent occupation of a buffer zone within Cambodia for an extended period of time.

However, if it were to happen that the enemy suddenly utilized a staging area, and there was a concentration of enemy troops and equipment obviously intended to be used against South Vietnam beyond the border, we would agree that the President, as Commander in Chief, has the constitutional authority to order his field officers to strike at and destroy such a base to protect American troops in South Vietnam. This would, however, be in the nature of a sudden strike and withdrawal operation.

I further agree with the Senator from Kentucky when he says that the adoption of the Byrd amendment would open up an exception so large that it honestly renders the Cooper-Church amendment meaningless.

The President could invoke the justification of acting for the purpose of defending American troops to cover almost any future operation that he himself might decide upon. That would be extremely unfortunate. That would permit our amendment to become another Tonkin Gulf resolution---if not even broader in conception---if the President were to decide later to use it for that purpose. . . .

Mr. COOPER. The Senator from Virginia asked about the Byrd amendment. Let me read it. I should like to place it in the Record. It reads as follows:

> On page 5, line 7, before the semicolon insert a comma and the following: except that the foregoing provision of this clause shall not preclude the President from taking such action as may be necessary to protect the lives of United States forces in South Vietnam or to facilitate the withdrawal of United States forces from South Vietnam.

The amendment has great appeal, because it speaks of protecting the lives of U.S. forces in South Vietnam. It will be argued and has been argued that Senators who vote against the amendment are not taking care to protect the U.S. forces in South Vietnam.

The Byrd-Griffin amendment cannot give the President any larger powers than the constitutional authority that he enjoys. What it would do, if it should be adopted by Congress, would be to approve in advance any action the President may want to take. His determination alone would justify it.

[Page S8766.] I want to make it clear that I am not talking in personal terms of the Executive, who is President Nixon. He is my President. I am a member of his party. I have supported him in his program for ending the war in Vietnam. But we have been through this procedure before, the procedure of giving authority to the President, who did not intend, I am sure, to extend the authority which is given him beyond that as expressed at the time, but which was extended.

This amendment is broader in its scope than the Tonkin Gulf resolution, so far as the protection of troops is concerned.

The Tonkin Gulf resolution has two parts, one dealing with protection of the troops, and the other dealing with protection of the freedom of the protocol states. The Tonkin Gulf resolution gave the President authority---I recall it because I read it just a short time ago---to protect troops, to repel an attack upon the troops, and to defend them. It was defensive---to repel an attack on our troops and defend them. This amendment is like the old, familiar barn door---wide open.

If some situation should occur, if the Thais go into Cambodia--- and the South Vietnamese evidently like Cambodia---and we find ourselves under some obligation to go into Cambodia and protect Cambodians or the Thais, I believe the commonsense and judgment of the Members of this body would be that the authority to do so would be the joint authority of the President and the Congress.

We do not take away from the President the opportunity to employ any course of action he wants to employ, but if the situation is beyond the defense of the Armed Forces let us say, "It is a joint responsibility and let us reason together and let us determine whether action should be taken." I do not see anything wrong with that. . . .

Mr. BAYH. [Page S8767.] Mr. President, as might have been expected, the fall of the neutralist Sihanouk government in Cambodia in early March of this year immediately raised the question of American assistance to the anti-Communist Lon Nol regime. Administration officials stated publicly that a request for military aid was being reviewed, but went further in saying that no American troops would be involved in Cambodia in accord with the President's Guam doctrine, which, as we know, was designed to try to shift security responsibility onto the nations of a given region.

Testifying before a House Appropriations Subcommittee on April 23, Secretary of State Rogers was asked about the extent to which the United States might be drawn into Cambodia. I think it is significant, in light of this discussion, to review his remarks. He said directly:

> We have no incentive to escalate. Our whole incentive is to de-escalate. We recognize that if we escalate and get involved in Cambodia with our ground troops, that our whole program (Vietnamization) is defeated.

The Secretary later restated the case against our involvement in Cambodia in much the same language before the Senate Foreign Relations Committee.

At the very same time the Secretary of State was cautioning against a wider war in Asia, we know now that contingency plans for U.S. military operations in Cambodia were being studied by the Secretary of Defense, the National Security Council, General Abrams, and

the President himself. In fact, it appears that at the time President
Nixon made his April 20 statement announcing the possible withdrawal
of 150,000 troops during the next year, he had reviewed the Cambodian
plans but tentatively deferred a decision.

The President's April 30 decision to invade Cambodia---taken after
consulation within the executive but without so much as a passing nod
to any congressional leaders---was a dangerous and irresponsible course
of action. I must say, at the risk of sounding as if I am personally
piqued at not being consulted, that this is not what I mean by a
passing nod to anyone in the legislative branch. I would not expect
the President of the United States to consult on this matter with the
junior Senator from Indiana, nor---at the risk of being disrespectful
---with our distinguished Presiding Officer, the senior Senator from
Ohio (Mr. YOUNG). It seems to me that he could have consulted with
the leadership of his own party and with the leadership of the relevant committees. But, as the record now shows, this did not happen.

Recent accounts of the decisionmaking process that led the President to authorize the Cambodian adventure serve only to confirm this
view. It seems that President Nixon gambled that by suddenly widening the war into Cambodia, his toughness would impress the North Vietnamese and the rest of the Communist world that the United States can
act vigorously, swiftly, and unpredictably.

If this was the message the President hoped to convey, it obviously was lost on the North Vietnamese, who indicated no greater willingness to discuss a negotiated settlement in the absence of a Presidential envoy at the Paris talks, and on the Russians, who continue
to expand their military and political influence in the strategic
Middle East. . . .

[Page S8768.] That the President's action has escalated and
widened the ill-fated Vietnam war already is apparent. The stepped-
up Communist activity around Phom Penh, the heavy fighting in Laos,
and the widespread and coordinated attacks within Vietnam itself are
early but clear signs of an impending confrontation throughout Indochina. The Vietnam war is fast becoming an Indochina war. . . .

[Page S8770.] Mr. President, one final thought on the amendment
offered by the Senator from West Virginia (Mr. BYRD). The Byrd exception to the Cooper-Church amendment provides that the amendment
shall not preclude the President from taking such action as may be
necessary to protect the lives of United States forces in South Vietnam or to facilitate the withdrawal of U.S. forces from South Vietnam.

If this is simply a restatement of the President's constitutional
powers as Commander in Chief, then it is unnecessary. As I pointed
out earlier in my statement, just as Congress cannot legislate restrictions on the President's constitutional authority as Commander
in Chief, it cannot expand those powers by statue. I recognize the
President's responsibility to protect our forces in the field, but
I do not believe he needs Congressional approval for this.

I believe he has the constitutional authority, in the first place.
It is interesting to note, Mr. President, that the amendment adopted
last year restricting our operations in Laos and Thailand carried no

such exception.   And yet for years, we have known that the Ho Chi Minh
Trail, running down through one corner of Laos, has been a major supply route and sanctuary.

On the other hand, if the Byrd exception is another Gulf of Tonkin resolution---a blank check from Congress approving in advance any
actions the President may take---then it is dangerous.

Such a gesture by the Congress can only serve to widen the war
and continue our unfortunate involvement.

All of us are concerned about protecting American fighting men.
It just seems to the Senator from Indiana, after a long period of
patience, that the best way to protect our American fighting men is
to end the war. . . .

Mr. JAVITS.   [Page S8777.] Mr. President. . . .

What needs to be defined is how the Congress is to exercise its
policymaking power with respect to war which is explicitly reserved to
it in the Constitution in consonance with the President's executive
or command authority as Commander in Chief.   The Constitution defines
this executive capacity of the President only to "take care that the
laws be faithfully executed."   The President certainly enjoys discretionary authority but it is the discretionary authority of an executive.   He does not have discretionary authority with respect to
warmaking in a policy sense.   This is a power granted to the Congress
under the system of checks and balances in the Constitution.

But, the adoption by the Senate of the Cooper-Church amendment---
an important piece in an emerging mosaic---would be a significant
historical milestone in asserting this authority of the Congress.   Its
historic significance may be further enhanced by the President's open
endorsement of the Byrd amendment.

Under these circumstances I see the Byrd amendment, in its effect,
as an effort to table the Senate's effort to reassert and to define
the constitutional responsibilities of the Congress as specified in
section 1, article 8, of the Constiution.   If the Byrd amendment is
adopted, it will set back a vital historic process---the assertion of
the responsibilities of the Congress in warmaking.   Also it will give new
momentum to a phenomenon which has aroused such grave concern in our
Nation in recent years---the exercise by the President of the warmaking power in the name of his authority as Commander in Chief.   Since
the first rumblings of World War II, we have seen this constantly expanding power of the President often due to abdication by the Congress
of its warmaking powers.   Throughout the past decade, this trend has
gained an ominous momentum.

It has reached the point where any effort just to check the expansion of Presidential power is regarded by some defenders of the
Presidency as an encroachment on the Office of the President.   Many
advocates of Presidential prerogative in the field of war and foreign
policy seem at times to be arguing that the President's "powers" as
Commander in Chief are what the President alone defines them to be.

I believe that passage of the Byrd amendment would amount to
Senate acquiescence in this position---that is, the [Page S8778.]

President enjoys such powers as Commander in Chief as he defines them to be. I believe that this could undermine our whole constitutional system and lead the Nation into grave new crises at home and abroad. . .

Mr. BYRD of West Virginia. [Page S8780.] Mr. President, I ask unanimous consent that I be permitted to modify my amendment 667 star print to read as follows:

> On page 5, line 7; before the semicolon insert a comma and the following: except that the foregoing provisions of this clause shall not preclude the President from taking only such action as is necessary in the exercise of his constitutional powers and duties as Commander in Chief, to protect the lives of United States forces in South Vietnam or to facilitate the withdrawal of United States forces from South Vietnam; and the President is requested to consult with Congressional leaders prior to using any United States forces in Cambodia if, as Commander in Chief, he determines that the use of such forces is necessary to protect the lives of United States forces in South Vietnam or to facilitate the withdrawal of United States forces from South Vietnam;

Mr. President, the specific changes which I would thus be making in amendment 667, if I am permitted to modify my amendment, would be as follows. I would suggest that Senators may wish to read the star print which is on their desks as I attempt to make the precise suggested changes clear.

I would modify amendment 667 to insert the word "only" after the word "taking" on line 3; to delete the words "may be" and insert in lieu thereof the work "is" on line 4; after the word "necessary" on line 4, insert a comma and the following language: "in the exercise of his constitutional powers and duties as Commander in Chief,"; and at the end of the present language on line 6 of amendment 667 delete the quotation marks and the period, insert a semicolon and add the following language:

> And the President is requested to consult with Congressional leaders prior to using any United States forces in Cambodia if, as Commander-in-Chief, he determines that the use of such forces is necessary to protect the lives of United States forces in South Vietnam or to facilitate the withdrawal of United States forces from South Vietnam:

Mr. President, that concludes the modification which I propose.

My modification, when taken together with paragraph (1) of the Cooper-Church amendment and language from the preamble of that amendment beginning with the word "unless" on line 3 of page 5, would then read as follows:

[Page S8782.] Unless specifically authorized by law
hereafter enacted, no funds authorized or appropriated
pursuant to this Act or any other law may be expended for
the purpose of---

(1) retaining United States forces in Cambodia except that the foregoing provisions of this clause shall
not preclude the President from taking only such action
as is necessary, in the exercise of his constitutional
powers and duties as Commander in Chief, to protect the
lives of United States forces in South Vietnam or to facilitate the withdrawal of United States forces from South
Vietnam; and the President is requested to consult with
Congressional leaders prior to using any United States
forces in Cambodia if, as Commander in Chief, he determines that the use of such forces is necessary to protect
the lives of United States forces in South Vietnam or to
facilitate the withdrawal of United States forces from
South Vietnam; . . .

Mr. BYRD of West Virginia. I view it as a limitation in this
respect: Without any language at all, without Cooper-Church, without
the Byrd amendment, but under the Constitution as it is presently
written, the President is Commander in Chief of the Army and Navy. I
think that he may use U.S. forces in Cambodia if he deems it necessary,
now, to protect the lives of American forces in South Vietnam, and I
do not believe that he is confined to that constitutional predicate
for the use of U.S. armed forces in Cambodia. I think he has additional legal authority under the Gulf of Tonkin language to so act.

But under my language, he would be confined to the constitutional
predicate insofar as we would express our sentiments here. We cannot
cut off or reduce his constitutional authority. . . .

[Page S8783.] I do not attempt to say in the language of this
amendment what the President's powers are. We do not attempt to interpret the President's powers. They are what they are, not by what
we say in this amendment but by what the Constitution says they are. . .

[Page S8784.] The Cooper-Church language says that after June 30
no more funds can be utilized for retaining U.S. Armed Forces in Cambodia unless hereafter specifically enacted by law. The language that
I have offered would simply say, "except" when the President himself
determines that it is necessary to act, in order to protect our troops
in South Vietnam, and so forth, and so forth.

Mr. FULBRIGHT. I do not see how the Senator can say that a recognition of what the President may do or want to do in the future is
automatically constitutional, that there is authority for it in his
role as Commander in Chief. I do not believe it is a fact. I do not
believe there is any support for it. Adoption of the Senator's amendment will be taken as a precedent that the Senate has so abdicated its
foreign policy role as in effect to be saying that the President may
do as he pleases.

There certainly would no longer be any need for a declaration of
war, because all the President would need to do as Commander in Chief

is say,"I think we ought to move into Mexico. These people are threatening our troops." The Senator's amendment would result in a complete distortion and abdication of the role of the Senate. . . .

[Page S8790.] This is the whole issue: Should the Senate abdicate its responsibility and say that as Commander in Chief the President can do as he pleases any time he can say that it is to protect the troops? Under the Byrd amendment, that would be all that he would need to say.

This is an absolutely new doctrine. I never ran across this when I was in school. I never ran across the matter of the powers of the President being such that he could invade a country if he says it is to protect the troops---a country with which we had not heretofore been at war. I do not think it is sound at all.

I think it would be a great mistake to put the Byrd language in the Cooper-Church amendment. The Senator may very well have the votes. If he is going to put something in the amendment, I would much prefer that he put in the language which does not go to the constitutional issue.

The Senator's amendment guts the Cooper-Church proposal.

It waffles around with these constitutional responsibilities and duties and leaves greater uncertainty. It is a very dangerous thing. . . .

Mr. BYRD of West Virginia. . . . [Page S8791.]

I have acted in good faith in trying to develop language which would meet the legitimate concerns of several Members of this body. I have sought to improve the amendment and in some way bring us at least part way toward the position that has been taken by the sponsors of the Cooper-Church amendment. I have tried to tighten up the original language of my amendment by tying it clearly to the constitutional authority, powers, and duties of the President---leaving aside entirely any legal authority which he may or may not have.

If the Senator feels that he would like to object to my unanimous-consent request I shall have to stay with the old language, and the Senate can vote on it. . . .

[Page S8793.] Of course, any language is subject to definition and interpretation by the lawyers and by everyone else. The language of the Cooper-Church amendment is not the last word in perfection---I say this with all due respect to the sponsors thereof---and it, too--- as I will soon attempt to demonstrate---can be subject to definition. But I believe that the verbiage of my amendment, when taken with my own statements and those of cosponsors of my amendment, leaves no room for doubt as to its intent and meaning. . . .

[Page S8794.] . . . as I say, paragraph (1) of the Cooper-Church amendment has troubled me from the beginning. I cannot cast a vote to tie the President's hands when it comes to necessary action to protect American troops in South Vietnam---and there are over 400,000 there now. Ask the fathers and mothers and sisters of those 400,000 American men in South Vietnam what should be done. They will say that they want to see their sons and brothers return home as soon as possible but, while they are there, protect their lives.

Mr. President, I had to introduce this amendment. I could not vote for the Cooper-Church amendment without it. . . .

(June 11, 1970)

[Page S8801.] Mr. President, I ask unanimous consent to modify my amendment No. 667, star print.

The Senators have a copy of the star print at their desks, if they will look at it and follow it as I read.

Mr. President, I ask unanimous consent to modify my amendment No. 667, star print, as follows:

> On page 5, line 7, before the semicolon insert a comma and the following: except that the foregoing provisions of this clause shall not preclude the President in the exercise of his constitutional authority, powers and duties as Commander in Chief, from taking only such temporary action as is clearly necessary to protect the lives of United States forces in South Vietnam or to facilitate the withdrawal of United States forces from South Vietnam, in which circumstances the President is requested to first consult with Congressional leaders; . . .

[Page S8802.] When I offered the amendment, the able Republican assistant leader immediately said that he would want to cosponsor it, and he did. So it is the Byrd-Griffin amendment, as the majority leader has said before. I merely wanted to emphasize the fact that this amendment grew out of my own concern and out of discussions with Senators likewise concerned about what may be the interpretation of paragraph (1) of the Cooper-Church amendment. It is said that my amendment would nullify the Cooper-Church amendment. My amendment does not touch paragraphs (2), (3), or (4) of the Cooper-Church amendment in any way whatsoever. I have indicated time and again that I would like to support those three paragraphs.

My amendment does not nullify paragraph (1) of the Cooper-Church language. It merely makes an exception, and that one exception is that when the President---in the proper exercise of his constitutional authority, power, and duties---determines it to be temporarily necessary to use U.S. Armed Forces in Cambodia for the protection of American troops in South Vietnam or to facilitate [Page S8803.] the withdrawal of those troops from South Vietnam, he may do so.

I came back to the Chamber yesterday, after working 2 days with other Senators and consulting my own conscience, and offered a modification of my amendment. I feel that every Senator should be accorded the right to modify the language of his own amendment. Of course, any Senator has a perfect right to object to a unanimous-consent request to modify an amendment. The Senator who has objected was acting within his rights. I had an opportunity to modify my amendment to my heart's consent prior to the time the Senate entered

into a unanimous-consent agreement. But after the passage of time, I
suppose one can see things that he did not know about or did not see
earlier. So it was after the passage of time and after much study
and consideration that I came to the Chamber and suggested a modification that I thought would meet the legitimate concerns of myself
and other Senators with respect to amendment No. 667.

Throughout the debate yesterday, I learned that there were those
who felt that the word "authority" should be put into the modification;
that it only made reference to the President's powers and duties, and
that we should include the word "authority." This was an inadvertence,
and so today I have added the word "authority" because I think it
should be in.

There were those who said if the Byrd amendment were adopted, it
would open the door for the President to make new commitments, or to
get into a new war, or to get involved in something permanent. I
thought those were expressions of legitimate concern. So today I have
offered to insert the word "temporary." "Temporary" is the opposite
of "permanent." So it reads:

> Shall not preclude the President in the exercise of
> his constitutional authority, powers, and duties as Com-
> mander in Chief, from taking only---

I stress the word "only"---

such temporary action as is clearly necessary. . . .

We say it must be "clearly necessary." What does "clearly necessary" mean? If it is clearly necessary for the President, upon the
advice of his generals and military and civilian advisers, to act for
the protection of American troops in South Vietnam, he should be able
to convince the congressional leadership that it is clearly necessary
to take action.

I continue with the language in the modification:

> clearly necessary to protect the lives of United States
> forces in South Vietnam or to facilitate the withdrawal
> of United States forces from South Vietnam, in which cir-
> cumstances---

I did not have this in my first amendment---

in which circumstances the President is requested to
first consult with Congressional leaders.

So we tried to go more than halfway in meeting the expressed objections to the Byrd amendment.

There are those who say that my amendment will gut the Cooper-Church amendment. It was said last night by one Senator, although facetiously, that he would prefer to have the first amendment because it would more clearly gut the Cooper-Church amendment.

But what are we looking for here? Are we looking for an issue, or are we looking for the enactment into law of meaningful language that will help avoid another Vietnam but which, at the same time, will make clear that the President can act, decisively and promptly, for the protection of American troops in South Vietnam?

The amendment makes clear that he cannot use it as a guise to get us into a new war, into a permanent war, into a new commitment. I use the word "guise" only because it has been used in discussions heretofore.

So here is an effort to meet the objections to close the gap and to come up with language--- . . . which might stand a slim chance of acceptance in the other body, once it is passed by the Senate. . . .

Mr. TYDINGS.   [Page S8809.] Mr. President. . . .

The amendment of the distinguished Senator from West Virginia (Mr. BYRD) will test whether the Senate is going to continue on this calamitous course. A "yea" vote will do just that. Or whether the Senate shall vote no and reassert for the good of the Nation its con-stitutional authority over the making of war and peace, and help end our involvement in the war.

The Byrd amendment grants to the President the authority unlimited in time, manpower, or expense to keep our troops in Cambodia in the name of protecting [Page S8810.] our forces in South Vietnam. It is said that this is necessary to reaffirm the President's right to pro-tect our troops against attack from Cambodia. But this rationale is the sheerest of folly.

For, as I have noted, our Constitution already gives to the Presi-dent the power to do just that---to defend against sudden attacks. Moreover, if history teaches us anything, it is that the President is all too aware of this power. The last thing Congress has to do is to remind him of it. Thus, on the basis of this rationale, the Byrd amendment is completely unnecessary.

But generally the acts of Congress are not interpreted as empty gestures. And I am concerned that the Byrd amendment will not be so interpreted. I am concerned that it could be used as another Gulf of Tonkin resolution. An open invitation to the President to take us into another endless war in Southeast Asia.

I am reminded of the wisdom of Lincoln. When President Polk started the Mexican War by sending American forces into disputed terri-tory along the Rio Grande, Lincoln wrote:

> Allow the President to invade a neighboring nation, whenever he shall deem it necessary to repel an invasion, and you allow him to do so, whenever he may choose to say he deems it necessary for such purpose---and you allow him to make war at pleasure. Study to see if you can fix any

limit to his power in this respect, after you have given
him so much as you propose.

I do not think the President intends to take us into a wider war
in Southeast Asia. But I am unwilling to exchange my own constitutional
responsibilities in this area for a ray of hope. If the **Vietnam** war
teaches Congress anything, it is that it **must no** longer neglect its
constitutional authority in this area. It must, as Jefferson said,
keep tight rein on the dogs of war.

Because the Byrd amendment would again relinquish those reigns
and give the President practically carte blanche authority to make
war in Cambodia, the Senate must reject this amendment. . . .

Mr. BYRD of West Virginia. . . . [Page S8811.]

We cannot add to the President's constitutional authority nor take
it away; but we can put handcuffs on it. We can prevent the proper
exercise of that authority, and I am afraid that paragraph (1) of the
Cooper-Church amendment, as now written, would do just that by cutting
off funds.

It is for that reason that I have offered the language in my
amendment, hoping to make it clear that the Cooper-Church amendment,
if enacted into law, will not attempt to preclude the proper exercise
of his constitutional authority, powers, and duties by the President
of the United States acting as Commander in Chief, if it becomes clearly necessary for the protection [Page S8812.] of the lives of our men
in South Vietnam to temporarily use ground forces again in Cambodia.

That is the purpose of my amendment. I hope that the Record will
be clear as to its intent and meaning. It is an effort to help all
sides. We all want to get out of the war, but we want also to protect
our men. Mr. President, the language as now written will never become law. Let us not suffer any illusions about that. The other
body will not accept it; or, if it does, the President would veto it,
and if he were to veto it, it would be impossible to get two-thirds
of both Houses to override his veto. So this language cannot become
law as now written. I am hopeful that if my language is adopted, it
might be somewhat more acceptable to the other body, and might have
better chances of enactment, because I do want to see the Cooper-
Church amendment enacted into law, if it can be amended as I have
sought to amend it.

Mr. President, I urge Senators to vote for **my** amendment. . . .

Mr. COOPER. . . . [Page S8815.]

In considering the two amendments, the Cooper-Church and the
Byrd-Griffin, it is important to do so in the framework of the war in
Vietnam and to analyze the purposes with which they are drawn, and
the consequences to which they could lead. . . .

It will be helpful to the Congress, to the President, to the
protection of American forces in Vietnam, to the objective of the
President's declared purpose of ending the war in Vietnam. It will
be reassuring to the people of the United States if the Senate shall

refuse to approve the Byrd amendment and if it shall approve the amendment offered by Senators CHURCH, AIKEN, MANSFIELD, and COOPER.

Whatever may happen to the amendment in the House of Representatives, at least the Senate will have met its responsibilities.

The VICE PRESIDENT. All time on the amendment has now expired.

The question is on agreeing to the amendment No. 667 of the Senator from West Virginia (Mr. BYRD) as modified.

Mr. CHURCH. Mr. President, have the yeas and nays been ordered?

The VICE PRESIDENT. The yeas and nays have not been ordered.

Mr. CHURCH. Mr. President, I ask for the yeas and nays.

The yeas and nays were ordered.

The VICE PRESIDENT. The yeas and nays have been ordered, and the clerk will call the roll.

ROLL CALL ON THE FIRST BYRD AMENDMENT*

[Page S8816.] The assistant legislative clerk called the roll.

Mr. GRIFFIN. I announce that the Senator from South Dakota (Mr. MUNDT) is absent on account of illness and, if present and voting, would vote "yea."

The yeas and nays resulted---yeas 47, nays 52, as follows:

[No. 153 Leg.]

YEAS---47

Allen	Eastland	Miller
Allott	Ellender	Murphy
Baker	Ervin	Pearson
Bellmon	Fannin	Prouty
Bennett	Fong	Russell
Bible	Goldwater	Scott
Boggs	Griffin	Smith, Ill.
Byrd, Va.	Gurney	Sparkman
Byrd, W. Va.	Hansen	Stennis
Cannon	Holland	Stevens
Cook	Hollings	Talmadge
Cotton	Hruska	Thurmond
Curtis	Jordan, Idaho	Tower
Dodd	Long	Williams, Del.
Dole	McClellan	Young, N. Dak.
Dominick	McGee	

                              NAYS---52

Aiken	Hughes	Packwood
Anderson	Inouye	Pastore
Bayh	Jackson	Pell
Brooke	Javits	Percy
Burdick	Jordan, N. C.	Proxmire
Case	Kennedy	Randolph
Church	Magnuson	Ribicoff
Cooper	Mansfield	Saxbe
Cranston	Mathias	Schweiker
Eagleton	McCarthy	Smith, Maine
Fulbright	McGovern	Spong
Goodell	McIntyre	Symington
Gore	Metcalf	Tydings
Gravel	Mondale	Williams, N. J.
Harris	Montoya	Yarborough
Hart	Moss	Young, Ohio
Hartke	Muskie	
Hatfield	Nelson	

                         NOT VOTING---1

                              Mundt

    Mr. BYRD of West Virginia. Mr. President, again I want to ex-
press my thanks to the sponsors, the cosponsors, and the supporters
of the Cooper-Church amendment. I thank especially those who participated in the debate last evening, the able Senator from Idaho
(Mr. CHURCH), the able Senator from Kentucky (Mr. COOPER), the able
Senator from Arkansas (Mr. FULBRIGHT), and other Senators who participated in that debate, who took the side of the opposition to my
amendment. I express my appreciation to them for the way they conducted their remarks and for the fine presentation they made with
respect to their objections to my amendment. They conducted what I
consider to be a very high level of debate on their part. . . .

                  THE MANSFIELD-DOLE AMENDMENT*

    Mr. MANSFIELD. [Page S8817.] Mr. President, the amendment that
is now at the desk and is the pending business needs no explanation.
The language is clear, to the point, concise, brief, and answers, I
believe, a doubt which has been in the minds of some Senators. I
think that without question that doubt will be removed.

    The modification reads as follows:

      Nothing contained in this section shall be deemed to
    impugn the constitutional power of the President as Com-
    mander in Chief.

    Mr. DOLE. Mr. President, will the Senator yield?

    Mr. MANSFIELD. I yield.

Mr. DOLE. The amendment offered by the Senator from Montana, the Senator from Kentucky (Mr. COOPER), the Senator from Vermont (Mr. AIKEN), and the Senator from Idaho (Mr. CHURCH)does, in large measure, answer some of the criticisms that have been raised with reference to the Church-Cooper amendment. I would hope that in a very few minutes we might discuss how the proposed amendment would relate to each of the four sections of the Church-Cooper amendment and what effect and bearing it would have. I should think that it would not take long to discuss the amendment and that there would be no reason why, so far as I know, we could not proceed to vote on it.

I would also ask the Senator from Montana whether he would have any objection to changing the word "impugn" to words "in any way modify." It would be a very minor change.

Mr. MANSFIELD. I would prefer to leave the language just as it is, not because of any pride of authorship, but because the amendment is a combination of the thinking of several Senators. I think the same objectives can be achieved. I would prefer to stand on the amendment as it is. . . .

Mr. HOLLAND. . . . . [Page S8819.] it appears to the Senator from Florida that the amendment as now proposed, since it applies to the whole of the Cooper-Church amendment as modified, would simply recognize the fact that the Commander in Chief has complete command of our Armed Forces, and it simply expresses the pious hope that the Senate be conferred with in the event of activities taken after June 30. Am I correct?

Mr. MANSFIELD. No. There is nothing pious about the hope. I do not think that is a very good word to use in relation to a very serious proposition which affects the welfare of this Republic and its policy overseas. This is a most serious matter, and those of us who have been advocating this and the majority of those who have been against the Cooper-Church proposal have looked upon it as a very serious matter.

What we say, in effect, in writing, is what both sides have said during the course of this debate. The question has been raised by those who are opposed to certain segments of the Cooper-Church amendment. The question has been answered in denial by those of us who favor the Cooper-Church amendment. What we do now is to put in writing what is the intent and the understanding on a matter which has never been questioned so far as the Senate is concerned, regardless of the sides the Senators were on. . . .

ROLL CALL ON THE MANSFIELD-DOLE AMENDMENT*

The PRESIDING OFFICER. . . . [Page S8829.]

The question is on agreeing to the amendment of the Senator from Montana (Mr. MANSFIELD) and other Senators. The yeas and nays have been ordered, and the clerk will call the roll.

The assistant legislative clerk called the roll.

Mr. KENNEDY. I announce that the Senator from Indiana (Mr. BAYH), the Senator from Maine (Mr. MUSKIE), and the Senator from Georgia (Mr. RUSSELL) are necessarily absent.

I further announce that, if present and voting the Senator from Indiana (Mr. BAYH) would vote "yea."

Mr. GRIFFIN. I announce that the Senator from South Dakota (Mr. MUNDT) is absent on account of illness.

The Senator from Colorado (Mr. ALLOTT), the Senator from Idaho (Mr. JORDAN), the Senators from Illinois (Mr. PERCY and Mr. SMITH), and the Senator from Vermont (Mr. PROUTY) are necessarily absent.

If present and voting, the Senator from Idaho (Mr. JORDAN) and the Senator from South Dakota (Mr. MUNDT) would each vote "yea."

The result was announced---yeas 91, nays 0, as follows:

[No. 154 Leg.]

YEAS---91

Aiken	Goodell	Montoya
Allen	Gore	Moss
Anderson	Gravel	Murphy
Baker	Griffin	Nelson
Bellmon	Gurney	Packwood
Bennett	Hansen	Pastore
Bible	Harris	Pearson
Boggs	Hart	Pell
Brooke	Hartke	Proxmire
Burdick	Hatfield	Randolph
Byrd, Va.	Holland	Ribicoff
Byrd, W. Va.	Hollings	Saxbe
Cannon	Hruska	Schweiker
Case	Hughes	Scott
Church	Inouye	Smith, Maine
Cook	Jackson	Sparkman
Cooper	Javits	Spong
Cotton	Jordan, N. C.	Stennis
Cranston	Kennedy	Stevens
Curtis	Long	Symington
Dodd	Magnuson	Talmadge
Dole	Mansfield	Thurmond
Dominick	Mathias	Tower
Eagleton	McCarthy	Tydings
Eastland	McClellan	Williams, N. J.
Ellender	McGee	Williams, Del.
Ervin	McGovern	Yarborough
Fannin	McIntyre	Young, N. Dak.
Fong	Metcalf	Young, Ohio
Fulbright	Miller	
Goldwater	Mondale	

NAYS---0

NOT VOTING---9

Allott   Mundt   Prouty
Bayh   Muskie   Russell
Jordan, Idaho   Percy   Smith, Ill.

So the amendment offered by <u>Mr. MANSFIELD</u> for himself and other Senators was agreed to.

(June 15, 1970)

<u>Mr. MILLER</u>. [Page S9011.] Mr. President. . . .

The other day, by a vote of 91 to 0, we adopted the Mansfield amendment, which says that the Cooper-Church resolution, whatever it says, whall not be interpreted to impugn the powers of the President as Commander in Chief. In a colloquy with the Senator from Idaho, who was managing the resolution at the time, I brought out from him--- and he was quite frank and fair about it---that the proponents of Cooper-Church have no intention whatsoever, under this amendment, to criticize the President for his action in the Cambodian sanctuary operation; and of course they could not, because he was taking the action as Commander in Chief.

I must say at this stage, with the Cooper-Church amendment here and with the Mansfield amendment having been adopted, I do not know what we have been doing for the last 5 weeks except having a lot of wind emanate from the Senate, making a lot of copy for the reporters to write about, and unduly delaying legislative programs this country needs very badly. . . .

THE SECOND BYRD AMENDMENT*

(June 22, 1970)

<u>Mr. COOPER</u>. [Page S9435.] Mr. President, after Byrd amendment No. 1 was defeated on June 11, several supporters of the Byrd amendment and of the Cooper-Church amendments expressed a desire to see in- cluded in the Cooper-Church amendment language recognizing the con- stitutional authority of the President as Commander in Chief to pro- tect the Armed Forces. Several Members, among them Senator <u>SPONG</u> of Virginia, Senator <u>PERCY</u> of Illinois, Senator <u>DOLE</u> of Kansas, made valuable contributions through amendments and discussion on the floor toward specifying recognized powers of the President to protect the Armed Forces of the United States.

I believe all agreed that it is difficult to specifically define these powers, for much depends upon the circumstances under which they would be determined. Nevertheless, the discussion pointed out that the powers are essentially defensive---to repel attack sudden and im- pending---to retaliate, to employ hot pursuit, and take other emergency action. The power of the President and the Congress overlap in a grey area, but I do not believe those who oppose the Cooper-Church amend- ment or those who support the pending Byrd amendment can correctly argue that the Executive has authority to engage in a new war for Cam- bodia, or extend the Vietnam war into Cambodia.

Senator BYRD has continued his work to develop an amendment which would recognize the authority of the President to protect the U.S. Armed Forces and he has done so in a very systematic and scholarly fashion. . . .

The amendment now pending is an amendment to the Mansfield amendment which was adopted on June 11 by the unanimous vote of those present.

I shall read the language of the Mansfield amendment:

> Nothing contained in the Section shall be deemed to impugn the Constitutional power of the President as Commander in Chief.

If the Byrd amendment is approved, his language will read as follows:

> Including the exercise of that Constitutional power which may be necessary to protect the lives of United States forces wherever deployed.

The original language of the Mansfield amendment is general. It recognizes the constitutional authority of the President---express and implied. The pending Byrd amendment would become a part of the Mansfield amendment, recognizing one of the constitutional powers of the President.

It is correct that the President of the United States has the constitutional authority to protect the Armed Forces of the United States around the world---wherever they are deployed. . . .

Mr. BYRD of West Virginia. . . . [Page S9437.]

Mr. President, I do not mean for the Byrd amendment to be interpreted as any advance approval for the President to enter into any new commitment or to enter into any new war.

Again, the able Senator from Kentucky states as follows:

> The distinguished Senator from West Virginia has stated in his very scholarly speech that he did not intend that his original Byrd amendment should be construed to provide authority to the President of the United States to engage the United States in a new war in Cambodia for Cambodia. . . .

That is correct. It was not the intention of the cosponsors of the original amendment that the amendment be construed to provide authority to the President to engage the United States in a new war in Cambodia for Cambodia.

Mr. President, the same is true with the amendment presently pending before the Senate. . . . on June 11, the Senate rejected, by

a vote of 52 to 47 the so-called Byrd amendment, No. 667, which I had
introduced in behalf of myself and Senators GRIFFIN, STENNIS, SCOTT,
HANSEN, DOLE, ALLEN, BAKER, HOLLINGS, GOLDWATER, and THURMOND.

That amendment reads as follows:

Except that the foregoing provisions of this clause
shall not preclude the President from taking such action
as may be necessary to protect the lives of United States
forces in South Vietnam or to facilitate the withdrawal of
United States forces from Vietnam.

The Byrd amendment, when added to the Cooper-Church amendment,
would then have read as follows, beginning at the comma on line 4 on
page 5 of H.R. 15628:

No funds authorized or appropriated pursuant to this
Act or any other law may be expended for the purpose of---

(1) retaining United States forces in Cambodia, except
that the foregoing provisions of this clause shall not preclude the President from taking such action as may be necessary to protect the lives of United States forces in South
Vietnam or to facilitate the withdrawal of United States
forces from Vietnam.

Following the defeat of my amendment No. 667, on June 11, the
able majority leader offered an amendment to the Cooper-Church amendment. Senator MANSFIELD'S amendment, adopted by a vote of 91 to 0,
was as follows:

Nothing contained in this Section shall be deemed to
impugn the constitutional power of the President as Commander in Chief.

Amendment No. 708, the new Byrd-Griffin amendment, is before the
Senate this afternoon, and a vote will occur at 2 o'clock thereon.
The amendment reads as follows:

On page 5, between lines 18 and 19, strike the period
and insert the following: , including the exercise of that
constitutional power which may be necessary to protect the
lives of United States armed forces wherever deployed.

This amendment, if adopted by the Senate, when added to the verbiage contained in the Mansfield amendment---and they must be read to-
gether---would read as follows:

Nothing contained in this section shall be deemed to
impugn the constitutional power of the President as Commander in Chief, including the exercise of that constitutional

power which may be necessary to protect the lives of
United States armed forces wherever deployed.

There are differences as well as similarities between the two
Byrd amendments: No. 667, which was rejected by the Senate a few
days ago, and No. 708, upon which we are about to vote.

Significant differences are as follows:

First. The first Byrd amendment contained the words "shall not
preclude the President from taking such action as may be necessary to
protect the **lives,**" and so forth. The words "such action" were intended by me to be grounded in the President's constitutional authority
but, as written, they were not confined to that authority. They very
well could have been interpreted to derive from the Gulf of Tonkin
resolution, Public Law 88-408. As a matter of fact, I think, in looking back, it could rightly be argued that they did not require any
specific legal or constitutional authority as an organic base. Rather,
they might have been interpreted as constituting a self-generating authority within themselves, because they authorized the President to
take "such action as may be necessary." The only qualifications upon
the action which could be taken was that it be an action considered
"necessary to protect the lives of United States forces," and so forth.
I am sure that neither I nor any of the cosponsors meant for the words
to be as broadly interpreted and as freewheeling as they might have
appeared, but, admittedly, that construction could have been placed
upon them were it not for the legislative history which the cosponsors
of the amendment laid down. The verbiage of the new Byrd amendment is
clear on this point in that it confines any such action to that which
derives from the President's "constitutional power." so that we get
clearly away from the Gulf of Tonkin resolution or any other wholly
statutory or self-generating authorization of power and we depend
alone upon the power and authority emanating from the Constitution to
be exercised by the President as Commander in Chief. . . .

[Page S9439.] Now, I want to make it clear beyond reasonable doubt
that the Byrd amendment is not intended to relieve the President
of the necessity of consulting with the Congress whenever it
is possible to do so before taking what might otherwise be a controversial action---even though he may have the constitutional power and
authority to do so. As I have said repeatedly, I believe that the
President's failure to consult with Congressional leaders in advance
of the April 30 Cambodian operation was an error of political judgment. It was a congressional relations mistake, and it subjected him,
quite rightfully, to some of the criticism which has been directed at
him following the action he took. I do not believe, however, that
his action to protect the lives of American servicemen in South Vietnam
was an abuse of constitutional authority, but that is a little bit beside the point. The point I am making here and now is that the President should consult with Congress about these matters whenever it is
possible for him to do so, and, in looking back, I think that it was
possible in respect of the Cambodian operation.

The Byrd amendment is not intended to relieve him in this regard.
I must be frank to say that I do not think he is bound, by the Constitution or otherwise, to consult with congressional leaders every
time he makes a tactical decision as Commander in Chief. For him to

be so bound would be to hamper and restrict him in the proper exercise
of his constitutional duty to protect the lives of American Forces.
In a critical emergency situation, he may have to act with great speed.
The element of surprise may be a vital factor. So, I do not view it
the constitutional prerogative of the Congress to require that the
President first clear every such action with the legislative branch,
because this could very easily compromise the success of any tactical
action designed to save lives of American Armed Forces. . . .

We do not intend it to provide a loophole for new commitments or
for entrance into new wars. But we do intend that it be a recognition
of that constitutional power and authority which it seems to me everyone should agree is reposed in the President to take action which may
be necessary to protect U.S. Armed Forces in perilous and dangerous
situations, and to do so without the requirement of consultation when
it would be impracticable and unreasonable to expect consultation.

Of course, it is the Commander in Chief who would decide when such
an emergency situation exists.

So, I think that the Byrd amendment rounds out the whole of the
equation. The Cooper-Church amendment goes a long way toward avoiding
new involvements in new wars without prior approval of Congress. But
the Byrd amendment, when coupled with the Mansfield language, fills
in the rest of the picture and recognizes the authority and duty of
the Commander in Chief to play his proper role as the protector of our
troops without undue, unreasonable, or impracticable restrictions
placed upon him in emergency situations which can and do arise in wars,
whether those wars be de jure or de facto, or whether those wars be
undeclared or formally declared. And frankly, I do not want any more
wars of either kind.

One final point should be made. It is wrong to say that the
Byrd amendment is unnecessary, and it is even a greater mistake to
imagine---as some have indicated---that it is meaningless. To do so
is to indicate that one has not carefully read and studied the amendment. It goes as far as the first Byrd amendment was intended by its
cosponsors to go, it achieves what the cosponsors of that amendment
endeavored to achieve, but, in my judgment, it is an improved amendment over that phraseology---an improvement which has come with debate,
with conference and with study. . . .

Mr. JAVITS. [Page S9442.] Mr. President. . . . this whole question of power is undefined, both as to that of the President and that
of Congress. We are defining it. The idea that we are defining it
to include whatever constitutional power is necessary to protect the
lives of U.S. Armed Forces, wherever deployed, is a very attractive
concept. But, question: A Commander in Chief can sacrifice 20 men
to save a million. That is the right which the amendment discusses.
But is there no limit on this whatever? Or is this another Gulf of
Tonkin resolution? I think we ought to know that. Suppose Congress,
in its majesty, does not assent to 6 years of war to save 50 American
troops. Are we conceding that the definition of the President's constitutional authority is solely what he defines it to be? That is
the question I ask the proponent of the amendment. Does he construe
this as a finding or definition by us which in any way excludes the
power of Congress, whatever it may be under the Constitution, to also
determine whether it does or does not wish to sacrifice whatever
lives may be necessary, as is often the case in war, in order to save

many more? What is the concept of the proponent of the amendment on this subject?

Mr. BYRD of West Virginia. Mr. President, Congress and the President share the war powers. The amendment clearly does not express our approval of any new commitment or new war.

Mr. CHURCH. [Page S9443.] Mr. President. . . .

In approaching the issue of the Cooper-Church amendment Senators should set aside the events of the long years of this war---and especially those of the last 2 months---and view the amendment as the institutional question it is. Make no mistake about it---the Senate as an institution is on trial here. I hope that in voting on the Cooper-Church amendment, the Senate will live up to the great expectations of the authors of the Constitution, who saw Congress as the people's bulwark against one-man rule.

Mr. President, in summary, if the Senate adopts the present Byrd amendment every substantive subsection of the Cooper-Church amendment, dealing with restrictions on the use of public funds, will remain intact. The Byrd addition to the Mansfield amendment explicitly recognizes the President's powers as Commander in Chief. These are not within the reach of Congress. Yet, money is within the reach of Congress, and the limitations imposed by the four subsections of the Cooper-Church amendment remain intact, operative, and whole.

The Cooper-Church amendment is a valid assertion of congressional power to prevent the United States from becoming engaged in a new war in Cambodia, for Cambodia. This was the original objective of our amendment 6 weeks ago and continues to be what we seek.

For these reasons, Mr. President, I see no objection to the amendment, in its new form, offered by the Senator from West Virginia. It is consistent with the action the Senate took more than a week ago when it adopted the Mansfield amendment by a unanimous vote of 91-0. I will, therefore, cast my vote in favor of the new Byrd amendment.

Mr. MANSFIELD. Mr. President, will the Senator yield?

Mr. CHURCH: I yield.

Mr. MANSFIELD. Mr. President, I wish to join my distinguished colleague, the senior Senator from Idaho, in what he has just said.

To me, what the Byrd-Griffin amendment does is in no way comparable to the Gulf of Tonkin resolution. If I had even the slightest suspicion that that would be the result of this amendment to the Cooper-Church amendment, I would vote against it unhesitatingly. . . .

ROLL CALL ON THE SECOND BYRD AMENDMENT*

The PRESIDING OFFICER (Mr. HOLLINGS). . . . [Page S9444.]

The question is on agreeing to the amendment, No. 708, of the Senator from West Virginia (Mr. BYRD).

On this question the yeas and nays have been ordered, and the clerk will call the roll.

The bill clerk called the roll. . . .

The result was announced---yeas 79, nays 5, as follows:

[No. 160 Leg.]

YEAS---79

Aiken	Goldwater	Moss
Allen	Gravel	Murphy
Allott	Griffin	Nelson
Anderson	Gurney	Pearson
Baker	Hansen	Pell
Bayh	Harris	Prouty
Bellmon	Hart	Proxmire
Bennett	Hartke	Randolph
Boggs	Holland	Saxbe
Brooke	Hollings	Schweiker
Burdick	Hruska	Scott
Byrd, Va.	Inouye	Smith, Maine
Byrd, W. Va.	Jackson	Smith, Ill.
Case	Jordan, N. C.	Sparkman
Church	Jordan, Idaho	Spong
Cook	Kennedy	Stennis
Cooper	Long	Stevens
Cotton	Magnuson	Symington
Cranston	Mansfield	Talmadge
Curtis	Mathias	Thurmond
Dole	McCarthy	Tower
Eagleton	McGee	Tydings
Eastland	Metcalf	Williams, N. J.
Ellender	Miller	Williams, Del.
Ervin	Mondale	Young, N. Dak.
Fannin	Montoya	Young, Ohio
Fong		

NAYS---5

Fulbright	Hughes	McGovern
Goodell	Javits	

PRESENT AND GIVING A LIVE PAIR, AS PREVIOUSLY RECORDED---1

Ribicoff, against.

NOT VOTING---15

Bible	Hatfield	Packwood
Cannon	McClellan	Pastore
Dodd	McIntyre	Percy
Dominick	Mundt	Russell
Gore	Muskie	Yarborough

So the amendment of <u>Mr. BYRD</u> of West Virginia (No. 708) was agreed to.

THE JAVITS AMENDMENT*

(June 26, 1970)

<u>Mr. JAVITS</u>. [Page S9970.] Mr. President, I send to the desk an amendment to the Foreign Military Sales Act, and ask that it be printed under the rule.

The <u>PRESIDING OFFICER</u>. The amendment will be received and printed, and will lie on the table.

<u>Mr. JAVITS</u>. Mr. President, the purpose of my amendment is to clarify the situation created by the adoption of amendment 708---the so-called second Byrd amendment.

I opposed amendment 708, as did the Senator from Arkansas (<u>Mr. FULBRIGHT</u>) chairman of the Foreign Relations Committee, because I feel that it has the unfortunate potential for being interpreted as Senate acquiescence in the concept of virtually self-defined power devolving on the President, as Commander in Chief, in the world of "undeclared" wars in which we now live.

My misgivings about the potential effect of the second Byrd amendment, as perhaps prejudicing a definition of the respective war powers of the Congress and the President as Commander in Chief, are shared by others within the Senate, and without.

The Cooper-Church amendment, in my judgment, is an historic move in the Senate to use the Congress' power of appropriations to affect warmaking power. I do not believe anyone has, or could, challenge the clear constitutional power of Congress over appropriations.

In a broader sense, however, the issue before the Senate and the Nation is a new and modern delineation in practice of the respective war powers of the Congress and the President, in the current circumstances. The basic constitutional war powers involved are those specified to the Congress in article I, section 8 of the Constitution, over and above the power of the purse which is not in any dispute whatsoever.

In my judgment, it is most important that Senate action should not have prejudiced the debate, and final delineation, of the policy war powers in dealing with the Cooper-Church amendment which relies on the appropriations power. Yet, I regret to say I believe that the second Byrd amendment has a very serious potential for prejudicing the final outcome of this most vital issue; hence the amendment I now offer.

For, whatever interpretation Senators may put upon the language of amendment 708, the crucial interpretation in practice will be the interpretation of the President who has the sole Executive power to implement the Foreign Military Sales Act.

The purpose of my amendment is to balance off the potentially prejudicial nature of the second Byrd amendment. The Byrd amendment reserves the broadest possible definition of Presidential power.

The problem that I found with it---and I was one of the very few, unhappily for me, who voted against the Byrd amendment---was that it tended to leave to the President the definition of the term "anywhere in the world," in determining what he could do with the Armed Forces of the United States. If a Marine guard's life in an embassy in Nepal, for example, were in danger, we were really saying to the President, "If you say that you have to engage in military operations to protect that man, we now construe your powers to mean that you can."

My amendment reserves in full the delineation of Congress' constitutional powers respecting warmaking. The net effect is to leave for future consideration a full and open disposition, unprejudiced either way, of the respective war powers of the Congress and the President. . . .

It is too important a matter to be disposed of through any controversial language which imperils, by definition, the division, and balance of the warmaking powers. . . .

Mr. BYRD of West Virginia. [Page S9971.] Mr. President. . . .

Certainly there was nothing meant in the language of the Byrd-Griffin amendment No. 708 which was meant to impugn the constitutional powers of Congress. As was stated so many times during the debate, nothing we could add to the language of the bill would in any way add to or detract from the constitutional powers of the President. It was only the fear that we might say something in the Cooper-Church language that would adversely affect or restrict the proper exercise of those constitutional powers by the President as Commander in Chief.

May I say, anent the Senator's reference to the President's power under the Byrd amendment---I believe the Senator indicated that we were leaving up to the President the decision as to when an emergency situation would arise which would necessitate action on his part to protect the lives of American troops. I think the President would have to make that determination.

Mr. JAVITS. Mr. President, would the Senator forgive me for interrupting?

Mr. BYRD of West Virginia. Yes. The Senator has the floor.

Mr. JAVITS. That was not my point. I agree with the Senator in that. The Commander in Chief does have broad executive and command authority. My point was, "How long, O Lord, and at what cost?"

Mr. BYRD of West Virginia. Once we agree, and I think all sides have agreed, that if there is a dire situation imperiling the lives of American troops, and it is so imminent that it would be impracticable for the President to consult with Congress, then he must act, because he has the constitutional authority and the duty to act, to protect the lives of our servicemen.

Once we open that door, once we admit that he has this power and authority, then I think it becomes academic, because who would decide when such an emergency situation has arisen? Certainly not the 535 Members of Congress, but only the Commander in Chief, under the Constitution, could and would make that decision.

That is what we were saying in the Byrd amendment. . . .

[Page S9974.] . . . Mr. President, I do not see any need for any large scale or extended debate on this amendment. . . .

I shall now refer to the language in the amendment offered by the senior Senator from New York: "Nothing contained in this section---" meaning section 47 of the Foreign Military Sales Act---"shall be deemed to impugn the constitutional powers of the Congress."

Who can quarrel with that? What are those constitutional powers of the Congress? They are set forth in paragraphs 11, 12, 13, 14, 15, 16, and 18 of section 8 of article I of the Constitution.

The warmaking powers of the President are set forth in paragraph 1, section 2 of article II of the Constitution. . . .

And when his amendment says, "constitutional powers of the Congress including the power to declare war and to make rules for the Government and regulation of the Armed Forces of the United States," it embraces all of the war powers of the Congress. . . .

Nothing we can do in the Senate by statute would amend the Constitution. The Senator is simply stating that the constitutional war powers of the Congress shall remain what they are now and what they have been for almost 200 years.

He is speaking of the war powers of Congress, and he states that they shall remain what they are. . . .

Mr. CHURCH. [Page S9992.] Mr. President, I, too, hope that the amendment offered by the distinguished Senator from New York will find unanimous favor with the Senate today. I could not vote against it, because a vote against it would be a vote against the Constitution. I could not vote against the Mansfield amendment, as modified by the Byrd amendment, because I believed a vote against it would be a vote against the Constitution.

Inasmuch as we chose to adopt the Mansfield-Byrd amendments, we should proceed, in the interest of balance, to adopt the Javits amendment, thus giving explicit recognition to the fact that the Constitution does confer certain powers upon the Presidency and certain powers upon Congress when it comes to warmaking.

As the Senator from New York has pointed out, Congress should proceed, in the coming months, to a more precise definition of these powers. As for now, however, I am happy to see that the Senator from New York has proposed this amendment. It brings back into proper equilibium our consideration of the Cooper-Church amendment. . . .

Mr. FULBRIGHT. [Page S9992.] Mr. President, I wish to pay my compliments to the distinguished Senator from New York for having thought of this language which I think puts the Byrd amendment into

proper perspective. I am one of those who were extremely disturbed
about the way the Byrd amendment would be ultimately interpreted.
There were those who believed it would have no effect at all; that it
was an innocuous repetition of what was obvious. But having seen how
other laws or resolutions have been distorted in the past, and taking
into consideration the circumstances of its attachment to the Cooper-
Church amendment. I was extremely disturbed about it, as I expressed
the other day.

So it gives me a great deal of satisfaction to see that the Senator from New York has brought in this additional amendment, which
restores, I think, the balance between the legislative and executive
branches, just as was contemplated by the Constitution itself.

As so often happens, if we carry on a debate long enough in this
body, no matter how confused the discussion may at times become,
sooner or later some Senator out of the 100 will have an inspiration
that will find a way to clarify the situation I think the Senator from
New York has done that in this case.

He has stated what is obviously true---that we do not intend to
impugn the proper role of the Senate in our constitutional system. . . .

Nearly everything we have done in the past year or so in this area
has been a groping by the Senate to try to reestablish a balance in
our constitutional system. . . .

Mr. GURNEY.   [Page S9973.] Mr. President, this amendment is offered in the whole context of the discussion we have had here in the
Senate during the past 5 or 6 weeks on the Cooper-Church amendment,
the Byrd amendments and the Mansfield amendment, all of which relate
to Southeast Asia on widening or contracting the war, the powers of
the President as Commander in Chief, and the role of Congress.

The questions asked the sponsor of the amendment so far have
been directed to the powers of Congress to declare war.

My question is this: the other part of the amendment states:

> Nothing contained in this section shall be deemed to
> impugn the Constitutional powers of the Congress including
> the power to declare war and to make rules for the govern-
> ment and regulation of the Armed Forces of the United States.

Now, as I say, this amendment in the context of the war in Southeast Asia. May I ask the Senator from New York what does he mean by
this language---

> Nothing contained in this section shall be deemed to
> impugn the Constitutional powers of the Congress including
> the power to declare war and to make rules for the govern-
> ment and regulation of the Armed Forces of the United
> States.---

insofar as this debate and the war in Southeast Asia is concerned?

Mr. JAVITS. I can explain that, I hope quickly. In the first place, my amendment closely parallels the Mansfield-Byrd language. More pertinently, it closely paraphrases the Constitution. That is what the Constitution says.

The Senator from West Virginia's amendment says that the President, as Commander in Chief, can react when the troops are endangered, wherever deployed. I agree. But there is a point at which that power ceases or, at least, the power of Congress comes into dominant play. I am not trying to define that point now. I am preserving our right to do it under the Constitution. That is all.

[Page S9993.] The amendment which has been offered by the able Senator from New York (Mr. JAVITS) reasserts the war powers of Congress under the Constitution of the United States.

I shall read, in part, the verbiage of the Javits amendment: "Nothing contained in this section---" again referring to section 47 of the Military Sales Act---"shall be deemed to impugn---" Webster defines the word "impugn" as "to assail, cast doubt upon, to question, or to deny." So, in reality, Mr. JAVITS is saying in this amendment that nothing contained in this section shall be deemed to question or cast doubt upon or to deny or assail the constitutional powers of the Congress.

What are those constitutional powers? The able Senator from New York goes on to refer explicitly to certain of those powers: He says: "including the power to declare war." That is a reference to paragraph 11 of section 8 of article I of the Constitution.

The Senator goes on: "and to make rules for the government and regulation."

That is a reference to paragraph 14 of section 8 of article I of the Constitution. The only change made in the precise verbiage of paragraph 14 by the Senator from New York in his amendment is in the words . . . "Armed Forces of the United States."

The Constitution makes reference to "the land and naval forces". . . .

In summation, the amendment offered by the able Senator from New York does nothing to affect the Byrd amendment, which has already been adopted by a roll call vote. The Byrd amendment went to the constitutional war powers of the President acting as Commander in Chief.

The Javits amendment goes to the war powers of Congress as set forth in the Constitution.

So, Mr. President, I wholeheartedly support the Javits amendment. I think it does bring a proper balance to the legislative history in connection with both amendments. I support the Senator's amendment. I hope that the vote thereon will be unanimous. . . .

ROLL CALL ON THE JAVITS AMENDMENT*

The PRESIDING OFFICER (Mr. CRANSTON). [Page S9994.] All time

having expired, the question is on agreeing to the amendment of the
Senator from New York. On this question the yeas and nays have been
ordered, and the clerk will call the roll.

The assistant legislative clerk called the roll. . . .

The result was announced---yeas 73, nays 0, as follows:

[No. 181 Leg.]

YEAS---73

Aiken	Fannin	McIntyre
Allen	Fong	Metcalf
Allott	Fulbright	Miller
Anderson	Gravel	Moss
Baker	Griffin	Muskie
Bellmon	Gurney	Nelson
Bennett	Hansen	Packwood
Bible	Harris	Pastore
Boggs	Hart	Pell
Brooke	Hartke	Percy
Byrd, Va.	Hatfield	Proxmire
Byrd, W. Va.	Holland	Randolph
Cannon	Hollings	Schweiker
Case	Inouye	Scott
Church	Javits	Smith, Maine
Cook	Jordan, N. C.	Spong
Cooper	Jordan, Idaho	Stevens
Cotton	Kennedy	Symington
Cranston	Long	Talmadge
Curtis	Magnuson	Thurmond
Dole	Mansfield	Williams, Del.
Dominick	Mathias	Young, N. Dak.
Eagleton	McClellan	Young, Ohio
Eastland	McGee	
Ervin	McGovern	

NAYS---0

NOT VOTING---27

Bayh	Jackson	Russell
Burdick	McCarthy	Saxbe
Dodd	Mondale	Smith, Ill.
Ellender	Montoya	Sparkman
Goldwater	Mundt	Stennis
Goodell	Murphy	Tower
Gore	Pearson	Tydings
Hruska	Prouty	Williams, N. J.
Hughes	Ribicoff	Yarborough

So Mr. JAVITS' amendment was agreed to.

DEBATE ON REPEAL OF THE GULF OF TONKIN RESOLUTION*

(June 22, 1970)

Mr. DOLE. Mr. President. . . . [Page S9445.]

Recent Senate debate has repeatedly emphasized the responsibility
of Congress to assume its obligations in the formulation and conduct
of foreign policy. While care should be taken to avoid actions which
would appear to limit or transgress upon the President's prerogatives
in this field, Congress, the Senate in particular, has a significant
role to play in establishing policy objectives and guidelines. By repealing the Tonkin Gulf resolution we can exercise our powers and fulfill our responsibilities in a positive and meaningful way. Having
provided the peg upon which the Vietnam escalation was hung, we can
make a start at exerting congressional influence and wisdom by removing that peg and clearing the way for other worthwhile achievements
in defining foreign policy and national priorities.

Several Senators addressed the Chair.

Mr. DOLE. Mr. President, I yield to the Senator from New York.

Mr. JAVITS. Mr. President, first, if the Senator is willing, I
would like to be joined as a cosponsor of his amendment.

Mr. DOLE. Mr. President I ask unanimous consent that the name of
the Senator from New York be added as a cosponsor of the amendment.

The PRESIDING OFFICER. Without objection, it is so ordered.

Mr. JAVITS. Mr. President, will the Senator yield further?

Mr. DOLE. I yield.

Mr. JAVITS. Mr. President, this Gulf of Tonkin termination measure was reported by the Committee on Foreign Relations, based upon a
measure introduced by the Senator from Maryland (Mr. MATHIAS),and the
Senator from Montana (Mr. MANSFIELD) and a measure introduced also by
the Senator from Rhode Island (Mr. PELL) and me.

This measure is eminently deserving and essential to what we are
about. The only really questionable point of difference on the Byrd
amendment---which we have just decided so overwhelmingly, and I understand it perfectly---is the question of what is the division of constitutional power between Congress and the President.

In view of the fact it is only the Gulf of Tonkin resolution which
stands in the way of a resolution of that question on the merits---be-
cause that is the only authority Congress has given, and the President
agrees it is obsolete and he is not using it; if President Johnson had
felt the same way our lives would have been simplified and he may have
been a candidate for President---I welcome very much the utilization
of the vehicle of this bill, which has taken so much debate already.
The Gulf of Tonkin resolution stands next in line.

Text of the
Gulf of Tonkin Resolution

Whereas naval units of the Communist regime in Vietnam, in violation of the Charter of the United Nations and of international law, have deliberately and repeatedly attacked United States naval vessals lawfully present in international waters, and have thereby created a serious threat to international peace;

Whereas these attacks are part of a deliberate and systematic campaign of aggression that the Communist regime in North Vietnam has been waging against its neighbors and the nations joined with them in the collective defense of their freedom;

Whereas the United States is assisting the peoples of southeast Asia to protect their freedom and has no territorial, military or political ambitions in that area but desires only that they should be left in peace to work out their own destinies in their own way; now, therefore, be it

Resolved by the Senate and House of Representatives of the United States of America in Congress assembled, That the Congress approves and supports the determination of the President, as Commander in Chief, to take all necessary measures to repel any armed attack against the forces of the United States and to prevent further aggression.

Sec. 2. The United States regards as vital to its national interest and to world peace the maintenance of international peace and security in southeast Asia. Consonant with the Constitution and the Charter of the United Nations and in accordance with its obligations under the Southeast Asia Collective Defense Treaty, the United States is, therefore, prepared, as the President determines, to take all necessary steps, including the use of armed force, to assist any protocol or member state of the Southeast Asia Collective Defense Treaty requesting assistance in defense of its freedom.

This resolution shall expire when the President shall determine that the peace and security of the area is reasonably assured by the international conditions created by action of the United Nations or otherwise, and shall so report to the Congress, except that it may be terminated earlier by a concurrent resolution of the two Houses.

Approved by Congress August 10, 1964

I hope very much the Senate will do what must be done to clear the decks and then we can deal with the Vietnam war on its merits. In that way we can proceed to the most critical question before our country: What is the definition of the power of the President and what is the definition of the power of Congress in respect of the power of making war.

I think the Senator from Kansas, especially because of his position on the Cooper-Church amendment, has rendered a real service in enabling us to terminate the Gulf of Tonkin resolution. I thank the Senator for adding my name as a cosponsor of the amendment. . . .

Mr. MILLER. Mr. President. . . . [Page S9447.]

I support the pending amendment to repeal the Gulf of Tonkin resolution. I want to remind my colleagues that back on March 7, 1968, while most of the Senators were present in this Chamber, we had a rather long discussion about the way the war was going and something about the Gulf of Tonkin resolution, which we had passed some years before.

As shown on page 5646 of the Record for the Senate on March 7, 1968, the distinguished Senator from Arkansas (Mr. FULBRIGHT) yielded, and I stated:

> Mr. MILLER. Mr. President, I thank the Senator.
>
> At the time we had before us the Gulf of Tonkin resolution I cast my vote in favor of it and I did so on the assumption that the military action taken by the President of the United States in the conduct of a war would be according to the best traditions of our military service. If at that time someone had told me that the conduct of a war after the Gulf of Tonkin resolution would be a prolonged war strategy, and if someone had told me that the Preparedness Investigating Subcommittee 2 years later would have found in 1966 that of the thousands of sorties flown over North Vietnam less than 1 percent would be directed at key chief of staff targets, I would not have supported the Gulf of Tonkin resolution.

Mr. President, there may have been reasons for the prolonged war strategy. No doubt there were. But, periodically and publicly, I called upon the former President to take the American people into his confidence and tell them why he was using a prolonged war strategy. I warned that the longer the war went on, the more casualties there would be and the more problems there would be. I regret to say that my plea never was heeded.

I feel the same way today as I felt at the time of the remarks I have just quoted from the Record. As a matter of protest to the way the war was conducted for nearly 5 years after the Gulf of Tonkin resolution, I propose to vote for the repeal of the Gulf of Tonkin resolution, which is the pending amendment.

There is another point to be made. There is some language in the

Gulf of Tonkin resolution with respect to which I would trust that
action on this amendment would not constitute a repudiation. In the
first place, we have a treaty on the books known as the SEATO Treaty,
and that is the supreme law of the land. It was duly negotiated and
ratified by a two-thirds vote of the Senate; and it is my understanding
that we cannot just out of hand repeal the SEATO Treaty, certainly by
a simple majority vote in the Senate. The Gulf of Tonkin resolution
recites that pursuant to the authority and the commitment made in the
SEATO Treaty, Congress resolves to support the President in whatever
his determination and his actions may be with respect to the situation
in Southeast Asia.

I recall that at the time this was being debated, the Senator from
Kentucky (Mr. COOPER) asked the manager of the Gulf of Tonkin resolution, the distinguished chairman of the Committee on Foreign Relations,
whether the authority granted in this resolution could lead to a war;
and the response from the distinguished chairman of the Foreign Relations Committee was: "That is the way I would interpret it."

With this legislative history, plus the wording of the Gulf of
Tonkin resolution, I do not have any question that there has been a
de facto declaration of war by Congress. The Constitution requires
that Congress declare a war, and what really counts is that Congress
express its will. The Constitution does not say that it has to be
a formal declaration, with a lot of ribbons on it. The Constitution
certainly makes clear that Congress must indicate its will, and that
was done with the overwhelming vote in favor of the Gulf of Tonkin
resolution, plus the legislative history to which I have just referred. . . .

Mr. ERVIN. . . . [Page S9449.]

The Gulf of Tonkin resolution was an exercise of one of our constitutional processes, the power of Congress to declare a state of
war. If we were to repeal that Gulf of Tonkin resolution, we would
repeal the authority Congress gave the President to put our troops in
combat in Southeast Asia.

The SEATO Treaty put no obligation upon the United States to do
that. So the Senator's amendment, if adopted, would be a repeal of
the authority of the President to command our troops in combat in that
area of the world. . . .

Mr. STENNIS. The Tonkin Gulf resolution was passed by an almost
unanimous vote in the Senate, and it was used by the President of the
United States as a basis for his action in Vietnam. And that action
was generally accepted as being within the purview of that language.

The resolution was not agreed to by everyone. There was dissent.
But for a long while there was no real effort made to change it or to
repeal it. And now, having gone for all these years, at least on a
partial basis for about 4 years by former President Johnson and for a
year and a half by the present President, President Nixon, it seems
to me that before the whole world and before a great majority of our
people, it is looked upon as at least constituting a major part of the
basis for the authority under which we have acted.

With respect to saying that that matter is a debatable question,

it seems to me, with all respect, that we would be far from exercising
a sound judgment if we were to jerk it up here now at the last minute,
after a fairly minor bill, the Military Sales Act, has been pending
here for all these weeks and add a major policy of this kind as an
amendment to a minor bill. It would jerk the rug out from under the
authority that has been exercised for all of these years, in a way,
and lives have been lost in battle under that authority. In part,
that resolution was at least the considered basis for the authority
for this war.

I am not trying to dodge the issue. We have a responsible committee that has weighed the evidence and considered this matter. The
committee respectfully made its recommendations and has come forward
with a responsible report on the resolution. It is certainly a debatable matter. It involves a major policy matter. As I say, we have
fought a war pursuant to this authority.

I respectfully submit that I hope the Senate will not consider
this as being so small a matter or so minor or so significant as to
warrant being added on as an amendment to the bill.

Frankly, my judgment would be that the President would not want
it handled in that way. However, I have no communication with the
White House. I do not speak for him. I do not know why all of a
sudden it is proposed here. However, apart from all those things, I
hope that the Senate will see fit to reject the amendment. . . .

Mr. COTTON. Mr. President, the Senator from New Hampshire has
carefully refrained from participating in this debate all these weeks.
However, he does want to say a word on this amendment.

The Senator from New Hampshire finds himself---with the great
respect that he has for the Senator from Mississippi---completely of
a contrary opinion.

Mr. President, 6 years ago at the request of the President of the
United States, the Senate, with rather brief debate, approved the so-
called Tonkin resolution. And that resolution has remained in effect
for 6 years as the only formal, official action on the part of Congress
in regard to the hostilities in South Vietnam, with the possible exception of some restriction in an appropriations bill regarding Laos.

Mr. President, the Senator from New Hampshire was present and
was one of 88 Senators to vote for that resolution.

The Senator from New Hampshire as long as 3 or 4 years ago publicly, in sackcloth and ashes, expressed his repentance.

If the Senator from New Hampshire were compelled to mention the
one vote that he regretted the most in the 16 years he has served in
the Senate, he would have to say that it was the vote he cast for the
Tonkin Gulf resolution.

I have been waiting now for 3 years for a chance to vote to repeal the measure.

It is no excuse or comfort for the Senator from New Hampshire to

say that 87 other Senators also voted in favor of the resolution. The
Senator from New Hampshire thinks they made the same mistake he did.
It is no excuse for any Senator to say that he did not realize or
understand that that resolution gave the approval of Congress to practically unlimited actions by the President of the United States.

We can all read. The resolution provided that the President could
take such measures as he saw fit to protect American interests in
Southeast Asia.

I suppose we, in reading that, fixed our attention on it and believed it had to do with action that would be taken in regard to the
attack on one of our naval vessels.

But the resolution went on to say, "to keep the peace in Southeast Asia."

In my book, it is not the unilateral duty of the United States of
America to keep the peace in Southeast Asia. In fact, I must say
frankly, with all due respect to my President, the present President,
that when I was listening to his news conference not long ago, I shud-
dered when I heard him---perhaps not calculatingly---refer to us as
the peacekeeper in Southeast Asia. . . .

Mr. DOLE.   [Page S9489.] Mr. President, it occurs to me this is
a very important amendment. The original Gulf of Tonkin joint resolution was enacted by Congress after brief debate. There was some reason for urgency at the time. Action on it was expedited through the
House and through the Senate. It was approved on August 10, 1964.
In effect, we have debated Southeast Asia, if not specifically the
Gulf of Tonkin resolution and its repeal, for over 30 days on this
floor, compared with 2 days when it was enacted in 1964, almost 6 years
ago. By virtue of the Gulf of Tonkin resolution, which I voted for as
a Member of the other body, and which every Member of the Senate who
was there at that time voted for as Members of this body, the war has
been escalated.

As I said at the outset, the present occupant [Page S9490.] of
the White House, President Nixon, has indicated no need for the Gulf
of Tonkin resolution. I would guess that the majority of the Members
of the Senate and the House of Representatives would indicate no need
for the Gulf of Tonkin resolution. I would say, in conclusion, that
the earlier we can repeal the Gulf of Tonkin resolution the better.

Mr. ERVIN.   Mr. President, will the Senator yield for a question?

Mr. DOLE.   I yield the floor.

Mr. ERVIN.   Mr. President, I ask that I be recognized.

The PRESIDING OFFICER.   The Senator from North Carolina is recognized.

Mr. ERVIN.   Mr. President, it is a most surprising development
that the President would seek to defeat the Cooper-Church amendment
which merely undertakes to put limits upon his power to wage war in
Cambodia and Laos, and then have his spokesmen propose to the Senate
an amendment which would not only take away his power to act in

Cambodia and Laos, but also take away his power to act in South Vietnam. That is exactly what this amendment does.

It is true that when Congress passed the Gulf of Tonkin resolution it inserted a section in which it said, among other things, that Congress could repeal the Gulf of Tonkin resolution by a concurrent resolution. Congress reserved the right to repeal by concurrent resolution. But here the proposal, instead of repealing it by concurrent resolution, would repeal it by an amendment to an act of Congress having no connection with the subject.

The Senate is getting itself in a rather perplexing state. . . .

I have stood by the President during this debate up to this point because Congress gave him authority to use the Armed Forces of the United States in combat in Southeast Asia, by the Tonkin Gulf resolution. Since article II, section 2 of the Constitution makes him the Commander in Chief of the Armed Forces of the United States, and Congress has authorized him to act as such in combat in Southeast Asia he had the authority to order the incursion into Cambodia as a part of his powers as Commander in Chief.

I do not know what the position of our boys in Southeast Asia will be if we repeal the Tonkin Gulf resolution, because the President of the United States has no power whatsoever to act as Commander in Chief in that part of the world with the exception of withdrawing the troops, if this repeal carries. It is true that he might have the inherent power to protect them as they withdraw. Manifestly, his power would extend no further than that. So why should the Congress becloud their situation by repeal of the Tonkin Gulf resolution?

I cannot view it as anything but intellectual and constitutional schizophrenia that the administration should stand here and fight the Church-Cooper amendment for all these weeks and then make through its spokesman the proposal on the floor of the Senate that the Senate repeal the only action taken by Congress which gives the President authority to use the Armed Forces of this country in combat in Southeast Asia.

This matter has no place as an amendment to this bill. The Foreign Relations Committee has reported a resolution, which is on the calendar, which is the orderly way to deal with this matter, and what is consistent with the Gulf of Tonkin resolution, which expressly reserves to the Congress power to repeal the Tonkin Gulf resolution by concurrent resolution of the Congress. That is the way the matter ought to be handled, and not in this unexpected way on the floor of the Senate at this late stage in the consideration of the pending measure. . . .

Mr. DOLE. . . . [Page S9495.] We have been debating the general issue of Southeast Asia and the effect of the Gulf of Tonkin resolution. The President has made it clear that he does not rely on the Tonkin Gulf resolution. The Senator from Arkansas and other Senators have made it clear that they do not rely on the Tonkin Gulf resolution now. It seems an appropriate time to act now.

I apologize if I have trespassed on the rights of any Member or any committee. That was not the purpose of my amendment. We were

debating a measure relating to the Tonkin Gulf resolution, not trying
to deal lightly with it. I may say the Tonkin Gulf resolution passed,
after a brief debate, by a vote of 88 to 2. Because of passage, the
war escalated until there were approximately 550,000 troops there.
Perhaps it was dealt lightly with at the time the resolution was
passed. I do not pass judgment on that. But now that we have expressed ourselves many times, why is it inappropriate to act now?
This is an appropriate time to pass on the proposition. If it fails,
we still have the concurrent resolution. This procedure will give
the President an opportunity, by appending his signature to it, to
affirm that he favors repeal of the Gulf of Tonkin resolution. . . .

Mr. FULBRIGHT. Mr. President, I cannot say any more than I have
as to why the Senator's amendment is inappropriate. It departs from
the usual procedure. The Senator from Florida made an eloquent argument for my position on the inappropriateness of it. I do not know
what I can say to add to what both the Senator from North Carolina and
the Senator from Florida have said. I can only conclude that the Senator has not listened very carefully and has not observed what the
proper procedures are. After he has been here a while, I think he will
come to appreciate the procedures of the Senate. One of the important
parts of the procedures of the Senate is following the committee procedure. In fact, following the proper procedure is very relevant to
our democratic form of government. One does not override the established procedures of a body like this and still reach any kind of result.

I do not blame the Senator, in view of his brief attendance here,
for not having learned all of the proper procedures. . . .

I do not know what more I can say to the Senator from Kansas---his
amendment does not accord with the proper procedure. . . .

No; there is no rule that one has to clear anything with me, but
all of the standing committees have a function to play in this body.
If the Senator will read the rules of the Senate, he will see each
committee has certain jurisdictions. The Senator can make any motion
he wants to. Of course he can. That does not mean we have to accept
it. I am not saying the Senator cannot make a motion. I am going to
move to table the motion, because the procedure proposed by the Senator is highly improper. . . .

The result was announced---yeas 15, nays 67, as follows:

[No. 161 Leg.]

YEAS---15

Allen	Fulbright	McCarthy
Anderson	Gravel	McGee
Bayh	Holland	Sparkman
Ellender	Hollings	Stennis
Ervin	Jordan, N. C.	Talmadge

NAYS---67

Aiken	Goodell	Pastore
Allott	Griffin	Pearson
Baker	Gurney	Pell
Bellmon	Hansen	Prouty
Bennett	Hart	Proxmire
Boggs	Hartke	Randolph
Brooke	Hruska	Ribicoff
Burdick	Hughes	Saxbe
Byrd, Va.	Inouye	Schweiker
Byrd, W. Va.	Jackson	Scott
Case	Javits	Smith, Maine
Church	Jordan, Idaho	Smith, Ill.
Cook	Kennedy	Spong
Cooper	Long	Stevens
Cotton	Magnuson	Symington
Cranston	Mansfield	Thurmond
Curtis	Mathias	Tower
Dole	McGovern	Williams, N. J.
Eagleton	Miller	Williams, Del.
Eastland	Mondale	Young, N. Dak.
Fannin	Montoya	Young, Ohio
Fong	Moss	
Goldwater	Nelson	

NOT VOTING---18

Bible	Hatfield	Muskie
Cannon	McClellan	Packwood
Dodd	McIntyre	Percy
Dominick	Metcalf	Russell
Gore	Mundt	Tydings
Harris	Murphy	Yarborough

So Mr. FULBRIGHT'S motion to table Mr. DOLE'S amendment was
rejected.

(June 24, 1970)

Mr. JAVITS. [Page S9660.] Mr. President, the Gulf of Tonkin resolution, it seems to me, is one of the keys to the argument now pre-
occupying the Senate with respect to the power of the President in
this war and future wars. Unless it is cleared from the books we will
not, and cannot, face the issue before the Senate and the country---the
division of the warmaking powers between Congress and the President.
If the President has the power to initiate undeclared war can Congress
"undeclare" such wars, as part of its constitutional power to declare
war? Can Congress stop a President other than by denying funds?

Perhaps the President could find funds in the Federal cupboard
and use them to support troops. There is always the great argument
that you would be depriving the men in combat who are in jeopardy of
the means to do their job. It would be an unfortunate course but it

may be the one we have to take if Congress does not resurrect the now atrophying policy war powers, so deliberately and explicitly reserved to it in the Constitution.

By clearing the decks of the Gulf of Tonkin resolution, we will have taken a step in dealing with a problem which American youth has so passionately and insistently demanded an answer on. That is: Who has the warmaking power? Can a President place us in a war---as we have been involved in a war since 1965 by a President---without public and congressional approval?

Unless this resolution is cleared from the books, President Nixon could subsequently make use of it, even though he says he is not now relying on it. It is there, and it gives him a lawful **cloak** of sorts for what he is doing, or might later seek to do. . . .

In the current debate we are writing a legislative record which history may deem as second in importance only to the deliberations of the Constitutional Convention itself. . . .

The Constitution divides and balances power. It deliberately tries to keep the power to get the Nation into war in the hands of Congress, as close to the people as possible, and away from the arbitrary exercise of Executive power.

We will only be able to face up fully to the truly historic challenge we now face when we have terminated the Tonkin Gulf resolution. This resolution, in addition to its legal implications, is a symbol of ill-considered congressional acquiescence in, and rubberstamping of, unlimited Presidential authority in warmaking. It wounds the wisdom of the Constitution. We are all agreed that it should be terminated. . . .

Mr. ALLEN. Mr. President. . . . [Page S9661.]

It is the opinion of the Senator from Alabama that the enemy in Southeast Asia, and our real adversaries, Red China, and Russia, will take great comfort from the fact that, in repealing the Gulf of Tonkin resolution, we are showing, to some extent, our withdrawal of authority for our presence in Southeast Asia; that we are withdrawing our authorization to see the war in which we are engaged in Southeast Asia brought to an honorable conclusion; and that we are lacking the resolve and determination to carry on this war to an honorable end. . . .

Mr. McGEE. Mr. President. . . . [Page S9669.]

Nor should we forget that nearly every Member of this body voted for the resolution on the one occasion when our judgment was requested. And while there have been numerous efforts by individual Members of the Senate to apologize for their vote several years later, I am not one of those who would be prepared to argue that we were either deceived or that we were just simple minded.

We voted then as we did because we believed it to be a wise statement of Senate judgment. And I think our honesty with ourselves should require us to say so now. But there is no resolution pending that permits us to do so.

Perhaps it does not strain the record too much at this late hour to suggest that, had the events in Southeast Asia gone more favorably after the Tonkin Gulf resolution was enacted, the Members of this body would be standing here on the floor yet today telling the world how they hand participated in the enlightenment which had resulted.

That is simply another way of saying that the Senate of the United States is at this time trying to play a trick on the past by appearing to undo something that some of the Members at least wish they had not done.

History can teach us many things. Among others, it ought to teach us the folly of trying to repeal history. That which is done is done. And for this body now to lend its efforts along with its oratory to the pending repeal measure at the very least can be rationalized only as a political charade in a context of "fun and games." The sad consequence of it is that in these particular times we can ill-afford such antics.

The second point is that to repeal the Tonkin Gulf resolution now becomes an act fraught with some mischief and perhaps even some serious negative consequences.

The mischief is that our people here at home may read into the action itself more than even its proponents ever intended. At the very least, it may be interpreted as a slap at the President of the United States. In this context, it could become a complication hampering his efforts to deescalate and disengage with responsibility in Southeast Asia. . . .

In my mind it is of questionable value for this body to be measuring the violations of constitutional intent from the past when we ought to be seeking a more modern and surely more enlightened procedure for the future. I realize that the newsworthiness of our present dialog seems to be far greater than would a scholarly and statesmanlike study of where we go from here. But the coverage or exposure or the popularity of the subject matter really is not the issue---and dare not be. . . .

ROLL CALL ON REPEAL OF THE GULF OF TONKIN RESOLUTION*

The PRESIDING OFFICER. [Page S9670.] The clerk will call the roll. . . . The assistant legislative clerk proceeded to call the roll. . . .

The result was announced---yeas 81, nays 10, as follows:

[No. 167 Leg.]

YEAS---81

Aiken	Bible	Cannon
Allott	Boggs	Case
Anderson	Brooke	Church
Baker	Burdick	Cook
Bayh	Byrd, Va.	Cooper
Bennett	Byrd, W. Va.	Cotton

YEAS-(Continued)

Cranston	Javits	Percy
Curtis	Jordan, N. C.	Prouty
Dole	Jordan, Idaho	Proxmire
Dominick	Kennedy	Randolph
Eagleton	Magnuson	Ribicoff
Fannin	Mansfield	Saxbe
Fong	Mathias	Schweiker
Goldwater	McGovern	Scott
Goodell	McIntyre	Smith, Maine
Gore	Metcalf	Smith, Ill.
Griffin	Miller	Sparkman
Gurney	Mondale	Spong
Hansen	Montoya	Stevens
Harris	Moss	Symington
Hart	Murphy	Talmadge
Hatfield	Muskie	Thurmond
Holland	Nelson	Tower
Hruska	Packwood	Tydings
Hughes	Pastore	Williams, N. J.
Inouye	Pearson	Williams, Del.
Jackson	Pell	Young, N. Dak.

NAYS---10

Allen	Fulbright	McGee
Bellmon	Hollings	Stennis
Eastland	Long	
Ervin	McClellan	

PRESENT AND GIVING A LIVE PAIR, AS
PREVIOUSLY RECORDED---1

Gravel, for.

NOT VOTING---8

Dodd	McCarthy	Yarborough
Ellender	Mundt	Young, Ohio
Hartke	Russell	

So Mr. DOLE'S amendment (No. 715) was agreed to.

U.S. TROOPS OUT OF CAMBODIA

(June 29, 1970)

Mr. GRIFFIN. [Page S10088.] Mr. President, a headline in today's Washington Star reads: "U.S. Finishes Cambodia Pullout."

When President Nixon announced the operation against the Communist sanctuaries in Cambodia, he promised that all American combat forces would be withdrawn from that country by July 1.

He repeated that promise several times---and now the promise has been kept 1 day ahead of time, according to an Associated Press dispatch from Saigon.

The dispatch says:

> The last American combat troops in Cambodia returned to South Vietnam this afternoon, in effect completing the U.S. withdrawal one day ahead of President Nixon's deadline.

The dispatch added:

> Still in Cambodia, but scheduled to leave by midnight tomorrow (and that this midnight tonight, our time) were a small number of advisers to some of the 39,000 South Vietnamese troops remaining there.

If those who have doubted, criticized, and lamented the President's decision continue to question the success of the operation, I have here the latest---and I suppose the last---summary of results of the Cambodian sanctuary operation.

Mr. President, I ask unanimous consent that the summary be printed at this point in my remarks.

Mr. President, this summary and the news dispatch indicating that all American combat forces are out of Cambodia, leave one question:

What is the need for the Cooper-Church amendment?

There being no objection,the material was ordered to be printed in the Record, as follows:

	Number	24-hour Change
Individual weapons	22,892	+32
Crew-served weapons	2,509[1]	-16[1]
Bunkers/structures destroyed	11,688[1]	+9[1]
Machinegun rounds	4,067,177	[2]
Rifle rounds	10,694,990	+97,420
Total small arms ammunition (machinegun and rifle rounds)	14,762,167	+97,420
Grenades	62,022	+984
Mines	5,482	+1
Miscellaneous explosives (pounds) (includes satchel charges)	81,000	[2]
Antiaircraft rounds	199,552	[2]
Motar rounds	68,539	[2]
Large rocket rounds	2,123[1]	-3[1]

[Continued on page 212]

	Number	24-hour Change
[Continued from page 211]		
Smaller rocket rounds	43,160	+574
Recoilless rifle rounds	29,185	[2]
Rice (pounds)	14,046,000	10,000
Man-months	309,012	+220
Vehicles	435	[2]
Boats	167	[2]
Generators	49	[2]
Radios	248	[2]
Medical supplies (pounds)	67,000	[2]
Enemy KIA	11,349	+17
POW's (includes detainees)	2,328	+1

Note: Figures do not include 70 tons of assorted ammunition.
[1]Field adjustment
[2]Unchanged

THE ISSUE OF MERCENARIES*

Mr. FULBRIGHT.   Mr. President. . . . [Page S10008.]

I wish to make some comments today on the subject of the experience we have had of paying foreign troops to fight in Vietnam.

This distortion of our values caused by the Vietnam war has not
been limited to the destruction of small countries in order to save
them. . . .

I am speaking first about the practice of paying extraordinary
individual overseas allowances to third country forces from Thailand
and South Korea, who are now fighting in South Vietnam.   Second, I
wish to discuss the negotiations, apparently underway between ourselves
and the Thais, on the amount of financial support we will provide them
if they enter the fighting in Cambodia.

I believe the time has come to stop the practice of making it
profitable for countries to send troops to fight wars we believe ought
to be fought in order to protect their countries.

The complete record of the Symington subcommittee makes clear
that neither South Korea, Thailand, nor the Philippines would have
sent troops to South Vietnam if they had not been able to tell their
individual soldiers they would get double or more their regular sala-
ries---plus American-style PX privileges, which is a very important
element if they "volunteered."   Whether, in the case of the Philippines,
the soldiers got that extra money is under investigation.   We agreed
to pay them and turned the money over to officials of their government.

It is not by chance that the State Department has required key
portions of the negotiations with these countries to be kept secret
by deleting from the record for publication.   The real story of the

use of mercenary forces in South Vietnam is a questionable practice on our already blotted record in this war.

At this point, I would like to place in the Record a table showing what the Philippine and Thai soldiers received from their own governments and what they received from ours. The Korean figures, which will become available when the Symington subcommittee record is published next month, show the same story.

I also have a table showing what we pay our soldiers and their overseas allowances, just by way of contrast, and I ask unanimous consent that both tables be printed in the Record at this point.

There being no objection, the tables were ordered to be printed in the Record, as follows:

	Monthly base pay and quarters allowances paid by Philippines	Monthly including per diem and overseas allowances paid by United States	Total
Brigadier general	305	210	515
Colonel	235	195	430
Lieutenant colonel	195	180	375
Major	153	165	318
Captain	125	150	275
1st lieutenant	102	135	237
2d lieutenant	90	120	210
Master sergeant	53	76	129
Sergeant 1st class	53	45	98
Corporal	43	36	79
Private 1st class/Private	43	33	76

	Monthly base pay paid by Thailand	Monthly overseas allowance paid by United States	Total
Lieutenant general	370	450	820
Major general	330	390	720
Special colonel	240	330	570
Colonel	190	300	490
Lieutenant colonel	140	240	380
Major	98	180	278
Captain	70	150	220
Lieutenant	50	120	170
Master sergeant	48	69	117
Sergeant	38	60	98
Corporal	33	50	83
Lance Corporal	30	45	75
Private	26	39	65

Note: Quarters and rations paid by United States.

U.S. PAY AND OVERSEAS ALLOWANCES

	Average[1] base pay	Overseas[2] allowances	Total
Lieutenant general	$2,426.70	$65.00	$2,491.70
Major general	2,180.20	65.00	2,245.20
Colonel	1,425.30	65.00	1,490.30
Lt. Colonel	1,209.30	65.00	1,274.30
Major	962.40	65.00	1,027.40
Captain	870.00	65.00	935.00
1st Lieutenant	731.40	65.00	796.40
Master sergeant (E-9)	903.60	22.50	926.10
Sergeant (E-5)	395.40	16.00	411.40
Corporal (E-4)	330.60	13.00	343.60
Private (E-1)	124.50	8.00	132.50

[1] U.S. Armed Forces are paid according to the number of years of service they have accumulated. Thus, there is a varying pay scale within each rank. The above figures were supplied by the Department of Defense based on the average number of years a person has served when he attains the given rank.

[2] In addition to the above amounts, which represent an allowance for "combat pay," the salaries of enlisted men serving in Vietnam are exempt from income tax and officers' salaries are exempt up to $500.

Mr. FULBRIGHT. Mr. President, I want to point out that a Thai lieutenant gets $120 a month from the United States and only $50 a month from his own country---if he serves in Vietnam.

Of course, he gets the same allowances by his own country if he serves in Vietnam. So we pay to the Thai lieutenant from our own funds twice as much as his country does to induce him to volunteer for service in South Vietnam.

The record shows that there is dissatisfaction among the Thai military who do not get a chance to receive the perquisites of a tour of duty in Vietnam. Those left behind to fight the insurgency in Thailand are paid only regular salaries---no bonus and they have no PX privileges.

[Page S10009.] This system leads to distortion of our values. The American people for years---unaware of the nature of the allowances---were continually told by their leaders that the Free World forces in Vietnam represented recognition that all Asian nations had a stake in the outcome in Vietnam.

That stake---it now turns out---was in good part money.

For that reason, I am opposed to the amendment submitted by the junior Senator from Michigan which would have the effect of removing the prohibition on paying allowances to allies to fight in Cambodia. I believe such payments also should be stopped now in South Vietnam and prevented in the future. . . .

[Page S10010.] How many of our citizens know that for American troops sent to Vietnam the highest monthly special combat allowance is $65 no matter what their rank? Yet at the same time the United

States pays almost twice as much combat pay to Thai and Korean officers in Vietnam as it pays to its own brave men who actually do
most of the heavy fighting.

The Senate has before it in section 3 of the Church-Cooper amendment language which simply says that before the United States uses its
taxpayers' money to pay allowances or other special funds to the Thais
or any other third country force going into Cambodia, the administration must come to the Congress---in the normal manner---and have such
a program authorized and funded.

If we are to give foreign allied troops combat pay twice as large
as that we give American troops, Congress should so decide.

Those who try to portray this Cooper-Church language as prohibiting Asians from helping Asians are distorting the facts.

There is nothing in the law today or in the Cooper-Church amendment that prevents the Government of Thailand---if it believes it is
in its interest---from sending its own forces into Cambodia to assist
the Cambodian Government. . . .

Mr. President, I believe it is time that we stop making mercenaries out of allies and allies out of mercenaries. We must prevent
our money from distorting the ability of countries to determine their
own national interests. We must stop deceiving ourselves as to what
our own interests are in Cambodia and in all of Southeast Asia. The
first step in this process should be to prevent Cambodia from becoming a profitable mercenary war for the Thais or anyone else. A
second step would be to apply the same policy to Laos and to Vietnam. . . .

THE GRIFFIN AMENDMENT*

Mr. GRIFFIN. [Page S10156.] Mr. President, the debate in which
the Senate is engaged is an historic one. It concerns the manner in
which the United States will meet its responsibilities as leader of
the free world. It concerns such questions as whether and how the
United States will use its influence to preserve peace and stability
in Asia and the Pacific.

It concerns the very heart of the Nixon doctrine.

Mr. President, I shall, upon conclusion of my remarks, offer an
amendment to subsection (3) which would modify the Church-Cooper language to make it read as follows:

No funds authorized or appropriated pursuant to this
Act or any other law may be expended after July 1, 1970
for the purpose of---

(3) entering into or carrying out any contract or
agreement to provide military instruction in Cambodia by
United States personnel or to provide United States personnel to engage in any combat activity in support of
Cambodian forces;

The operative change in the amendment to subsection (3) is to insert the words "by United States personnel" in two places.

The purpose of the amendment is to make clear that the United
States would not be enjoined by the Church-Cooper language from assisting non-Communist nations in Asia which stand prepared to cooperate in
lending support to a neighboring country in dire need, in this case,
particularly Cambodia.

The amendment we offer would not authorize anything, but it would
modify the broad language of subparagraph 3 of the Church-Cooper amendment, which goes far beyond the "mercenary" issue; it would actually
nullify the Nixon doctrine so far as Cambodia is concerned.

Indeed, if the Church-Cooper language as now presented, were to
be enacted into law, the so-called Nixon doctrine would apply to all
non-Communist nations in Asia except Cambodia.

It is understandable that the sponsors of the Cooper-Church language do not want American forces to become involved in Cambodia.
Obviously, the Church-Cooper amendment was precipitated by the temporary incursion ordered by President Nixon to clean out Communist sanctuaries inside the Cambodian border.

Many people who have been reading about the Church-Cooper amendment are laboring under assumption that it deals only with the use of
American forces in Cambodia. Well, it does deal with the use of
American forces in Cambodia, but what many people in and out of the
Senate have overlooked is that the Church-Cooper language goes much
further. Indeed, it seeks not only to preclude the use of American
troops in Cambodia but the Church-Cooper language [Page S10157.] says
in effect that we cannot help any other country in Asia which is willing to come to the aid of Cambodia.

As the Church-Cooper amendment now stands, and I refer particularly
to subparagraph (3), it defeats its own purpose.

I know that those who support the Church-Cooper language are
trying to guarantee that indirect involvement in Cambodia by the United
States will not lead to direct involvement of the U.S. forces. But it
goes too far. . . .

It is self-defeating for two reasons.

First,it is in the interest of the United States that the non-
Communist nations of Asia be able to carry the primary burden of their
own defense. In practical terms, this would be impossible if those
who receive U.S. military assistance are not allowed to turn to one
another for aid and support.

Second, to enact subparagraph 3 as it now stands would set a precedent that will give alarm to our friends and allies elsewhere around
the world whose mutual cooperation we have been encouraging for the
past 25 years.

In the President's statement at Guam in mid-1969, and in his report to the Congress on U.S. foreign policy for the 1970's, Mr. Nixon
observed that we look to Asian nations to increasingly assume the
primary responsibility for their own defense. He said:

This approach requires our commitment to helping our partners develop their own strength. In doing so, we must strike a careful balance. If we do too little to help them . . . they may lose the necessary will to conduct their own self-defense or become disheartened about prospects of development. Yet if we do too much, and American forces do what local forces can and should be doing, we promote dependence rather than independence. . . .

I realize the sponsors of the Cooper-Church language want us to disconnect ourselves in such a way from Asian efforts at collective self-defense that we will not become directly involved in Cambodia. I respect their intentions.

But as the amendment now stands, it would mandate abdication of our responsibility, and it would discourage our friends from shouldering theirs.

On the other hand, our amendment recognizes American supportive responsibility, and would enable us to carry it out in a way that makes clear to other countries that the direct burden for their defense rests with them and not in the United States.

This brings us to the second reason why the language of subparagraph 3 of the Church-Cooper amendment is so broad as to be self-defeating. As I said earlier, to enact the amendment as it now stands would set a precedent that will give alarm to our friends and allies elsewhere around the world whose mutual collaboration we have been encouraging. . . .

[Page S10158.] Discouraging our friends from helping one another is no way to bring peace to Asia; nor does it make it easier to bring American men home. . . .

If section 3 of the Church-Cooper language were enacted without amendment, it would mean that our friends among the Asian and Pacific powers would have their hands tied, specifically with relation to Cambodia. And the effects could be more far reaching than that.

If this is to be the American response when an Asian nation comes to the aid of another Asian nation, we will certainly not be building or encouraging the self-reliance that is so desperately needed.

Our amendment is designed to protect the basic intent of the Nixon doctrine, and support individual and collective efforts by the countries of the region to defend themselves. . . .

There are some who will say that the United States intends to hire mercenaries to act as proxy warriors. They point to the fact that during the previous administration arrangements were made under which the United States agreed to meet the operating expenses of certain units in Vietnam. They argue that the previous administration, in order to fly more flags in Vietnam, paid for units which otherwise would not have been sent.

Nothing of that kind is contemplated by this administration with respect to Cambodia. What our amendment seeks to do is to keep the door open so that if other nations in Southeast Asia wish to assist

Cambodia they can do so without being penalized by the loss of U.S. economic and military assistance, in accordance with the Nixon doctrine.

It should not be overlooked that the foreign forces which the United States may in the past have helped to support South Vietnam were brought there at a time when the United States was rapidly building up its military presence. Whatever economic or military aid the present administration may provide today to friendly nations in Southeast Asia, would come at a time when we are rapidly reducing our military presence in Southeast Asia.

It is essential to keep in mind that other countries in the area, such as Thailand, have a direct national interest in aiding Cambodia. If Cambodia should fall to Communist aggression, who will say that neighboring countries such as Thailand would not be in grave danger?

If one man's mercenary is another man's patriot, then clearly much depends upon which side of the coin we examine. . . .

Mr. CHURCH. [Page S10160.] Mr. President, it has been argued that the adoption of the Griffin amendment is necessary if the United States is to implement the so-called Nixon doctrine. I find this argument difficult to grasp. The President himself, on November 3, in the course of an address to the Nation, defined the Nixon doctrine as follows: "In accordance with this wise counsel---" said the President---

I laid down in Guam three principles as guidelines for future American policy toward Asia. First, the United States will keep all of its treaty commitments. Second, we shall provide a shield if a nuclear power threatens the freedom of a nation allied with us or of a nation whose survival we consider vital to our security. Third, in cases involving other types of assistance, we shall furnish military and economic assistance when requested, in accordance with our treaty commitments, but we shall look to the nation directly threatened to assume the primary responsibility of providing the manpower for its defense.

Now that is the definition of the Nixon doctrine according to its author, Mr. Nixon. He carefully applied the doctrine to those countries to which we are presently committed by treaty. In his explanation, he referred twice to our treaty commitments. He carefully avoided reference to countries not aligned with us.

No treaty commitment, of any kind, is owed to Cambodia. We have assumed no obligation for the defense of that country, formally or informally. There is no mutual defense treaty between the United States and Cambodia; neither is there any Executive agreement. Every Senator has acknowledged, throughout this debate, that we have no obligation to Cambodia. Cambodia, therefore, falls outside of the scope of the Nixon doctrine, as defined by the President himself.

Second, President Nixon stated that his Guam pronouncement was a policy declaration that the United States would only furnish military assistance to those Asian governments willing to fight for themselves.

Listen to the President's own words:

> But we shall look to the nation directly threatened
> to assume the primary responsibility of providing the
> manpower for its defense.

Are we now going to convert a valid policy of providing arms and
equipment to a country that is willing to defend itself into something
quite different? Is this to become a policy of hired guns and paid
mercenaries, labeled the Nixon doctrine? That, I suggest, is the
effect of the amendment offered by the Senator from Michigan. At the
very least, it is a gross distortion of what the President has said
his own doctrine is. And at the very worst, it is a total departure
from the best traditions of American foreign policy. It also raises
questions which we think the Congress should consider if American
support for mercenaries is to become our policy toward Cambodia.

There are reasons why we feel so strongly. The previous administration did not consult with Congress in regard to agreements the
United States made with Asian countries whereby their troops were
hired at a profitable price to fight in South Vietnam.

In some instances, it has taken Congress years to find out about
those agreements. It was the insistent investigatory effort of the
Symington Subcommittee which enabled us to discover what was taking
place in countries such as Laos; which enabled us to ascertain that
large sums of money were paid to the Philippine Government for 2,500
troops sent to Vietnam, yet never fought there, and have now returned
home. Many millions of dollars were involved, much of which was
siphoned off in ways that have never been explained.

Throughout this unfortunate period, Congress remained ignorant of
these secret agreements made with the Philippine, Korean, Lao, and
Thai Governments. Only years later, left to our own investigatory
devices, did we find out what had been done in secret dealings.

That may be the way some Members of the Senate view the conduct
of constitutional government. That may be the demeaning role some
Members want the Congress to play. If it is, then we no longer are
the legislative body fashioned by the Constitution of the United States.

When Congress is not even informed of such dubious aggrangements,
let alone asked to consent, the President is being allowed to usurp
congressional power. We should confess our error, and correct our
practices before congressional power wastes away.

[Page S10161.] The Cooper-Church amendment would not prohibit the
hiring of mercenaries, if that is to be the American policy in Cambodia.
Our amendment would prohibit that policy from taking effect without
the Congress being first informed by the President and without his receiving congressional consent. . . .

One of the most unsavory aspects of the history of warfare---man's
seemingly prime occupation---is the role of the mercenary. By briefest
of definitions, a mercenary is a "hired gun." This is not a pretty
label, but it is an accurate one.

Hiring mercenaries has been practiced by expansionist city-states and nations as far back as written records serve the historian.

The doleful list of mercenary involvement is a long one:

The Romans, in their lust for empire, employed Aegean bowmen and Carthaginian cavalrymen.

The imperious Persian king, Darius, had his Greek mercenaries.

The French had their Swiss mercenaries in the frightful Thirty Years War of Religions. Actually, the Swiss were quite bipartisan about the matter. They rented themselves out to all sides during this war, thereby, as one historical account phrased it, providing Switzerland and "an important source of foreign exchange."

The Turks employed Albanian mercenaries on their westward lunge for empire.

The British had their continental mercenaries to subjugate forcibly the Irish.

But as we approach the 200th anniversary of our Nation's founding, the one mercenary example that should be particularly hateful to us Americans was the use of Hessian mercenaries by the British during the American Revolution. In Massachusetts, in New York, in New Jersey, the Colonies to the South, thousands of Hessians fought General Washington's troops. As in most cases of mercenaries, the bargain was a bad one for the British. The Hessians did not fight very well. And the use of mercenaries was a goad that buttressed the determination of the English-speaking American colonists---revolutionists really---to fight more determinedly for their cherished independence.

The Senate will vote tomorrow on the Griffin amendment, which will permit this country to employ combat troops of third-party nations--- mercenaries---to fight in Cambodia in support of the Lon Nol government without Congress being informed and without benefit of congressional participation or consent. At the same time, the United States will be embracing a marked characteristic of past empires---the hiring of mercenary armies.

The Griffin amendment, moreover, casts the most serious pall over the Nixon doctrine. Rather than furnishing weapons to Asian governments whose citizens are willing to do their own fighting, the Griffin amendment would convert the Nixon doctrine into a policy of American-financed wars by proxy.

Is the Nixon doctrine to be an acceptable and valid program of provisioning Asian governments with supplies and equipment with which to defend themselves? Or is the watchword of the Nixon doctrine to become "Hessians Unlimited"?. . .

The Congress, and particularly the appropriate committees of both Houses, have the right---in fact the responsibility---to be informed about, to review and to pass judgment on any agreements that precede the sending of third-country forces into Cambodia financed by U.S. funds.

The effect of the amendment by the distinguished Senator from

Michigan (Mr. GRIFFIN) would be to permit the administration to enter into any agreement, pay any price, and cover up whatever deal is struck with any country that sends combat troops or advisers into Cambodia.

We have heard a good deal of misleading talk that this section of the Cooper-Church amendment would prevent "Asians from fighting Asians," or that it would prevent our giving arms to countries which wish to aid Cambodia.

Neither of these is true.

The amendment would in no way stop Thais or South Vietnamese trainers or combat forces from going to the aid of the Cambodian Government provided their own governments pay the salaries and allowances of their own forces.

Let me emphasize that last phrase, for it is in the nub of this argument---provided their own governments pay the salaries and allowances of their own forces.

It is not an overstatement to say that we have made it profitable for the individual Thai, the individual South Korean and---before they left---the individual Philippine officer and enlisted man to serve in South Vietnam.

I want to emphasize that we do not pay the basic salaries of any of their forces in South Vietnam. We therefore do not---as some have tried to say---make it possible for them to go. Rather, we make it profitable.

At this point, I ask unanimous consent to have printed in the Record a table prepared for the Symington subcommittee by the Department of Defense which compares the base pay of Thai officers and enlisted men, as paid by their own government, with the special supplementary allowances paid to them by the United States. In every case, the allowance paid by the United States is above, and in some cases more than double, the individual's base pay.

There being no objection, the table was ordered to be printed in the Record, as follows:

ROYAL THAI ARMED FORCES (RTARF) PAY AND
ALLOWANCES FOR THAI PERSONNEL IN VIETNAM

That Government fiscal costs, including RTARF pay, allowances and benefit schedules for overseas service, are set forth below. Pursuant to an agreement with the Thai Government, the United States covers the costs of certain of the items listed, the others being paid by the RTG with no USG reimbursement.

The Thai Government pays without reimbursement base pay for Thai troops in Vietnam and numerous standard Thai allowances, e.g., hazardous duty pay, combat pay, education, transportation discount, etc., and other costs not specifically associated with service in Vietnam.

The United States has agreed to cover certain additional costs connected with the Thai Government's sending and maintaining these troops outside of Thailand.
These include overseas allowances based on normal Thai
overseas rates, death and disability benefits and a
mustering-out bonus. While the Thai troops are in Vietnam, the U.S. also provides quarters and rations and
other support in the logistical area (e.g., transport,
ammo, etc.). The overseas allowance is paid in military
payment certificates in South Vietnam. The death and
disability benefits and the mustering-out bonuses are paid
in baht in Thailand.

All data below are presented in dollar equivalents on
a monthly basis. A conversion rate of B20 equal $1 has been
used.

RTARF PAY AND OVERSEAS ALLOWANCES IN VIETNAM

[Per Thai regulations and expressed in U.S. dollar
equivalent on a monthly basis]

	Base pay (paid by Thailand)	Overseas allowance (paid by United States)	Monthly total
Lieutenant general	$370	$450	$820
Major general	330	390	720
Special colonel	240	330	570
Colonel	190	300	490
Lieutenant colonel	140	240	380
Major	98	180	278
Captain	70	150	220
Lieutenant	50	120	170
Master sergeant	48	69	117
Sergeant	38	60	98
Corporal	33	50	83
Lance corporal	30	45	75
Private	26	39	65

Note: Quarters and rations paid by United States.

DEATH AND DISABILITY (1-TIME PAYMENTS) PAID BY
UNITED STATES

Enlisted men	$2,500
Noncommissioned officers	3,500
Officers	5,500

In the case of disabilities, these rates were scaled
downward according to the nature of the disability.
Mustering-out bonus of $400 per volunteer.

Source: "United States Security Agreements and Commitments
Abroad---Kingdom of Thailand Hearings," Senate Foreign Relations Subcommittee on U.S. Security Agreements and Commitments Abroad, pt. 3,
p. 842.

Mr. CHURCH. I would also note that the allowance paid to Thai officers exceeds the combat pay allowance given U.S. officers serving in Vietnam.

There are other personal U.S.-paid benefits given these Thai troops---some of which, like $400 mustering-out bonuses---are in the published record. Still others---at the request of the State Department---are classified.

There are other ramifications to this question of paying bonuses to foreign troops and thereby making out-of-country adventures profitable to them.

The practice has distinct political disadvantages both to the United States and to the country involved.

In Thailand, for example, where there is a minimal---but persistent---insurgent movement, the allowances to troops going to Vietnam works a morale problem within those forces that stay home. Thai army elements must fight at home against alleged Communist insurgents for half the pay---or less---that their comrades get fighting Communists in South Vietnam. . . .

Mr. SCOTT subsequently said: [Page S10165.] Mr. President, I have heard so many references to mercenaries by those who are opposed to the Griffin amendment.

The Griffin amendment simply permits Asians to help Asians and clarifies the fact that there should be no legislative amendment to an Executive doctrine, the Guam doctrine.

The Griffin amendment, after all, is in keeping with our desire to remove the American presence as soon as may be possible from Southeast Asia. We cannot remove the Asian presence from Southeast Asia. They will be there after we have gone.

They have a right to defend themselves. They have a right to concerted action among themselves as to how they will defend themselves.

We engage here in a lot of semantics. The current semantic phrase is mercenaries. I want to say this about the so-called mercenaries: In World War II when the Poles went to Scotland and then into Western Europe for the liberation of Western Europe; were they mercenaries?

When the free French returned to the land of their birth, were they mercenaries? When Eisenhower took the armed forces of our allies into Normandy, was that an invasion, or was that an act meeting with the approval of the free peoples of that territory?

When the United Nations decided to repel aggression in Korea, the Turkish forces went there. No one called the Turks mercenaries, even though the other word for mercenaries, "Janizaries," originates from the Turkish language.

When the British troops went to Korea, no one called them mercenaries.

Why do we call Asians who want to help other Asians mercenaries?

That is not good enough.

This is a good amendment. It would clarify the bill. It would make the Cooper-Church amendment a great deal more palatable to some supporters, but above everything else, why do we indulge in phrases like mercenaries when, in all due sincerity, I do not think we mean what we say.

What we are saying is that we do not want Asians to help Asians. And if we do not let Asians help Asians, we will leave the Americans on the hook, stuck there indefinitely, to help the Asians.

We have a choice. We cannot have it both ways. And I would rather have the Griffin amendment.

Mr. COOPER. Mr. President, our amendment does not prohibit the use of other nationals in Cambodia. It says, "If you want to use them, pay for them."

There is no prohibition in the amendment against the use of other nationals without the advance approval of the United States.

Mr. SCOTT. Mr. President, as I understand the amendment, without the Griffin amendment, it would not be possible for the United States to conduct its aid to Thailand if the Thais were to assist the Cambodians.

There is no American in Cambodia tonight. And that is good. I hope it is never necessary for us to go back. But I still think we ought not to tie the hands of the Thais now or in the future if the Thai government, a sovereign nation, wishes to go to the aid of the Cambodians. It is a neutral country.

I do thank the distinguished Senator from Kentucky. . . .

ROLL CALLS ON THE GRIFFIN AMENDMENT*

(June 30, 1970)

The PRESIDING OFFICER. . . . [Page S10264.]

The question is on agreeing to the amendment offered by the Senator from Michigan (Mr. GRIFFIN). On this question the yeas and nays have been ordered, and the clerk will call the roll. . . .

The result was announced---yeas 47, nays 46, as follows:

[No. 190 Leg.]

YEAS---47

Allen	Bible	Cotton
Allott	Boggs	Curtis
Anderson	Byrd, Va.	Dole
Baker	Byrd, W. Va.	Dominick
Bellmon	Cannon	Eastland
Bennett	Cook	Ellender

YEAS- (Continued)

Ervin	McClellan	Sparkman
Fong	McGee	Stennis
Goldwater	Miller	Stevens
Griffin	Murphy	Symington
Gurney	Packwood	Talmadge
Hansen	Pearson	Thurmond
Holland	Percy	Tower
Hruska	Prouty	Williams, Del.
Jackson	Scott	Young, N. Dak.
Jordan, Idaho	Smith, Ill.	

NAYS---46

Aiken	Hatfield	Muskie
Bayh	Hollings	Pastore
Brooke	Hughes	Pell
Burdick	Inouye	Proxmire
Case	Javits	Randolph
Church	Jordan, N. C.	Ribicoff
Cooper	Kennedy	Saxbe
Cranston	Magnuson	Schweiker
Eagleton	Mansfield	Smith, Maine
Fulbright	Mathias	Spong
Goodell	McCarthy	Tydings
Gore	McGovern	Williams, N. J.
Gravel	McIntyre	Yarborough
Harris	Metcalf	Young, Ohio
Hart	Montoya	
Hartke	Moss	

PRESENT AND GIVING A LIVE PAIR, AS
PREVIOUSLY RECORDED---1

Long, for.

NOT VOTING---6

Dodd	Mondale	Nelson
Fannin	Mundt	Russell

So Mr. GRIFFIN'S amendment No. 716 was agreed to.

Mr. MANSFIELD. Mr. President, I move to reconsider the vote by which the amendment was agreed to. . . .

Mr. DOLE. Mr. President, will the Chair advise me whether we are voting on a motion to table or a motion to reconsider?

The PRESIDING OFFICER. The Senate is voting on whether to table the motion to reconsider the vote by which the amendment was agreed to. On this question the yeas and nays have been ordered, and the clerk will call the roll.

The legislative clerk proceeded to call the roll.

The PRESIDING OFFICER. (Mr. GRAVEL). Senators will please take seats. The roll call has been suspended until there is decorum in

the Chamber.   Senators will please be seated.   Every Senator is aware
of all the interest in this vote.   It is the desire of the Chair that
no mistakes be made by the clerks.

The Senate will be in order.

The call of the roll was resumed and concluded.

The result was announced---yeas 46, nays 47, as follows:

[No. 191 Leg.]

YEAS---46

Allen	Ervin	Packwood
Allott	Fannin	Pearson
Anderson	Fong	Percy
Baker	Goldwater	Prouty
Bellmon	Griffin	Scott
Bennett	Gurney	Smith, Ill.
Bible	Hansen	Sparkman
Boggs	Holland	Stennis
Byrd, Va.	Hruska	Stevens
Cannon	Jackson	Talmadge
Cook	Jordan, Idaho	Thurmond
Cotton	Long	Tower
Curtis	McClellan	Williams, Del.
Dole	McGee	Young, N. Dak.
Dominick	Miller	
Eastland	Murphy	

NAYS---47

Aiken	Hollings	Muskie
Brooke	Hughes	Pastore
Burdick	Inouye	Pell
Case	Javits	Proxmire
Church	Jordan, N. C.	Randolph
Cooper	Kennedy	Ribicoff
Cranston	Magnuson	Saxbe
Eagleton	Mansfield	Schweiker
Fulbright	Mathias	Smith, Maine
Goodell	McCarthy	Spong
Gore	McGovern	Symington
Gravel	McIntyre	Tydings
Harris	Metcalf	Williams, N. J.
Hart	Mondale	Yarborough
Hartke	Montoya	Young, Ohio
Hatfield	Moss	

PRESENT AND GIVING A LIVE PAIR, AS
PREVIOUSLY RECORDED---1

Byrd of West Virginia, for.

NOT VOTING---6

Bayh	Ellender	Nelson
Dodd	Mundt	Russell

So the motion to table the motion to reconsider the vote by which the Griffin amendment was agreed to was rejected.

Mr. DOLE. Mr. President, a parliamentary inquiry.

The PRESIDING OFFICER. The question is on the reconsideration of the vote.

Mr. MANSFIELD. Mr. President, I ask for the yeas and nays.

The yeas and nays were ordered. . . .

[Page S10265.] The result was announced---yeas 49, nays **46**, as follows:

[No. 192 Leg.]

YEAS---49

Aiken	Hatfield	Muskie
Bayh	Hollings	Pastore
Brooke	Hughes	Pell
Burdick	Inouye	Proxmire
Case	Javits	Randolph
Church	Jordan, N. C.	Ribicoff
Cooper	Kennedy	Saxbe
Cranston	Magnuson	Schweiker
Eagleton	Mansfield	Smith, Maine
Ellender	Mathias	Spong
Fulbright	McCarthy	Symington
Goodell	McGovern	Tydings
Gore	McIntyre	Williams, N. J.
Gravel	Metcalf	Yarborough
Harris	Mondale	Young, Ohio
Hart	Montoya	
Hartke	Moss	

NAYS---46

Allen	Ervin	Packwood
Allott	Fannin	Pearson
Anderson	Fong	Percy
Baker	Goldwater	Prouty
Bellmon	Griffin	Scott
Bennett	Gurney	Smith, Ill.
Bible	Hansen	Sparkman
Boggs	Holland	Stennis
Byrd, Va.	Hruska	Stevens
Cannon	Jackson	Talmadge
Cook	Jordan, Idaho	Thurmond
Cotton	Long	Tower
Curtis	McClellan	Williams, Del.
Dole	McGee	Young, N. Dak.
Dominick	Miller	
Eastland	Murphy	

PRESENT AND GIVING A LIVE PAIR, AS
PREVIOUSLY RECORDED---1

Mr. Byrd of West Virginia, against

NOT VOTING---4

Dodd   Nelson   Russell
Mundt

So the motion to reconsider was agreed to.

Mr. BYRD of West Virginia addressed the Chair.

The VICE PRESIDENT. The Senator from West Virginia is recognized.

The Senate will be in order.

Mr. BYRD of West Virginia. Mr. President, I ask that the Chair state to the galleries the provisions in rule XIX which preclude demonstrations of approval or disapproval upon the announcement of a vote.

The VICE PRESIDENT. The Chair advises the occupants of the galleries that they are guests of the Senate and they must not in any way applaud or show approval or disapproval of the action of the Senate. If the galleries show any discourtesy or action, the Chair will feel compelled to have the galleries cleared.

The clerk will call the roll.

The assistant legislative clerk proceeded to call the roll. . . .

The yeas and nays resulted---45 yeas, 50 nays, as follows:

[No. 193 Leg.]

YEAS---45

Allen	Eastland	Murphy
Allott	Ervin	Packwood
Anderson	Fannin	Pearson
Baker	Fong	Percy
Bellmon	Goldwater	Prouty
Bennett	Griffin	Scott
Bible	Gurney	Smith, Ill.
Boggs	Hansen	Sparkman
Byrd, Va.	Holland	Stennis
Cannon	Hruska	Stevens
Cook	Jackson	Talmadge
Cotton	Jordan, Idaho	Thurmond
Curtis	McClellan	Tower
Dole	McGee	Williams, Del.
Dominick	Miller	Young, N. Dak.

NAYS---50

Aiken	Cranston	Harris
Bayh	Eagleton	Hart
Brooke	Ellender	Hartke
Burdick	Fulbright	Hatfield
Case	Goodell	Hollings
Church	Gore	Hughes
Cooper	Gravel	Inouye

NAYS-(Continued)

Javits	Metcalf	Saxbe
Jordan, N. C.	Mondale	Schweiker
Kennedy	Montoya	Smith, Maine
Long	Moss	Spong
Magnuson	Muskie	Symington
Mansfield	Pastore	Tydings
Mathias	Pell	Williams, N. J.
McCarthy	Proxmire	Yarborough
McGovern	Randolph	Young, Ohio
McIntyre	Ribicoff	

PRESENT AND GIVING A LIVE PAIR, AS
PREVIOUSLY RECORDED---1

Mr. Byrd of West Virginia, for.

NOT VOTING---4

Dodd	Nelson	Russell
Mundt		

The VICE PRESIDENT. On this vote the yeas are 45 and the nays
are 50. The amendment is rejected. A motion to reconsider is not
in order. . . .

THE JACKSON AMENDMENT*

Mr. COOPER. [Page S10267.] We agreed that the purpose of our
subsection (3) is to prohibit combat activity over Cambodia by U.S.
forces in support of Cambodia.

The Senator has moved to amend the amendment by inserting the
word "direct" before the word "support." I am not questioning the
Senator's statement. But I want to get the Senator's interpretation.

Are we leaving the doors open? Could the United States so use
its Air Force above Cambodia, while not directly, but indirectly on
doubtful missions, over Cambodia, for the purpose of supporting the
Cambodian forces?

Mr. JACKSON. My amendment narrows the issue in language that I
think is clearly unequivocal. I shall repeat what I said in my opening statement. My amendment makes unequivocal the prohibition on providing direct air support to Cambodian forces. I will read what I
said in offering the amendment:

> I offer this one-word change, not with a view to
> making a substantive change in the Cooper-Church amend-
> ment, but, rather, to incorporate in the amendment itself
> what we take to be the principal objective of its spon-
> sors---that we refrain from activity that could lead to
> getting bogged down in Cambodia. Direct air support to
> Cambodian forces might lead us down that path. Air activi-
> ties, however, aimed primarily at the defense of our forces

in Vietnam, and the forces of the South Vietnamese, would
be consistent with my understanding of the intention of
the Cooper-Church amendment.

What I am saying here is what I understood to be the intent of the
sponsors. All I am trying to do is make the language definite and
certain.

Mr. COOPER. As the Senator from Arkansas noted, it appears from
the newspapers that the United States is providing air support for Cambodian forces.

Mr. JACKSON. Direct air support.

Mr. COOPER. At this moment I do not know whether this is correct
or not. I simply wish to ask if the Senator's amendment would in any
way approve in advance such activity?

Mr. JACKSON. My amendment would clearly and unequivocally prohibit it because the situation to which the Senator refers relates to
support exclusively of Cambodian forces. The amendment would not prohibit support for non-Cambodian forces.

Mr. COOPER. I understand they may be closely merged.

Mr. FULBRIGHT. Mr. President, will the Senator yield?

Mr. JACKSON. I yield.

Mr. FULBRIGHT. There is one point the Senator raised I had not
thought of and that is the business of the Ho Chi Minh Trail in protection of our own forces. To illustrate the point, let us assume
the South Vietnamese become more and more excited over the prospect
of taking Cambodia and pursue on their own an aggressive campaign
throughout Cambodia. Will we, without congressional approval, give
them close tactical air support if they begin to move all over Cambodia?

Mr. JACKSON. The present Cooper-Church amendment does not prohibit that. That is my understanding. . . .

We cannot do what has been done in the past---providing direct
support. I do not want to get bogged down in Cambodia.

Mr. FULBRIGHT. But we could get bogged down as satellites of the
South Vietnamese.

Mr. JACKSON. We could get bogged, no matter what.

Mr. FULBRIGHT. And if we do, Congress should have a voice in the
matter.

Mr. JACKSON. This amendment does help clarify what I understand
is the situation.

Mr. FULBRIGHT. I agree up to that point. When the Senators
mention the South Vietnamese that is another question. If they are
determined to stay there, as Mr. Ky says they are, are we going to
give them close air support without the approval of Congress?

Mr. JACKSON. I hope they do not stay there.

Mr. FULBRIGHT. Now they are beginning to say they are going to stay. The Senator does not want us to stay with them, does he?

Mr. JACKSON. I do not want the South Vietnamese, the ARVN forces, to stay any longer than is necessary to protect their forces in withdrawing from Cambodia. I am not going to be a party to a further campaign in support of Cambodia.

Mr. FULBRIGHT. That is what I want to make clear.

Mr. DOLE. Mr. President, will the Senator yield?

The VICE PRESIDENT. All time of the Senator from Idaho has expired. The Senator from Washington has 10 minutes remaining.

Mr. JACKSON. I yield 3 minutes to the Senator from Kansas.

Mr. DOLE. Mr. President, I support the amendment of the Senator from Washington.

Mr. President, I think it has been made clear in debate that they would have that right to make air strikes and keep the Vietnamization program on in Cambodia to protect American forces schedule. But who will make the decision as to whether it is direct? Is that decision to be made by the Senate or the generals? Who makes that determination?

Mr. JACKSON. This would have to be an executive decision by the President exercised through his chain of command. Congress runs into differences on the problem of the authority of the President as Commander in Chief and the responsibility of Congress to provide the funds to support the Armed Forces.

The point I am making is that there could be some very close cases where U.S. action might be construed as direct support of Cambodian forces and others where it would be protection of American forces. . . .

This could result from many situations, especially on the battlefield. But at least we have a responsibility to try to make our position as clear as we can and that is what I am trying to do. In the end it would, of course, be necessary for Congress, upon appropriate investigation, to decide whether they want to make another change. . . .

ROLL CALL ON THE JACKSON AMENDMENT*

[Page S10268.] The assistant legislative clerk called the roll.

The result was announced---yeas 69, nays 27, as follows:

[No. 194 Leg.]

YEAS---69

Aiken	Ervin	Montoya
Allen	Fannin	Murphy
Allott	Fong	Packwood
Anderson	Fulbright	Pastore
Baker	Goldwater	Pearson
Bayh	Gravel	Pell
Bellmon	Griffin	Percy
Bennett	Gurney	Prouty
Bible	Hansen	Randolph
Boggs	Hartke	Scott
Burdick	Holland	Smith, Maine
Byrd, Va.	Hollings	Smith, Ill.
Byrd, W. Va.	Hruska	Sparkman
Cannon	Jackson	Spong
Church	Jordan, N. C.	Stennis
Cook	Jordan, Idaho	Stevens
Cotton	Long	Symington
Cranston	Magnuson	Talmadge
Curtis	Mansfield	Thurmond
Dole	McClellan	Tower
Dominick	McGee	Tydings
Eastland	McIntyre	Williams, Del.
Ellender	Miller	Young, N. Dak.

NAYS---27

Brooke	Hughes	Moss
Case	Inouye	Muskie
Cooper	Javits	Proxmire
Eagleton	Kennedy	Ribicoff
Goodell	Mathias	Saxbe
Gore	McCarthy	Schweiker
Harris	McGovern	Williams, N. J.
Hart	Metcalf	Yarborough
Hatfield	Mondale	Young, Ohio

NOT VOTING---4

Dodd	Nelson	Russell
Mundt		

So Mr. JACKSON'S amendment was agreed to.

DEBATE: THE FINALE*

Mr. MANSFIELD. [Page S10270.] Mr. President, it is said that the House of Representatives will not approve Cooper-Church should it pass the Senate. It is said that if Cooper-Church clears the Congress, in all probability, it will be vetoed by the President.

Whether these predicates are true in whole or part or not true

at all remains to be seen. I hope they are not true. True or not,
however, they do not and cannot detract one iota from this vote today.

The Senate cannot answer for the President. The Senate cannot
answer for the House. The Senate can speak only for the Senate. In
the vote on Cooper-Church, today, Senators will most assuredly do so,
as individuals and collectively. What is said will be most significant, in my judgment, to the future of this Nation.

Cooper-Church is a response to a pattern of Executive actions in
Southeast Asia which has been evolving for years and which has now
raised constitutional questions regarding the responsibilities of the
Senate in the gravest questions which confront the Nation---the questions for war and peace. It is a pattern whereby the Congress was
first invited to join with the executive branch, as in the Tonkin
Gulf resolution, in delineating a policy, presumably for peace in Vietnam. Therefore, the Congress discovered it had joined in a strategy
which led to war. The Congress was carried along into the ever-
deepening military involvement in Vietnam.

At first, it was maintained that we had endorsed this course by
passing the Tonkin Gulf resolution. Then, several years ago, the
executive branch decreed that Congress had not really been needed to
legitimize the course. With or without Congress, it was contended,
the executive branch could pursue whatever military measures were appropriate under the unilateral powers of the Presidency.

So, the grip of death and destruction which is Vietnam was fixed
ever more tightly not only on Southeast Asia but on the neck of this
Nation. All the while, Congress has been progressively excluded, even
from consultation, on the decisions which have sustained this tragic
involvement year after year after year.

A few weeks ago, the matter was brought to a head by the investi-
ture of Cambodian border areas with a massive U.S. military incursion.
The executive branch, unilaterally, decreed this advance of our forces
across an international border. The executive branch, unilaterally,
decreed that Cambodia should be added to the Vietnamese theater of
war. Congress was not privy to the decisions which led to this expansion. The Senate leadership was not consulted in either party.
The committees of the Senate were not consulted. The advice of the
Senate was not sought. The consent of the Senate was not requested,
nor was it given.

According to those responsible, the military operation in Cambodia has been a great "success" and U.S. forces have now been withdrawn. May I say that, notwithstanding my view of the initial action,
the President is to be commended for insisting that the withdrawal be
completed by his military commanders by June 30. That decision, at
least, has had some limiting effect on what was undertaken.

We are advised that great quantities of war material have been
seized in this successful operation in Cambodia. Great destruction
has been visited on hostile military bases. Thousands of hostile
Vietnamese are reported killed.

These reports, I am sure, are carefully compiled by the computers.
They are, undoubtedly, some sort of a measure of "military success."
What they do not measure is what the success will yield in the end.

The fact is that the road into the quagmire of U.S. involvement in Indochina has been lit with the fires of an endless succession of military successes. These other successes---5 years of successes---I am
sure, were all accurately computed and reported in their turn, but the
war goes on---deeper and deeper into Southeast Asia.

     Nevertheless, we may take the assurances of those responsible
that Cambodia was a great military success, the greatest of the war.
We may take these assurances notwithstanding the fact 339 Americans
died in Cambodia and 1,501 were wounded. We may take them even
though great segments of Cambodia which were once free of Vietcong and
North Vietnamese are now serving as bases of operations for these
forces. We may take these assurances, even though this newest success
has led to a new U.S. aid commitment at an initial cost of millions in
equipment and supplies and, apparently, a commitment of U.S. air support and bombing runs in Cambodia; all this new expenditure of lives
and resources will take place in Cambodia, in an area where 4 months
ago this Nation spent no resources on aid and its forces were not engaged. Nevertheless, we may take the assurances of the success of
this adventure. We may take them even though it must be asked, who
will now pay to maintain the new government in Cambodia? Who will see
to its survival? Even though it must be asked how much beyond the
points of its bayonets does the influence of this government extend
among its own people?

     We may take these assurances if, for no other reason, than that
there is no relevance in a military postmortem at this time. The degree of success of the Cambodian operation is not involved here today.
How can it be involved when the necessity for Cooper-Church was con-
ceived before the beginning of the operation in Cambodia? What is
involved here is whether the Senate wants to try to inhibit new involvements of this Nation abroad, without prior consultation with the
Senate and without sanction from Congress---in Cambodia or elsewhere
in Southeast Asia or the world. . . .

     [Page S10271.] Reject Cooper-Church and, in my judgment, the Sen-
ate will have acquiesced in an indefinite continuance of the involvement in Southeast Asia and in a relentless accretion in U.S. casualties
and cost in Indochina. That is, I know, not wanted by the President.
Nor is it wanted by any Member of the Senate. But that is what we are
going to get. That is what the people of this Nation, in my judgment,
are going to get. The end of this involvement will remain, as it is
now, nowhere in sight.

     Reject Cooper-Church and, I say in all soberness, it would be
wise for the Senate to anticipate other Cambodias and other Vietnams,
elsewhere in the world. They may be expected under any kind of administration.

     Cooper-Church is not a guarantee of noninvolvement in Cambodia
or anywhere else. It is an attempt; it is not a certainty. However,
if it passes, we will have made clear, at least, that the Senate is
prepared to try to act with the President to forestall other Vietnams
which the President---any President---may be under pressure to undertake.

     If it passes, we will make clear, at least, the Senate's resist-
ance henceforth to the pattern of enlarging involvement in Southeast
Asia. We will make the Senate's position clear, irrespective of party

considerations here and irrespective of the views of the House or the
President. I say that most respectfully because, as do we, they have
their own responsibilities in this matter and may see them differently. . . .

To be sure, it is devoutly to be hoped that the House will concur
in Cooper-Church and that the President will sign the bill of which
it is a part. Indeed, in my judgment, the greater the cooperation
among the three elected parts of this Government, in this connection,
the greater the chance of finally extricating this Nation from this
hydra-headed war in Southeast Asia.

In my judgment, therefore, it is of the greatest significance
that Cooper-Church is not designed to conflict---and it is not---**with**
the President's constitutional Powers as Commander in Chief. Rather,
it is designed to permit the constitutional powers of both Congress
and the President to be meshed in a common effort to extricate the
Nation from the misbegotten situation in Southeast Asia. By passing
Cooper-Church, in my judgment, the Senate will have begun to move this
Government, beyond words, toward the end of the U.S. involvement in a
tragic and mistaken war, toward the restoration of this Nation's tranquility and well-being. . . .

Mr. McGEE. [Page S10272.] Mr. President, I want to say at this
late hour that I still think we are missing the point, that the many
weeks we have spent on this amendment should be addressed to the real
problem before the Senate: How do we update the role of the Senate
in the latter half of the 20th century to exercise its responsibility
in foreign policy in a nuclear age?

In a day when some people think we can only afford a limited war
if we have to test strategic areas, where else can we find the answer
to that but by a searching inquiry now?

We have a penchant in this country for looking backward. We spent
30 years trying to avoid World War I after it was over. We spent over
20 years after the fact trying to avoid World War II. Now we are trying to find out who is to blame for Vietnam.

I believe that we should be worrying about what we should be and
can be doing in a Burma crisis, an Indian crisis, or a Near East crisis.
I would therefore hope that the Committee on Foreign Relations, on
which I serve, will turn its energies, resources, and good judgment
into a searching exploration of a modern role for the Senate, in concert with the President of the United States, in projecting future
crisis decisions in the field of foreign policy. . . .

Mr. THURMOND. Mr. President, I rise in opposition to the Cooper-
Church amendment.

Passage of the Cooper-Church Amendment today by the U.S. Senate
would be a blow to the struggle of free men in Cambodia who are being
murdered daily by Communist forces from North Vietnam. Its effect
could bring down the new government of Cambodia. This would be followed by the positioning of Communist forces along the borders of
South Vietnam and Thailand which adjoin Cambodia. While many Americans feel this amendment would merely prevent the further introduction
of U.S. troops into Cambodia it goes much further in that it also prohibits U.S. help to any other country in Asia which is willing to come

to the aid of Cambodia. Thus the Senate would be waving the white
flag of surrender over Cambodia under the cloak of reassuming the
warmaking powers of the Congress. While it is may belief the House
of Representatives will never accept this amendment, the psychological
effect will be a repudiation of the Nixon doctrine which called upon
our Asian allies to stand together in their own defense: I favor
giving arms and other necessary aid to those Asian countries under attack by Communist forces as the surest means of permitting the reduction of U.S. military personnel in this area. At the same time such
a policy would enable the soldiers of Asia to possess the means to
successfully defend their own soil from Communist attacks. The passage of this amendment will also shake our allies in Asia and likely
weaken their resolve to stand up to Communist forces. In this respect
it is dangerous and could possibly be disastrous. The Senate would in
effect be casting Cambodia into the jaws of Communist expansion and,
if engulfed, South Vietnam and Thailand could follow. . . .

     [Page S10285.] . . . my opposition today to passage of the Mili-
tary Sales Act in its present form rests on the crippling amendments
affixed to the bill by the Senate Foreign Relations Committee. While
I support military sales and credits to our allies abroad, the bill
is replete with unwise amendments. These amendments, including the
Cooper-Church amendment, repudiate the Nixon doctrine of providing
sufficient military arms to our allies in Southeast Asia and encouraging them to provide for their own defense. A number of Senators
have stood on the Senate floor and stated it is not important to the
United States who governs in Southeast Aisa. Several have gone so
far as to state that a Communist government in South Vietnam would
promote tranquility in that area on grounds the North Vietnamese con-
querors would not submit to Red China. Such reasoning is devastating
to the hopes of free men everywhere and encourages the forces of oppression, thereby prolonging the murder of innocent people. The removal of U.S. fighting men from Southeast Asia is one thing, but restricting aid to local forces opposing Communist invaders is quite another. This trend in the Senate reveals the frustrations of the Vietnam war and could mark the beginning of a return to a fortress America
policy which would doom the struggle of freedom-loving people throughout the world.

     Mr. MANSFIELD. Mr. President, I ask for the yeas and nays on the
bill.

     The yeas and nays were ordered.

     The PRESIDING OFFICER. The bill is open to further amendment.
If there be no further amendment to be proposed, the question is on
the engrossment of the amendments, and the third reading of the bill.

     The amendments were ordered to be engrossed and the bill to be
read a third time.

     The bill was read the third time.

     The PRESIDING OFFICER (Mr. ALLOTT). The hour of 4 o'clock has
arrived. The bill (H.R. 15628) having been read the third time, the
question is, Shall it pass?

     On this question the yeas and nays have been ordered, and the
clerk will call the roll.

The bill clerk called the roll. . . .

ROLL CALL ON THE COOPER-CHURCH AMENDMENT*

The result was announced---yeas 75, nays 20, as follows:

[No. 196 Leg.]

YEAS---75

Aiken	Gravel	Moss
Allott	Griffin	Murphy
Anderson	Harris	Muskie
Baker	Hart	Packwood
Bayh	Hartke	Pastore
Bellmon	Hatfield	Pearson
Bennett	Hollings	Pell
Bible	Hruska	Percy
Boggs	Hughes	Prouty
Brooke	Jackson	Proxmire
Burdick	Javits	Randolph
Byrd, Va.	Jordan, N. C.	Ribicoff
Byrd, W. Va.	Kennedy	Saxbe
Cannon	Long	Schweiker
Case	Magnuson	Scott
Church	Mansfield	Smith, Maine
Cooper	Mathias	Smith, Ill.
Cranston	McCarthy	Sparkman
Curtis	McGee	Spong
Dole	McGovern	Stevens
Eagleton	McIntyre	Symington
Fong	Metcalf	Tydings
Fulbright	Miller	Williams, N. J.
Goodell	Mondale	Yarborough
Gore	Montoya	Young, Ohio

NAYS---20

Allen	Fannin	Stennis
Cook	Goldwater	Talmadge
Cotton	Gurney	Thurmond
Dominick	Hansen	Tower
Eastland	Holland	Williams, Del.
Ellender	Jordan, Idaho	Young, N. Dak.
Ervin	McClellan	

NOT VOTING---5

Dodd	Mundt	Russell
Inouye	Nelson	

So the bill (H.R. 15628) was passed. . . .

The title was amended, so as to read: "An act to amend the Foreign Military Sales Act, and for other purposes."

Mr. FULBRIGHT. Mr. President, I move that the Senate insist upon
its amendments and request a conference with the House, and that the
Chair be authorized to appoint the conferees on the part of the Senate.

The motion was agreed to; and the Presiding Officer (Mr. ALLOTT)
appointed Mr. FULBRIGHT, Mr. SPARKMAN, Mr. MANSFIELD, Mr. CHURCH,
Mr. AIKEN, Mr. CASE, and Mr. COOPER conferees on the part of the
Senate.

Mr. President, I ask unanimous consent that the bill be printed
and passed, so that Senators may be informed of the many changes.

The PRESIDING OFFICER. Without objection, it is so ordered.

Mr. FULBRIGHT. Mr. President, I wish to commend the distinguished
Senator from Idaho (Mr. CHURCH) for his great patience and wisdom in
handling this bill. This bill has been under consideration for nearly
8 weeks---I think it will be 8 weeks on Thursday. This is one of the
most arduous and difficult bills we have had this year. The Senator
from Idaho has done an outstanding job and has handled it with great
tact and wisdom and has been most conscientious in his attendance. I
believe the effect of his management and the cooperation of the Senator from Kentucky (Mr. COOPER) has been very beneficial to the work
of the Senate. I commend both of them.

Mr. MANSFIELD. Mr. President, having spent over 7 weeks on this
one piece of legislation, it is impossible to single out any particular
Senator for commendation; the Senate as a whole has participated in a
truly historic event. The issue of the separate responsibilities of
the Congress and the executive branch have never been more fully ex-
plored; the final action on this bill marks a significant breakthrough
in the reassertion of the responsibilities of the Senate in the essential decisions affecting the foreign policy of this country as well
as the issue of war and peace.

The Senator from Idaho (Mr. CHURCH) who managed this bill along
with the Senator from Kentucky (Mr. COOPER) must however be mentioned.
The long hours spent in shepherding this bill to passage demonstrated
a dedication to duty and principle that sets a noble example to every
public official.

To the Senate as a whole I wish to express my appreciation, grat-
itude and pride for the level of the debate during these weeks and for
the cooperation afforded the leadership while these issues were before
us.

FINAL TEXT OF THE COOPER-CHURCH AMENDMENT

In concert with the declared objectives of the President of the United States to avoid the involvement of the United States in Cambodia after July 1, 1970, and to expedite the withdrawal of American forces from Cambodia, it is hereby provided that unless specifically authorized by law hereafter enacted, no funds authorized or appropriated pursuant to this act or any other law may be expended after July 1, 1970, for the purpose of--

(1) retaining United States forces in Cambodia;

(2) paying the compensation or allowances of, or otherwise supporting, directly or indirectly, any United States personnel in Cambodia who furnish military instruction to Cambodian forces or engage in any combat activity in support of Cambodian forces;

(3) entering into or carrying out any contract or agreement to provide military instruction in Cambodia or to provide persons to engage in any combat activity in support of Cambodian forces; or

(4) conducting any combat activity in the air above Cambodia in direct support of Cambodian forces.

Nothing contained in this section shall be deemed to impugn the constitutional power of the President as Commander-in-Chief, including the exercise of that constitutional power which may be necessary to protect the lives of U.S. armed forces wherever deployed.

Nothing contained in this section shall be deemed to impugn the constitutional powers of the Congress including the power to declare war and to make rules for the government and regulation of the armed forces of the United States.

CAMBODIA

INTERLANDI ©1970, LOS ANGELES TIMES

"So long, buddies—I hope it was worth it!"

PART IV

Conclusion

Debate is not policy. Yet in the long run few policies are effective that cannot withstand testing in the crucible of debate. The Senate debate on Cambodia provided a vehicle for detailed evaluation of presidential alternatives in Southeast Asia and critical analysis of executive-legislative relations. Though sometimes described by observers as a filibuster, in this case there was little evidence of the negative aspects usually associated with a fulibuster. The extended debate was fluid rather than rigid; constructive rather than negative; germaine rather than irrelevant. Roll-call votes revealed considerable shifting of positions, and party lines were crossed frequently enough to belie charges that members of the debate were "obstructionist" and "doctrinnaire." That little other significant business passed the Senate during this period is an indication of the importance and exceedingly complex nature of the central issues demanding the Senate's continuous attention.

The Cambodian debate, culminating in approval of the Cooper-Church Amendment, is significant as a statement of proposed public policy and as legislative history; despite the American predilection for fundamental written charters on all levels of government, the content of policy is shaped, for the most part, outside Constitutional clauses and provisions. In this situation divergent interpretations of the Constitution provoked the interaction that becomes the primary material of which public policy is made. The sharing of war powers between the executive and legislative branches, difficult enough in a formally declared war, finds few Constitutional guidelines in a protracted undeclared conflict such as Vietnam. Few serious commentators on the war in Southeast Asia can afford to neglect the materials comprising the full record of the Cambodian debate. Executives, legislators, scholars, and concerned citizens will find in future years the Cambodian debate a "bench-mark" in understanding the nature of the dilemmas facing American foreign policy at the beginning of the 1970s. Its contemporary importance, however, lies in its place in the broad evolving pattern of a newly-sensed senatorial "declaration of independence"---the protest against unilateral presidential decision-making.

The Cooper-Church Amendment may be viewed as a "half-way house" along the arduous road to the development of an activist Senate aimed at a more effective balancing of Presidential and Congressional power. As with his nominations of judges Clement Haynsworth and G. Harrold Carswell to the U.S. Supreme Court, President Nixon refused to compromise on the Cooper-Church Amendment---his opposition was adamant and implacable. These three major presidential defeats in the Senate raised issues beyond party allegiance, for in each instance party lines were crossed. The common threads---the lack of prior consultation about Cambodia or the nominations with appropriate Senators,

and the President's refusal to dilute his assertions of executive
powers---were the factors contributing most heavily to the final results. Together, the Senate's actions on these three occasions may
presage a newly awakened Senatorial determination to shape national
policy rather than merely to acquiese to policy made elsewhere.

It would be foolhardy to view the Cooper-Church Amendment as
heralding an overall revision of American foreign policy. What it
does suggest, however, is that the Senate is under continuing pressure
to take a more positive role in national security and foreign policy
issues. The Cambodian debate legitimatized re-assessment of the
nation's commitment to Vietnam and the neighboring nations of the
Southeast Asian mainland. Equally significant was its highlighting
of serious deficiencies in the procedures and mechanisms of inter-
branch relationships. The tensions and mutual suspicions between
Chief Executive and Senate, when combined with the weak legal and
psychologically negative aspects of undeclared major wars, place great
strain on many of the traditional assumptions of American government.

Despite outward appearances the Cambodian debate was not the
occasion for a "trial" of presidential war powers. To the contrary,
it was the future of the Senate and its credibility as a consultative
body that were at stake. The ultimate issue was not the Presidency
but the Senate itself. It was in the process of baring its own
frustrations and aspirations that the Senate questioned presidential
policies. In undeclared wars (and few future conflicts will be formally "declared") is the Senate doomed to sit in the audience while
the principal actors---the President, the Pentagon and the intelligence
agencies---occupy the central stage?

The implications of the presidential decision to send American
forces into Cambodia were clearly a challenge to whatever claim the
Senate felt it had in shaping the contours and content of American
foreign and military policy. Lacking any pretense to consultation
with the Senate President Nixon, moreover, based his unilateral decision on his Commander-in-Chief powers rather than on the Gulf of
Tonkin Resolution which President Johnson used to support his Vietnam
policy. To the increasing restiveness of the Senate anti-war coalition,
the Chief Executive was staking out claims on a wide Constitutional
front outside any Congressional authorization. It was feared that
this would bring about dangerous and adverse consequences for the
checks-and-balance system. If the Senate was ever to make any counter-
claim of its own, it had to be done immediately due to the rapidity
with which events were unfolding. Senators were well aware that executive precedent is as compelling in the formulation of policy as is
legislative history.

Claims to power must be based both on one's image of oneself and
upon the calculation of the strength of the adversary. Any realistic
claim of the Senate to powers and influence allegedly aggrandized by
the executive branch since the turn of the century had to be based
upon a new "frame of mind" in the upper chamber. The Cooper-Church
Amendment was the test deciding the credibility of the Senate's claim
to share in the fundamental responsibilities of foreign affairs and
military policy.

As the debate evolved it revealed deep Senate dissatisfaction
with its access to information. Admittedly the complexity of national

security matters is almost unmanageable, but the lack of adequate information and data makes any attempt to assert claimed power little
more than illusion. Senate knowledge of the exact state of American
commitments to the nations of Indochina, and indeed throughout Southeast Asia, is often dependent upon vague and highly selective information which executive agencies are disposed to dispense. Such selective information is hardly an adequate base for Senatorial decisionmaking since it is usually formulated to buttress earlier executive
decisions. Any effective Senatorial claim to increased influence must
be based upon a vastly improved intelligence-information system under
the sole jurisdiction and authority of that chamber, and specifically
designed to serve uniquely legislative rather than executive needs.

Proponents of the Cooper-Church Amendment manifested an intense
suspicion not only of "hard data" and information supplied by the
military but reflected a serious loss of confidence in executive interpretations of that material. To many Senators the conclusions
reached and acted upon by key executive decision-makers were not supported by evidence presented for their justification.

The spirit of the Cooper-Church Amendment undercuts presidential
authority to make the "Guam Doctrine" self-executing. Unilateral
presidential actions for new ventures where existing commitments are
not formal and precise may prove to be increasingly self-defeating.
Congressional consultation and evaluation may be the condition for
support of any American military or logistical presence in the fringe
areas outside the irreducible commitments recognized by Congress as
essential to the nation's security. On this issue the Cooper-Church
Amendment has implications far beyond Cambodia.

Realistically, the Cooper-Church Amendment reflects a model of
"the desirable" rather than what exists as effective policy. It represents the Senate's sense of "ought"---it is a statement of ethics
as much as a governmental document. It is not law and may never be
written into the nation's statute books; it is not binding on President or any executive subordinate to the Chief Executive. It is,
however, an important policy statement on the upper chamber's posture
in a controversy of global dimensions. The Senate cannot speak or
act for the House of Representatives nor the President. It can only
speak its own collective mind, but in so doing it is fulfilling its
alloted Constitutional role.

The future of the Cooper-Church Amendment as effective law is
hardly promising. The Military Sales Bill to which the Amendment was
added was returned to the House of Representatives by the Senate in
early July 1970. In a roll-call vote the House, in effect, rejected
the Cooper-Church Amendment as drafted following less than one hour
of debate. Any future version of the Amendment must consequently
emerge as the product of a joint House-Senate conference committee.
Chances are remote that it will bear close resemblance to the Senate
version. For this reason President Nixon has chosen to virtually
ignore the Amendment.

The Senate, like the President, has many weapons in its Constitutional arsenal. The Cooper-Church Amendment is directly tied into
Senate policies in future executive-legislative relationships. From
this perspective the Senate has not won, nor has the President lost,
the big battle. The skirmishing is just beginning if the Senate is
truly determined to gather strength unto itself. The Cooper-Church

Amendment cannot be regarded as a one-time accomplishment but will in all probability emerge as one of a series of executive-legislative confrontations shaping the future of the nation.

The Cooper-Church Amendment, as passed by the Senate, reflects the compromise so essential to the American system of government. Many of the modifications adopted were aimed at conciliatory language. The final text of the Preamble was suggested by the original co-sponsors of the Amendment---Senators Cooper and Church---in order to allay apprehensions that the Amendment was a wide frontal assault upon Presidential veracity. The Preamble as revised expresses shared Presidential-Senatorial objectives concerning the July 1 deadline for the withdrawal of American forces from Cambodia. Thus the presidentially determined schedule was taken by the Senate as its own. Withdrawal is mutually desired by the President and the Congress, and throughout the Amendment the language has been so drafted as to avoid antagonistic and unilateral declarations of legislative initiative through the usurpation of executive powers.

In the same vein, the Mansfield-Dole Amendment, adopted by unanimous vote, expressed the Senate's intent that the Constitutional powers of the president as Commander-in-Chief should not be impugned by any provisions of the Cooper-Church Amendment. The heart of this Amendment---its four substantive sections---are carefully circumscribed by language which, in effect, re-affirms the separation-of-powers doctrine. The language of the Mansfield-Dole Amendment was balanced by the Javits Amendment reflecting Senate concern that Congress, no less than the President, had legitimate Constitutional responsibilities in foreign and military affairs. Consequently, nothing in the Cooper-Church Amendment was designed to impugn Congressional power and authority. This was too significant to be left to inference or implication.

The Second Byrd Amendment was passed as an extension of the Mansfield-Dole Amendment. It expanded the first narrowly-defeated Byrd Amendment which dealt only with Presidential power to protect U.S. troops in Vietnam. The language as adopted recognizes the Constitutional authority of the president to protect American forces wherever they may be deployed throughout the world.

It is in the language of the four substantive sections of the Cooper-Church Amendment that the Senate takes its stand undiluted by concern for conciliation. The intent of the Senate is expressed precisely and clearly. In successfully adhering to his withdrawal deadline, however, the President avoided direct confrontation with Senate policy; the full impact and influence of the Cooper-Church Amendment is therefore untested and prospective. Nevertheless, its place in American history is already assured. It marks the first time the Senate has ever voted to impose limitations on spending funds for military operations while the nation was engaged in war.